THE MACMILLAN COMPANY
NEW YORK · BOSTON · CHICAGO
DALLAS · ATLANTA · SAN FRANCISCO

MACMILLAN AND CO., LIMITED
LONDON · BOMBAY · CALCUTTA
MADRAS · MELBOURNE

THE MACMILLAN COMPANY
OF CANADA, LIMITED
TORONTO

THE CROSS
AND
THE ETERNAL ORDER

A Study of
Atonement in Its Cosmic Significance

BY

HENRY W. CLARK, D.D.

Author of "The Philosophy of Christian Experience,"
"The Christian Method of Ethics," "Liberal Orthodoxy," etc.

WITH A FOREWORD BY

PROFESSOR C. H. DODD, M.A., D.D.

Norris-Hulse Professor of Divinity in the University of Cambridge

91022

NEW YORK

THE MACMILLAN COMPANY

1944

Copyright, 1944, by

THE MACMILLAN COMPANY

All rights reserved—no part of this book may be
reproduced in any form without permission in writing from the publisher, except by a reviewer who
wishes to quote brief passages in connection with a
review written for inclusion in magazine or newspaper.

First Printing

A WARTIME BOOK

THIS COMPLETE EDITION IS PRODUCED
IN FULL COMPLIANCE WITH THE GOVERN-
MENT'S REGULATIONS FOR CONSERVING
PAPER AND OTHER ESSENTIAL MATERIALS

PRINTED IN THE UNITED STATES OF AMERICA
BY THE VAIL-BALLOU PRESS, INC., BINGHAMTON, N. Y.

FOREWORD

This book has its place within the high debate upon the interpretation of the work of Christ, or the doctrine of the Atonement, as it was set in motion by the Reformation divines, and continued by their successors for three centuries and more. It is with the classical exponents of evangelical theology that Dr. Clark reckons, explicitly or by implication. The renewed interest in that theology in recent years will secure him a wider and readier reading, probably, than he would have found, say, thirty years ago. No reader, I think, with any lively awareness of the problems, can fail to be carried along by the argument, rigorous and closely knit as it is, or to recognize the gravity, subtlety, and religious insight with which it is developed. The conclusions have philosophical as well as theological import; for Dr. Clark, unlike some others of those who are leading us back to the springs of evangelical theology, refuses to separate religious belief from *Weltanschauung*. The thesis which he presents demands and deserves deliberate and critical consideration. Without presuming to anticipate the results of such consideration on the reader's part, I venture to commend the book as one in which I have found both stimulus to thought and fresh illumination upon its great theme, and, what is more, the touch of a wise and deeply devout spirit

C. H. DODD

PREFACE

It was with utmost hesitancy that I began to write this book, hovering in a "strait betwixt two." Cause sufficient for hesitancy there was; for there must always be fear lest the most sacred themes should be touched with too coarse or rough a hand; and the theme of these pages is assuredly one of the most sacred in all the world. There was also the greater fear induced by the haunting warning that they must be clean who handle the vessels of the Lord. For that matter, the book was commenced many years ago and then, under the stress of the indicated hesitancies, laid aside. If it be a mark of presumption that the hesitancies were at last overcome, presumption brings its penalty, now that the final words are set down, in a feeling of profound disappointment and self-reproach. Disappointment, because much of even the writer's own poor thought has refused to be run into the moulds of clear and adequate expression; self-reproach—intensified into shame—because the high experiences which the study compels the writer to set before his readers remain little more than a name to the writer himself. So soiled and tattered one's own garments, compared with the white robes one bids others wear! Yet perhaps pages so begun and so ended may have some little truth to teach, if sincerity and reverence have gone to the making of them; and this much at least I would humbly claim.

The book is not controversial or critical except incidentally here and there; and when it has become so, it is with real reluctance that I have permitted it to drift upon the controversial or critical line. It has not been altogether avoidable. For when the development of ideas which I have tried to sketch has come within sight of or into touch with ideas at variance with my own, the fact could not be ignored. If at any point it became clear that opposing views would suggest themselves to a reader's mind, I was under compulsion to render a reason for the faith that is in me and to meet the implied challenge. And I confess that such occasions became more numerous than I could have wished. But I repeat that the book is not *primarily* controversial or critical. At any rate, it is not as starting from, or as built round, other theories that it has been planned. And hence there is comparatively little reference to other books on the topic, even to those best known. I should not however like it to be supposed that these, as well as not a few less well known, have not been read with care. Yet, having read them, I have wished that anything I might say should be based—I dare not say upon realized experience—but at any rate upon glimpses of and aspirations after an experience which is far, far off indeed, but yet so illuminated that its outlines, though not the full richness of its content, can be discerned plainly enough to quicken desire; and an experience whereof in the soul's rare exalted moments the fringes may be touched. For so based, the book's pages should possess a stronger appeal than a merely critical or speculative discussion can ever possess for those who want their religious thinking to point a direct pathway to something beyond itself, and who say

> 'Tis life, whereof our nerves are scant,
> Oh life, not death, for which we pant;
> More life, and fuller, that I want.

I am aware that the treatment is upon occasion somewhat of the "sermonic" type, with something of the pulpit appeal. I do not know that this is a thing of which I need be ashamed. Indeed, it was inevitable. Upon this theme, if upon any, the theologian necessarily becomes the evangelist, and preaches most of all to himself. I have said something of the kind in the body of the book. For all the while, that Figure stands in view, with its appeal, "Is it nothing to you, all ye that pass by?" How can anything written about that appealing Figure be itself other than an echoed appeal, implicit always, explicit when the frequent moment permits or calls?

That portion of the book written after its resumption (the larger portion) has been prepared under circumstances which made the writing hard. I do not say this by way of deprecating criticism in advance. But it may serve as some sort of apology for certain blemishes which are probably to be found, and may at least excuse me from the accusation of carelessness. In the twilights which descend upon one as one treads certain valleys of human experience, one's sight is apt to become blurred; and there may be many a raggedness about the garments in which I have dressed the thoughts I peered at, and fancied I caught, in the half-dark—this quite apart from their essential truth or error. I do not know. I must take the verdict upon it, whatever the verdict be, offering only such excuse as the above facts may provide.

My cordial thanks are due, and are hereby offered, to Professor C. H. Dodd, M.A., D.D., for his kindness in writing the foreword to this volume.

NOTE.—It may be well to mention, though I do so with reluctance, that the first chapter of this book appeared in the *London Quarterly Review* under the title "The Standpoint for a Doctrine of the Atonement," so far back as 1910. I state the fact because in a book published a number of years later one or two points of that article were made in phrases not very remotely resembling mine.

The book has had to be reduced somewhat from its intended length to meet publication requirements. Consequently some matters which, though not of primary importance, are nevertheless very relevant have had to be left undealt with, and others have received briefer treatment than I should have liked. Readers to whom such points may occur are asked to believe that they have not been overlooked. Nothing essential to the main argument has been omitted.

H. W. C.

BROXBOURNE, HERTS

CONTENTS

consequence of Christ's work, but being manifested in it, and God has His "small-scale" action against sin within this "large-scale" work.

1. There must be no divorce between theology and philosophy, as has too often been the case, and even soteriology must be fitted into a philosophical scheme. 2. This book has been an attempt to reconcile theological and philosophical thinking in such a way that both receive and exercise their full rights. 3. The claim is that the Christian view of the world-order, based on Paul's "thought-series," provides what non-Christian philosophy cannot offer, namely the "final fact" of the "eternal order" and, over and above that, the *"final fact of the final fact"* when God shall be all in all.

THE CROSS AND THE
ETERNAL ORDER

CHAPTER I

THE STANDPOINT

It may sound startling to say that the worth of any doctrine of the Atonement cannot be rightly estimated, nor any doctrine of the Atonement properly framed, unless we seek to do these things from a standpoint outside our own experience. Yet the saying contains a very real and essential truth. In one sense, of course, it would be quite impossible to perform such a task: we cannot march up to this or any other question divested of the general ideas and mental habits wherewith experience has taught human nature to work. Nor, indeed, would aught be gained if such a thing could be done. But when we say that, in framing a doctrine of the Atonement, we must take a standpoint outside our own experience, it is meant that we must not, in our search for the material of the doctrine, for hints and suggestions from which the doctrine is to be wrought out, confine ourselves to the moral relations between man and man as human history and experience know them, or to the processes whereby those moral relations, if once impaired, are set right again. The point to be emphasized, in brief, is that since the Atonement is, by its very nature, a transaction, an event, whatever we prefer to call it, wherein something from *beyond* human experience touches upon and enters *into* human experience, something more than human experience itself must be explored if the key to the transaction or the event is to be found. All that has taken place *within* the moral history of the world is manifestly insufficient to furnish an explanation of something that starts elsewhere; and we must strive, as we carry on our doctrinal search, for a standpoint in that larger order wherein the Atonement, whatever the ultimate theory of it may be, had its initiation, and out of which its processes took their rise.

In this preliminary chapter no particular doctrine of the

Atonement is in view. It is desired only to justify this idea as the one with which we must set out and the one on which any doctrine of the Atonement must be founded—the idea that the Atonement cannot be properly dealt with except as we deal with it from a standpoint outside of our own experience—and to note one or two things the idea involves, one or two consequences that follow in its train.

I

We may start from the almost universally admitted fact that the death of Jesus on the Cross has something entirely special about it, and is in some way or other quite apart from the whole order of martyrdoms—from the order of even the greatest and sublimest martyrdom that history has known. And an almost universally admitted fact this may justly be termed. Even those who reject anything that could be called a "transcendental" theory of the Atonement, who hold the death of Christ to be only the perfect example of self-sacrifice for Right and Truth, or who in any way find its *raison d'être* simply in the spiritual inspirations that come forth from it and in the moral ardours which it kindles in the minds and hearts of men—even they confess, for the most part, that the Cross marks an event entirely unique in the process of the ages, altogether unclassifiable under any of the terms that suffice to cover the rest of history's content. In some way, they assert, the sacrifice of Jesus has a quality possessed by no other, and hence its power. An altogether special intention lay behind it, and an altogether special effect flows from it. Some few, certainly, do not shrink from declaring boldly that Calvary saw simply martyrdom at its highest degree, and nothing more; and these are wholly logical and consistent in interpreting what was done on Calvary by analogies, and according to the categories, that serve for other events of a similar kind. They would, in fact, be illogical and inconsistent if they did anything else. But they are only few; [1]

---

[1] Outside Unitarianism, that is. Unitarianism is not here within our purview, which includes only those who hold Christ's special Divinity as an article of their faith.

and in their case one can only wonder that they can lightly sever themselves from the instinct which has maintained itself so strongly entrenched in the historic Church throughout the long procession of the centuries; wonder, next, that the atmosphere of Calvary (if one may use the phrase) does not penetrate them more adequately; and then pass on. The majority, at any rate, admit that here, in the Cross of Christ, the world saw an event which has not had even a distant blood-relation, as it were, among all the events of time. The death of Jesus is almost universally held to have differed, not only in the degree but in the essential quality of its working, from the death of all others who have given their lives for the good of men. Indeed, while some few theories of the Cross, when strictly interpreted, reduce its operation to what might be called ordinary levels, the framers of them seem to strain language for the purpose of making it appear that this is not what they really intend to do after all. One overhears them at war with themselves. If at one moment they find a sufficient explanation of the Cross in the lines along which moral influence, as men in their mutual relationships know it, does its work, at the next moment they admit that only because in the Cross there is something wholly exceptional are they attempting to explain it at all. It was—even they admit—something entering into human experience from beyond. In some wholly unique fashion the Cross was the touch of God's mind and God's hand upon the moral and spiritual history of the world.

2

It is necessary to realize what is involved in this fact—if it be admitted as a fact, and if the practically universal feeling alluded to be held as just. It comes really to this—the Atonement belongs primarily to what, speaking in human fashion, we may venture to call the history of God, rather than to the history of man. Its result for man, whatever that may be, is to lead to some result for God in the way of restoring to Him a perfectly ordered world; and since this ultimate object must have been present in God's own mind as the initial impulse out of which the Atonement came, it is by attempting to ascertain how the Atonement furthers this result for God that its *rationale* must be sought. And when it is declared that the investigator must survey the Atonement from a standpoint outside his own experience, what is meant is that he must seek to take the standpoint of God. Of course, the same thing is true of other points of Christian doctrine—of every point of Christian doctrine, in fact, wherein some special interposition of God in the ordinary processes of world-development is implied. The doctrine of the nature of Christ, for instance, can be properly examined only when we inquire how the sending of One who was God's Son in a sense entirely unique could have formed a part of, or could have repaired, the working out of the plan that dwelt in God's own mind from before the foundation of the world; when we attempt to ascertain in what way the coming of a divine Christ could have been related (not only by its patent historical connections but as a dynamic force furthering the divine Will) to what had gone before and to what came after in the position of things between God and man. It is not as an isolated phenomenon, but as part of the eternal dynamic through which God's Will works itself out, that the nature of Christ must be surveyed. We cannot understand aright how a divine Christ could be a help to man unless we seek to understand also, and primarily, how a divine Christ could be a help to God.

It is from God, then, and from God's unchanging plan and purpose as affected by the condition of man, that we have to start our inquiries when we deal with any alleged special activity of God in human affairs. Of the Atonement, therefore, we may say the same thing, *mutatis mutandis,* as of the nature of Christ. In formulating any theory of the action and the effect of the Cross we have to inquire, primarily, whether the theory assists us to see how the Cross moves the world further along towards the fulfilment of God's eternal intention. We have to realize how the Atonement, in setting man right with God, sets God right with Himself—is, as it were, a re-assertion of the purpose God eternally entertained. We have to see the Cross falling into line, not with the past history of the world, but with the other movements of that unchanging Will out of which the previous history of the world came (except so far as human sin diverted it from its appointed path) and which the subsequent history of the world was meant to express. It is as part of a larger sequence whereof the previous world-history, the Atonement itself, and the subsequent world-history, are all sections—unified by the changeless purpose wherein they all inhere and on which, so to say, they all lie back—that the Atonement is to find its place; and in its function in the larger sequence must its secret be sought and found. It comes out of, and at the same time conserves and furthers, the one original Idea. The problem is, How? Assuming the changelessness of God's Will, and assuming that man's condition was not in accordance therewith, what was there in the Cross to make that changeless Will effective once more? How did the Cross harmonize, or reharmonize, the world-process into which it was thrown with the original Idea dwelling in the mind of God? How did God, through the Cross, readjust the effect of the world-process upon Himself and upon the working out of His Will? What was the Atonement *for Him?* These are the directions in which the inquirer must look. We cannot realize what the Atonement is for man without first realizing what it is for God. It is God's point of view that we must endeavour to take.

This, it must be conceded, means that the full and final significance of the Atonement is probably not for us to know. We are necessarily unable to see the whole sweep of things as God sees it; and it is impossible, without doing that, to penetrate into *all* the adjustments which the Atonement makes for God in the eternal movement, or to grasp in its *entirety* the method whereby it works them out. We cannot by any effort so thrust out the boundaries of our horizon as to compass what God sees, and cannot, consequently, *perfectly* understand how the Atonement, or any other interposition of God in the moral history of the world, arises out of His estimate of the moral situation, creates new possibilities of bringing it back into harmony with His Will. But that is no reason why we should not reach at least a partial comprehension; and when we admit that the ultimate secret is not for us, we by no means acquiesce in that counsel of despair which so many offer, to the effect that all speculation about the Atonement had better be left alone, and man's attitude towards it be confined to a simple taking of its benefits. Even if the thing were possible, the suggested attitude would have too much of a superstitious savour. But, as a matter of fact, the counsel is self-contradictory. If the Atonement came forth from God as an essential part of the dynamic through which God seeks to readjust the moral history of the world to Himself in rectitude, man must know something of the nature of the dynamic and of the method by which it works, if he is to lay himself beneath its power. To say that the Atonement is to be accepted without being in any wise understood, is to make it a mere fact in history to which credence has to be given, and not an actual dynamic at all. So far as possible, therefore, man must strive to push back the door behind which the significance of the Atonement is hidden, even though at the end of his striving he can but set it a little way ajar. Fully admitting that the *ultimate* meaning of the Atonement cannot be known in all its length and breadth and depth and height, we nevertheless claim that it is a proper subject for reverent human thought. If we cannot take God's standpoint in fulness, we can at least press some few steps upward and make some feeble approach toward the attainment of God's wide and august view.

3

In seeking to frame some theory of the Atonement, we have, then, to take, so far as is possible to us, the standpoint of God Himself. If there be any validity in the practically universal sentiment which puts the death of Jesus in a category by itself, this necessity is forced upon us. Yet it is often forgotten. It is quite inconsistent with an admission of the uniqueness of the Cross, in the sense indicated, to make human experience the test of any doctrine of the Atonement, or to frame a doctrine of the Atonement solely out of the material which human experience supplies. But this is precisely what is often done. An action alleged as having been wrought by God on and for man becomes suspect if no parallel action can be pointed to as wrought by man on and for man. And when positive construction of doctrine is attempted, it is with the same pre-suppositions underlying the attempt. It is from a survey of right as man has rendered it to his fellow-men, of wrong as man has committed it against his fellow-men, of reconciliation as it has been brought about between man and his fellow-men—it is from this survey that sufficient material is thought to be gathered for an exposition of right and wrong and reconciliation as between man and God. You have only, when you are seeking to interpret the Cross, to give a sort of cosmic flavour to the terms which serve you for the less ambitious purpose of describing the reception of a returned prodigal in an earthly home, or the heroism of a man who goes down on a sinking ship that others may be saved. It is only a matter of superlatives instead of the lower degrees. What passes between man and man gives, in essence, the secret of what passes between man and God. And even apologists for what may be called "orthodox" theories of the Atonement have not seldom condoned the error, indeed committed it themselves, by playing in tentative and half-timorous fashion with analogies drawn from the sacrifices which man makes for man, and using them as testimonials to commend—although confessedly they cannot describe—the sacrifice made by God when He gave His Son, and the sacrifice made by the Son Himself when He became obedient unto death, even the death of the Cross. The moral history of humanity is too frequently accepted as giving the lines for a doctrine of the moral relations between humanity and God.

All this would be very well if the Cross were merely an event *within* the history of the world, an item in a self-developing process through which man has attained his present spiritual stage. The explanation of the Cross might then be legitimately sought among, and taken as suggested by, other events of the same class as that to which it would then belong. Necessarily, it would have to fall into line. Produced by the same forces as other events, it would be covered by the same formula—at any rate, the same formula would form the basis of the calculation by which the total of its significance is worked out. But, by the hypothesis, the operation of the Atonement is *upon* human evolution, not *within* it. It is not itself a part of that evolution: it is a force which was thrown upon the stage from beyond to quicken the process of spiritual evolution when it lagged, and to repair it when it broke down. It is not something that happened in this world that is being surveyed when we endeavour to penetrate the meaning of the Cross: it is something that happened in the *relations* between this world and a higher—and moreover, something whose beginning and initiative is in that higher world, not in this. It was not this world putting itself right with the higher: it was the higher world putting this world right with that higher world itself. It was not the taking of an unassisted step upward by the spiritual evolution of man: it was the grasping of that spiritual evolution, lamed and disorganized as it was, by a hand from above. Whatever, in the Atonement, happened *within* the world happened only because something happened—previously, or simultaneously, or both—*beyond* the world. In the examination or construction of any doctrine of the Atonement, therefore, the question whether the history of the world has itself produced or evolved anything like what the doctrine suggests becomes irrelevant altogether. And the formularies which cover the processes of ordinary spiritual growth, spiritual recuperation, spiritual movement, cannot help us here. The event with which we are dealing is not in the class wherein these processes are ranked. It ranks in another order of things—not the order of happenings in this world, but the order of the *relations* between this world and another. And the investigator who looks upon the moral relations between man and man as an adequate source of material for a doctrine of the moral relations between man and God is forgetting the primary condition on whose fulfilment his investigation depends. He is forgetting that the investigator must set himself in thought *outside* the process of human evolution, and must endeavour, as he makes his doctrinal construction, to survey the

Atonement from a standpoint in that larger sum of things to which it belongs.

4

Starting from an admission of something distinctive in the death of Jesus, we cannot, then, consistently limit the material of our constructive doctrine of Atonement to the moral history of man. But how is it, it may be asked, that this is precisely what is done by not a few? The question is worth reply; for in meeting it, we come upon another point which it is necessary to make.

What lies beneath the tendency just spoken of—the tendency to make moral relations between man and man the source or standard of a doctrine concerning moral relations between man and God—is probably this. From anything that appears to be exceptional, an isolated phenomenon among the general sum of things, an event unclassifiable and without kindred, the human mind is apt to sheer away. Yet so soon as men attempt, starting from the unevadable consciousness of something entirely special in the death of Christ on the Cross, to formulate a doctrine of that death's significance, they of course find themselves announcing just such an unclassifiable and isolated event—find themselves openly and explicitly avowing what previously consciousness held unvocal and implied. Straightway protest arises within them. Although they cannot escape from the initial feeling that the Cross of Christ stands alone, they hesitate to assent to any theory (notwithstanding that such a theory is but the logical exposition or expansion of the initial feeling itself) wherein that exceptional character of Calvary's sacrifice is made to stand out clear. Thereupon they travel back—forgetting the inconsistency involved in so doing, the faithlessness to the very instinct which originally impelled them to their doctrinal search—to the ordinary moral history of the world, looking there for something which, if it cannot exactly parallel, may at least suggest or adumbrate or somehow be brought into intimate relation with, the moral process wrought out at the Cross. The human mind shrinks from accepting, or incorporating in the system of belief to which it says "Amen," any doctrine wherein some wholly singular and unrelated fact or event is implied. What is alleged to have happened only once is, for that very reason, touched with suspicion when it applies for a certificate in the courts of the mind of man.

In attempting any constructive doctrine of the Cross the investigator must, besides remembering the necessity of taking so far as possible the standpoint of God Himself, remember also that the exceptional character of the Atonement-process, as some doctrine under construction or examination may describe it, is no argument against it. From the indicated standpoint, the standpoint of God Himself, things may become reasonable which are—not of course unreasonable but at least non-reasonable—in the sense of not being positively and ascertain-ably conformable to anything within the stretch of human life: as Pascal put it, "the last proceeding of reason is to recog-nize that there is an infinity of things which are beyond it" : [2] one need not fear to say, at any rate, that an event which is quite abnormal to the experience of man may be wholly normal to God. It is not suggested that what is unjust upon earth can by any possibility be just in heaven; and if the objections fre-quently made against certain Atonement theories (objections based upon the offence given by those theories to the sense of right in man) can be sustained, then the theories against which they are launched must go. But, on the other hand, when we are endeavouring to take God's point of view, a doctrine is not to be waved aside merely because it tells of some process, alleged to have taken place at the Cross, for which neither in man's dealings with man nor in God's other dealings with man can a parallel be found. The mind must be prepared to accept the exceptional if upon its merits the exceptional can claim to be approved as true. In the matter of the Cross and its meaning, if we start from our initial consciousness that the death of Jesus contains something never held in man's sublimest martyrdoms, we must follow the road. And the road leads us first, as we

[2] *La dernière démarche de la raison, c'est de connaître qu'il y a une infinité de choses qui la surpassent. (Pensées, xiv. 1.)*

have seen, to a definite endeavour to take the standpoint of God; and then, still following the straight path, we come inevitably to an acceptance of the exceptional as a possible thing. For the whole of that human experience, with all its moral facts and possibilities, whereto the objector against an Atonement which has something exceptional in it would limit our search for doctrinal material—the whole of that human experience itself comes out of a larger life with other possibilities in reserve. We admit this by our very attempt to take God's point of view— admit it, in fact, by acknowledging the existence of God at all. The effort to stand with God is really an effort to pass beyond human experience as we know it to that out of which human experience came, and out of which, similarly, something else may come. The whole of human experience, with its moral facts and processes and possibilities, is itself but *one* realized possibility out of all the possibilities inhering in God. And God may surely see fit to project, into the midst of that one realized possibility, the realization of *another* possibility, starting, so to say, from another point within Himself. And this is simply what a unique Atonement—an Atonement which cannot be brought into a relation of likeness with any other known moral process—implies. Entirely abnormal as such an interposition would appear to any observer whose horizon is bounded by the limits of human experience and whose thought refuses to transcend them, to God Himself it would be but a normal outputting of His Will and power, as normal as that other outputting whereby human experience itself came to be. And they who seek to take God's standpoint, to raise themselves in thought to that infinite sum of possibilities whereof human experience is one (but *only* one) manifestation, must at once perceive that such an interposition is a possible thing. A doctrine which speaks of an Atonement whereto no parallel can be found is not discredited thereby. The uniqueness of a suggested process of Atonement is, from this standpoint, no matter for surprise. In fact one may go further than this, and say that the uniqueness of a suggested process of Atonement is a recommendation of the doctrine which suggests it rather than the reverse. For if there be such a thing as Atonement at all in any real sense (that is, if the instinct which sees something quite special in the death of Jesus be valid) it marks the coming of something *into* human experience from *beyond*. And it must surely be a fundamental consideration upon the theme that there can be nothing else like the Atonement so wrought out—except on the supposition, which probably no one would seriously advance, that the higher world has more than once interposed under similar circumstances, to correct the failure of this. The inquirer, as he frames his doctrine of the Cross, must be prepared to give credence to a fact, an event, a process, which stands entirely alone. Nay, if he rightly realize the conditions of the problem, it is precisely to some such unique fact or event or process that he will expect to be led when his thought has reached its goal.

It may be objected that this concession to the exceptional gives *carte blanche* to unregulated speculation, and permits any doctrine, however extravagant, to shelter itself under the protection of the idea of a fresh activity of God. The objection calls for at least a word. As a matter of fact, it cannot hold good if what was previously said be borne in mind. There is still a very definite test whereby every doctrine must stand or fall, a definite standard of judgment to which every doctrine must be brought up and whose requirements it must fulfil. There is still a background into which our doctrine of Atonement must fit, though a larger background than that afforded by human experience and its limited range. So far is this method of taking the standpoint of God, spite of its open door for the exceptional, from allowing speculation to run riot, that we find ourselves, in adopting it, confronted by most binding rules.

In this way. Let some of the phrases previously employed be for a moment recalled. It was said that in formulating any theory of the Cross, we have to inquire, primarily, whether the theory assists us to see how the Cross moves the world further along towards the fulfilment of God's eternal intention. It was said that it is as part of a larger sequence whereof the previous world-history, the Atonement itself, and the subsequent world-history, are all sections (unified by the changeless purpose wherein they all inhere and on which they all lie back) that the Atonement must be viewed. It was said that the Atonement must be seen as coming out of, and at the same time conserving and furthering, the one original Idea. Here are surely tests and safeguards enough. What it all implies is this—that whatever was done at the Cross, although it is not to be brought into a relation of actual *likeness* with anything in the previous moral history of man, is to be viewed as a real dynamic pushing on or restoring the ascent of spiritual development which that moral history ought to have climbed, and did not climb. There must be discernible in the Atonement-process, when any theory ventures to formulate it, the reassertion of that original Will which the life of man ought to have fulfilled and did not fulfil—and there must be discernible, not only the reassertion of that original Will, but an indication of the method whereby through the Atonement-process that Will comes again to its own. A relation, therefore, there will be between the moral history of man and the process wrought out at the Cross, though a relation of likeness it certainly is not. It is not enough that an Atonement theory should point to an event wherein God is supposed to have made some magic pass across the moral disasters of the world, and that in yielding himself to the Atonement's power man should simply be taken as believing that such a magic pass has been made. It is not enough that God should be proclaimed as having done something isolated and special before the eyes of men, and that men should be asked to look back upon it and bow their heads. And it is not to be denied that theorizing about the Atonement has sometimes been too much upon these lines. Something isolated and special the Atonement assuredly was; and not into a relation of actual *likeness* with anything in the moral history of men can it be brought. But a real relation, nevertheless, there must be—not a relation of likeness, but such a relation as is implied in the fitness of the Atonement-process to bring back the moral history of man into *its* first-intended fitness once more. The Atonement is to be connected with man's moral history, not directly, but through that eternal Idea to which both belong and out of which both emerge—man's moral history only partially, inasmuch as it has taken alien elements into its being, and the Atonement perfectly, inasmuch as it is that eternal Idea exerting and expressing itself once more and seizing upon man's moral history in its failure and its fall to draw it back to the line over which it was meant to run. Falling back upon another phrase previously used, we may say that human experience was the realization of *one* of the possibilities inherent in God, the realization being, however, impaired and spoilt by the intrusions of sin: the Atonement was the realization of *another* of the possibilities inherent in God; but the realization of the second was projected into the sum of things only in order that the intention behind the attempted realization (speaking after the fashion of men) of the first might still be fulfilled. And a theory of the Cross must endeavour to show how this is so. That is the theory's test. The theory, accordingly, must establish and vindicate in the Atonement-process a dynamic consonant with a Will which had been in part thwarted in the process of human experience, but which would not admit defeat. There must be present to us, when we endeavour to formulate our doctrine of the Cross, the background of the one eternal Idea. Human experience came out of that Idea and betrayed its own call, fell from the ordained line. Then, out of that same eternal Idea, organically connected with it as changed instrument with unchanged intention, came the Cross—a veritable dynamic, the appropriately adjusted dynamic, so to speak, to bring the process of human experience back to the true line and enable the eternal Idea still to claim its rights, and to work itself out and to win. A worthy theory of the Atonement must not only assert that this is so, but must attempt to indicate *how* the Cross fulfils this function in the eternal economy of man's relations with God. And since it is within the limits thus suggested that every theory of Atonement must move, no fantastic speculation can find place; and the unique and special fact whereof a doctrine of the Cross may speak must of necessity be discerned as part and parcel of one great unity after all.

If this be borne in mind, then, while allowing scope for all the greater possibilities of doctrine implied in taking the stand-

point of God Himself, we nevertheless guard ourselves against
extravagant and rash surmise, find a finger laid upon our lips
when we tend to talk too loudly, and provide ourselves with a
stringent test whereby every doctrine of the Cross must stand
or fall.

5

One brief word remains to be set down. Nothing has hitherto
been said as to the method of treatment adopted by the New
Testament Scriptures in dealing with the significance of the
Cross. The emphasis has simply been laid on this—that in
formulating any theory of Atonement we must endeavour to
take, so far as is possible, the standpoint of God. But this, let
it be noted at the end of this preparatory chapter, is precisely
what the New Testament does. It is always in terms of the
everlasting Will and Idea that the New Testament writers seek
to interpret the significance of the death of Christ; and it is
always as something accomplished by God, started freshly out
of God, started and accomplished in order to rescue the earlier
process of things back into consonance with the changeless purpose out of which first it came, that the Atonement-process
stands out in their thought. Thus the investigator of to-day
will first of all rejoice to find this confirmation of the method
whereto, following his primary instinct, he is driven; and will
then be profoundly conscious (theories of inspiration quite
apart) that what the New Testament writers have set down is
not to be lightly dismissed, since those writers have thus taken
the one and only way to a serious dealing with their theme.

This it is, indeed, that gives the Scripture its weight, its grip,
its power. The reproach sometimes levelled against the New
Testament writers by men of our later day—the reproach of
subjectivity—is nothing less than grotesque. They used the
language of their times, of course; but if that be a fault, it is a
fault to which all times are liable. No time can employ the
tongue of a century ahead; for that tongue is as yet unknown.
But subjective, in any real sense, the New Testament writers

certainly were not. On the contrary, they were delivered from themselves, brought out into a large place. The New Testament is pre-eminently distinguished for that elevation of mood, that largeness and breadth of view, which come from transcending the limitations of human experience and lifting oneself up to what may with reverence be called the experience of God, and surveying all things from a lofty platform there. It is, in fact, precisely the New Testament method we need to recover if we are going to do any worthy work in doctrinal construction upon such topics as this. Many of our modern methods are a curious contradiction—a curious blend of daring and cowardice. Daring they may be in the sense that they do not shrink from renouncing the great heritage left to us by the inquirers of the past, and bidding us start out upon our pilgrimage of thought as it were without staff or script except such as we can fashion impromptu out of casual materials that have just been discovered. But the value of daring like this is questionable, to say the least. And cowardly some of these methods certainly are, in that they will not venture upon the flight to a peak outside of limited human experience; in that they allow themselves to be fascinated by the mere process of human moral evolution itself, and will not look beyond the brackets enclosing it for something greater out of which perchance it came, and out of which something else, to further and set it right, may be found to have come also; in that they refuse in brief, to take the standpoint of God. *These* are the subjective methods; and subjective the New Testament methods are not. The Scripture writers looked at things *sub specie æternitatis,* in the true and proper meaning of the phrase. They tried to see things as God sees them. They viewed the world-process, not in itself, but in its relation to God. We shall need once more to do the same. And it may be that the modern investigator, as he does this, will find that the holy men who, as the Scriptures claim for them, were moved by the Holy Spirit, were indeed moved by the Holy Spirit of truth— that by them the one best word was said—that all he has to declare when his thinking is done was declared by them (perhaps in the speech of their own day, but none the less truly and forcefully for that) long ago.

Chapter II

GOD'S PROBLEM IN REDEMPTION

We seek, then, to take, so far as is possible to us, the stand-point of God. And the question immediately facing us as we seek to take it is—as has in fact already been suggested—"What must God's provision for Atonement really contain and convey in order that it may rectify and redeem, in God's own sense of rectification and redemption, a morally failing world?" The Cross of Christ is God's supreme ministry of salvation—granted. But when we set ourselves to search for something which shall stand to our minds as its *rationale,* we are (if we fully understand the conditions of successful seeking) brought up against the fact that we cannot explain what God has done in the Cross of Christ without a preliminary understanding of what He had to do. God made His redeeming love effectual in the death of Jesus Christ. Yes, but what did redemption mean—what did the term involve—for God? What was it that, as between God and man, redemption really had to accomplish? That is a fundamental question which no inquirer ought to shirk; and any investigation of the significance of the Cross which does not face it begins, so to say, too far down the line, and is consequently vitiated, or at any rate may be so, from its start. Theorizing about the Atonement too often runs in a direction precisely the reverse of the true and proper one; and the theorizer, having constructed or evolved or hit upon some conception of what the Cross might conceivably mean, argues back to an idea of the world's moral situation, and of what that situation called for from God's hands, which the conception is sufficient to cover and meet. The true and necessary order of things is surely to ascertain what God had to do (of course one has to speak after the manner of men) before we construct a

17

formula interpretative of what God has done. What then is the problem of redemption for God? That is the inquiry which in this chapter we shall try to meet.

I

But in order to estimate God's "problem" in the matter of redemption, a preliminary question must be encountered. We have to drive our minds a step yet further back, and apprehend so far as possible what God's intention, lying behind all human history, originally was; for it is out of a frustration of that original intention which man has brought about that the problem of redemption rises up. To answer the inquiry, "What must God do to put right the sin of the world?" we must first of all answer the other inquiry, "What precisely was it that the world's sin put wrong? What was the divine idea it contradicted, the divine plan it foiled, the divinely-appointed operation whose working-out it checked?" The problem of redemption is really the problem of restoring something which has broken down; and the whole method of restoration must necessarily be conditioned by what that something is. In fact, the entire question of Atonement (of course only so far as its theoretical treatment, not the practical use and experience of it, is concerned) must start from a philosophical platform. In dealing with sin, God seeks to restore that "wholeness" of things, that perfect moral and spiritual structure of the universe, whereinto His relations with man enter as a most essential part, and which just at that most essential point has been broken through. It is from the midst of that originally-intended "wholeness" of things, from the midst of that designed perfect moral and spiritual structure, therefore, that the problem of sin and of God's dealing with it must be estimated, if its measure is to be rightly taken. Only thus can we come to understand what the problem is *for God*. The new problem created for God by human sinfulness (if one may employ such terms) is conditioned, as to the nature and incidence of its demand upon God's resources, by the nature of God's earlier and now violated design. Our view of God's attitude towards, and God's necessary work upon, a failing humanity will depend in great part upon our view of that whole world-process whereof man is, or ought to be, the crown; and the value of our view of the first will depend upon the correctness and fulness of our view of the second.

Forgetfulness of this is frequently the initial mistake whereby theories of forgiveness and atonement are vitiated, even when in measure the "standpoint of God" is felt for; and God's present "problem" of putting things right is misapprehended, not to say belittled, because God's ultimate and original "plan" is not grasped. It is possible to make some endeavour at taking God's standpoint, and yet to be unprepared for a sufficient dealing with the atonement problem, inasmuch as the endeavour may carry us no further than to the platform of God's feeling as affected here and now by single acts of human sin, rather than to the platform of God's original energizing Will as affected by sin's long contrary energizing in the history of the world. And to be carried only thus far is to forget that there is an essential distinction between God's standpoint and man's, to take them as being in effect one and the same. It is with this partial endeavour that not a few theories of redemption rest content. They seek to stand with God *in* the world, but not *before* the world, not realizing that you cannot truly do the second unless you have done the first. Take, for instance, the theory to which allusion has already been made; for although the examination of it is reserved for the chapter following this, it may serve to illuminate the present point. "God has only to forgive as man forgives," it is said, which is in effect to say that no "problem of redemption" exists for God at all. But you cannot say this—certainly you cannot advance it off-hand as being a self-evident axiom and as exhausting the entire theme—unless you have in your thought drawn God in from the place where He sits as the *source* of the entire world-process, initiating and maintaining it for a purpose specially and exclusively His own, and have planted Him wholly *within* that world-process and made Him (what man is, but

what God assuredly is not) a mere contributory to it or a mere
factor in it rather than its author and its source. "God has only
to forgive as man forgives," it is said. But to assume this is to
assume that wrong from man to man is the same as wrong from
man to God—the same not merely in its nature, but in its issues
and effects; that God's position in regard to the world, so to
say, is affected by sin which man commits against God in precisely the same way as man's position in regard to the world is
affected by sin which man commits against man. And this, in its
turn, is to forget that God is not merely in the world, but outside it and before it, with a final purpose in regard to it which
everything in it (man's relations to man included) were meant
to subserve. God acts in the world-process—true; but all His
action in the world-process is conditioned by the original Will
which moved Him before the world-process began; and treatment which may be adequate and proper in respect of a moral
situation lying between two parties, each of whom is set *within*
the limits of that world-process, need not necessarily be either
proper or adequate when the moral situation, however superficially similar it may be, lies between a member of the world-
process and the Will out of which the world-process came. For
the superficial similarity between the two situations hides a
great difference, when all is said. In the setting right of moral
relations between man and man, no question of giving restored
validity and effect to an ultimate purpose is directly involved;
while this is exactly what *is* involved in the setting right of
moral relations between man and God. Of this something more
must presently be said. But to toss the phrase, "God has only to
forgive as man forgives," lightly against the problem is to
ignore the difference, fundamental and far-reaching though it
be. For the most part, they who make easy play with the phrase
and think to settle the problem of forgiveness by the facile
repetition of it, are content with their method only because they
have not put themselves in thought with God outside of and
before the world, entered into and realized the purpose for
whose fulfilment the world was made, understood how the sin
of man has made that purpose go haltingly towards its goal,

and thus measured the magnitude of the redemptive work which God has had to do. They are content, not having viewed the situation thus, with what seems to get over the momentary difficulty—a thing that mere "forgiving as man forgives" is of course enough to do. The mere theism which sees as the only factors in the moral problem a God of fatherly kindness in contact with a manhood which has not treated that fatherly kindness as it ought may well construe the immediate need in such wise as to make that simple formula suffice. The problem of spiritual restoration and repair is, under the circumstances, quickly stated and easily solved, though the very ease of the solution might suggest that the statement was incomplete. To let thought go for its start no further back than to the point of a God of fatherly love in contact with a sinning world leads to asking no more than this, "What will be God's feeling, *as it were at the moment,* things being as they are?" And as the obvious reply, under the conditions, will be that God must wish for the re-establishment of tender and sympathetic relations between Himself and alienated man, the formula of "God forgives as man forgives" suggests itself at once as giving the obvious programme for God to carry through. But by this method the whole problem is viewed from too low a level and in too narrow a range; and the solution so attained fails adequately to cover the case. Once thought goes further back for its point of start, back to the eternal purpose and Will which were antecedent to the world—once thought realizes that it is in its frustration of that eternal purpose and Will that the disturbance of tender and sympathetic relations between man and God finds its significance and importance—then thought will also perceive that what restores those tender and sympathetic relations must also do more. It must set that eternal purpose and Will on the road to fulfilment again; and the correction of the *immediate* situation must bring the correction of the *larger* situation too. And although to assert this may not be at once to discredit the formula "God forgives as man forgives," it is at least to prevent a calm assumption of its validity, to put it on its trial, and to supply a test which it must face. If it is to hold its ground, it must show that it possesses the secret, not alone of the relief of the immediate position, but of the victory of the eternal purpose and Will. For God's dealing with the moral problem as *we* see and know it must be directed upon re-securing the temporarily-checked success of His original and ultimate idea as *He* saw and knew it in the founding of the world; and so no theory of what God must do in order to put right the sin of the world can have value or soundness unless it be based upon, and fitted into, an understanding true as can be achieved of what it was the sin of the world put wrong.

What then was God's original intention behind the world-process, the intention which that world-process was meant to carry out? What was the relation which God desired to sustain to the world, the relation which God desired the world to sustain to Him, the action which God desired to put into the world-process and carry through by its means, the reaction (so to term it) which God desired the world-process to have upon Him? The reply to the inquiry must emphasize this at the outset—if for no other reason, for the sake of sound philosophy —that God's intention pointed to something more than the initiating of a history in which God was to take continued interest, the creation of a humanity on which God would direct a kindly glance while it played its part. The position is not even adequately described by saying that God held within His thought certain hopes and purposes for the men He made, that He was ready to offer men counsel and help for the fulfilling of these same hopes and purposes, that His interest was so intensely personal as to involve joy for Him in men's success and pain for Him in men's failure, that He intended to be ever present in the midst of history with suggestion and inspiration and revelation and command, and that He wished humanity to be mindful of all these and of the God from whom they came. Such an answer to the question may certainly satisfy the mental and moral restlessness of a moment, but it cannot satisfy the requirements of a mind searching for a formula which will so to say go round all things and bind them up as a whole, leaving no ungathered threads or ragged ends. All the things said above are true, of course, and all the phrases used above hold good; but it is possible to say all these things and to use all these phrases without touching the heart of the case. They give us nothing more than a God and a world set over against each other, or set side by side if that phrasing be preferred, the first watching the second in sympathetic love; and great as that conception is, its formula does not come sufficiently near to ultimates to satisfy the requirements of thought when thought is seeking for the fundamental relation between God and the world He made. The simple theism, previously alluded to, which sums up the entire matter of that relation as one of fatherly kindness surveying with beneficent interest the fortunes of man, while it does undoubtedly seize upon *one* of the facts of the situation, cannot claim to do more; and it must not, because it reads off a single aspect of the present relation between God and man, be allowed to put itself forward as translating the entire ante-temporal divine idea. Indeed, that it cannot do this is clear enough.

For it does not answer to what, in respect of that idea, the mind requires. It has no suggestion of such an ultimate unity between Creator and creature as that idea must have foreseen, decreed, and provided for. Its utmost suggestion along that line is a suggestion that man *came from* God; but of man's return *to* God—otherwise than in the metaphorical sense of faith and love and moral sympathy—it cannot speak. It does not contain within itself (as a satisfying translation of the ante-temporal idea must contain) any indication of the way wherein the God who projected the world-process out of Himself is to draw it, or the final fruit of it, back into Himself again, so remaining in the future eternity as in the past, not only God over all, but God *all in all*. A God interested in and loving a world—a world watched and loved even by a God—there is in this no hint of a movement which reveals its meaning and secret by returning upon the Source whence it emerged; or of a fundamental and all-inclusive oneness which the world's separate existence seems for a while to contradict only in order that in the final stages of the world's development it may be the more clearly emphasized once again; or of an Eternal which first puts the temporal forth out of itself and at last receives it back; or of an ultimate consummation in which but one essential thing, with all other things held within it, shall be left. Yet from start to finish of its quest for a fundamental conception of God's relation to the world and for a final formula embodying that conception on which it may settle down, thought must be making provision for these things. Unless it does so, it will fail to satisfy its own most imperative requirement; for it is an irresistible demand of thought itself that when at last it reaches its ultimate aim and "sees the whole," it shall perceive a veritable unity, not merely correspondences or connections or harmonious relationships. It cannot answer to this demand if it starts from a theory which takes God's intention in the starting of the world-process as having been simply the creation of a humanity for which He would cherish certain hopes and for which He would preserve a changeless love. That still leaves God and man—however closely drawn together by ties of feeling and sympathy—apart in essential life for evermore: it does indeed view the temporal as coming out of the Eternal, but not as falling back, otherwise than figuratively and by the stretch of responsive love or eager desire for moral likeness, into the Eternal again; and thus thought, as it seeks to trace for the entire world-process a road which shall at length bring it back to its starting-point and so settle it down into its home, is left wondering and questioning still. To speak of God as having created the world in order that He might sustain affectionate relations with mankind does not offer any sufficient suggestion as to an underlying *raison d'être* or a final destiny for the world. Emotion, sensibility, the yearning for a strengthening companionship and love, may be satisfied with a formula such as this; and in many of life's most frequent experiences it is as bread to the hungry or as the shadow of a great rock in a weary land. But it does not follow that an idea which seems all-sufficing just when some one particular need has grown clamorous within us or one particular pain is tearing us asunder is really ultimate, though the temptation to take it so is strong. It is as something far deeper and larger than this that God's original intention for the world must be read, if we are to know true mental content and rest. In brief, to think of God's relation to the world as summed up in the terms interest and love, let the significance with which we invest the terms be raised to as high a temperature as they may, is to mistake, or at least to minimize, God's fundamental idea and purpose in regard to the world—and by consequence, to put ourselves at the wrong angle for estimating those restorative ministries which God must perform when once His fundamental idea and purpose have been foiled.

Put in positive instead of negative fashion, it is into some such statement as the following that the matter shapes itself. God's original intention for the world contemplated a development—not merely a *condition,* but a *development*—and, further, a development which should in the end return upon its starting-point in God Himself. Not, indeed, *backward* by the road it came—which would not be development at all; but *forward* by a path bending round and up to make the circle complete. That is, the long process of evolution, projected by God out of Himself with the first creative *fiat,* having emerged at last upon the stage in which man at the same time embodies and controls it, was thenceforth to be continued and concluded by man's actual *movement into God.* (This last phrase should be borne in mind. It is the key-phrase here. For man, *movement* rather than *development* is the word; and through the *movement* of manhood—its movement *of* itself *out of* itself—the *development* of the entire system of things as God ordained it is brought about. This will become clearer presently.) It was to such a movement, and to its issue, that the divine idea looked on. And if we seek to fill in this bare outline, it is not difficult so to do. It involves something over and above more frequent thought, or more constant obedience, or more profound sympathy, passing from man to God. It involves much more even than closer likeness between God and man. These things mean nothing beyond development *within* personality; and for personality *movement*—let it be said again—movement of itself *out of* itself into God, is the key-phrase, the key-idea. The

supreme demand upon man, the demand made upon man because God is what He is and man is what *he* is, was concerned
with more than man's mood, disposition, action, or even character as the word is commonly understood. All these things
would count, of course, but they would count because according
as they were right or wrong they would help or hinder the ascent
into God of the personality, the essential life, which was behind
them all and in which they inhered. But the supreme demand
was that life in man should make a new attachment of itself
to life in God; that the life which was already divine in that it
had come *from* God should become divinely re-made by passing
of its own free choice *to* God, *into* God, once more and, still by
its own free choice, continuous or ever renewed, remaining
there. In brief, man's ultimate destiny would be fulfilled when
he had learnt, and when he lived by, the lesson that his will
was only his to make it God's. For the will carries the whole
man; and the poet's familiar saying really declares that our
personality is only ours to merge it in God's. Of course this does
not mean that we are interpreting God's original purpose as
having pointed to the annihilation of human self-hood. A personality which by its own choice and act drops itself into God
and keeps itself in God is necessarily conscious of itself still; but
it is henceforth conscious of itself as *in God;* and it knows that
it is moment by moment being made by the God-life in which it
is enwrapped. It is all the more, not all the less, itself through
that constant surrender which is now the one calling wherewith
it is called. One must take whatever risk of misunderstanding
may lie in saying that not even the term "goodness" exhausts
God's idea and intention for the world and for man. Not even
goodness, without life's conscious and constant self-derivation
from a consciously-formed and constantly-maintained identification with God—had such a thing been possible—would have
satisfied the divine ideal. Not even a sinless development of
humanity *within humanity's own boundaries,* had such a thing
taken place, would have fulfilled all the demand—though one
must go on, having said this, to say that such a sinless development of humanity would have contained within itself a con-

sciousness that the crown of development lay, not in life developing itself, but in life entering into the eternal life, as it were re-entering it at a different door from the one whence it had long ago emerged, and going out no more. What God wanted was the return of a life-development to its source, His own "planted-out" life coming back to Him again, a progress of character which should at last become something more than a progress *in* character and should lead man outside of and beyond himself to live as from fresh sources in God. Thus—to use phrases employed before—would the whole temporal movement reveal its meaning and secret by returning upon the Source whence it emerged, and thus would the God who projected the world-process out of Himself draw it, or the final fruit of it, back into Himself again, so remaining, through the future eternity as in the past, God all in all.[1]

But then it was, of course, at the end of a long, long journey that the temporal process would attain the goal. And this means —if we vision human history to ourselves as we may dare to think God's will ordained its course, this means that as age succeeded age man would both grasp more firmly the *fact* that it was in God he was to find his life and more completely and steadfastly fix himself in the receptive *attitude* called for if the fact were to be a fact indeed. Slowly the fact would grow clear, as human eyes sought to scan the why and wherefore of things, and human minds struggled to stable ground from out of perplexity's shifting, tossing seas. Here and there, at various points along the embankment of mystery blocking man's range of sight, the embankment would crumble, and little by little lanes of vision would be opened from this world to the other and the higher, until at last, the many narrow lanes of light combining into one broad illuminated road with the heart of things blazing in glory at its end, the God who is the beginning and

---

[1] The Eternal Son as provider of the dynamic whereby this life-movement was from the beginning to be maintained, not merely of a dynamic whereby the life-movement was to be restored after it had been checked, will be spoken of later on. (See Chapter VI, section 4.) The topic is held over in order to avoid complicating the treatment at this stage. The reader is asked to bear in mind that it will be dealt with at the indicated place.

the end of all the worlds would stand clear, offering to make Himself one with man if man were only willing to be one with Him. And parallel with that growing revelation from the side of God would go on a growing concentration from the side of man, concentration turning to consecration, and consecration itself becoming more and more nearly identification, at any rate more and more nearly a passionate desire for it, as time went by: for the clarifying, emphasizing, fulfilling, of that self-identification with God, accepted as the ultimate meaning of things, everything that established itself within man's nature —all his loves and tendencies, instincts and habitudes, qualities and attributes of every order—would harmoniously work; and so little by little man would grow into power to become God's son, and would draw nearer to that final glory wherein his own destiny and God's desire would alike be crowned,—the glory of a life which with every pulse-beat does but fix itself more firmly into God, and in which every thought and every action follows upon and represents some movement of the God-life wherein it is set. Such a historic process, leading to such a goal, was what God contemplated before history began; a process slow, perhaps, as indeed such a process must be if it is to have any moral quality or value, and is to stand for the intensifying of a spiritual consciousness on man's part rather than to be imposed upon man by an arbitrary influence acting from without; but a process sure and straight to its end. A veritable *move-ment* of personality that should at length carry it out of itself into God and hold it there for ever—that, we may say, was the ante-temporal divine intention and idea.

To make the statement complete, it should be added—although the thing is so self-evident as to need no argument —that it was in the interest of God's holiness, and in order that holiness might be the constitutive essence of man's life as it has been from all eternity the constitutive essence of God's own, that this divine intention and idea was entertained in the divine mind and proceeded as operative (so far as God's part in its fulfilment is concerned) from the divine power. It was from a holy God that the creative process emerged: in creation, as in all else, holiness was at the same time the energizing power and the ultimate aim: the life which God sent forth from Himself was to be finite holiness seeking to expand itself more and more into the boundlessness of infinite holiness; and the final return of that life, by voluntary self-surrender, into the life of God was to be a partially-realized potentiality for and yearning after holiness settling itself for holiness' sake back into the holiness which had originally given it birth. But, as has been said, in respect of all this argument is not needed. Mere affirmation, in order that the statement of the case may be formally complete, is all that is required. For God Himself, life *is* holiness: according to God's intention and idea, the life-movement which bore man on its bosom—and which, when man came not only to be carried on it but to control it, was to be returned into God—was to be made in the interest of holiness and for holiness' sake, and, as it had holiness for its origin, was to have holiness and the triumphant glorification of holiness for its goal.

2

With all this in mind, we can form a true conception as to what the world's failure has been, and as to what God's "problem," in respect of the failing world, really is. The world—or rather let us at this stage say humanity—humanity has failed because that life-movement in and through which humanity should have been borne back into God has been checked, and this by humanity's own choice and fault. Man, instead of realizing (and acting on the realization) that life in him fulfils its destiny only as, for its supreme and constant employment, it submits and adjusts itself to the life that is in God, permitting itself to be ceaselessly remade thereby, has preferred to live *as in and from himself*. He has forgotten that his highest fate is not fulfilled by a development *within* himself, but only by carrying the *whole* of himself into God for God to enfold and continuously to re-make by the enfolding. Then, with man living in and from himself rather than in and from God, there have

established themselves within him qualities of character, constituents of his moral make and substance, which are alien to
that God (and to that God's holiness) in and from Whom man
has refused to live, and which, having found entrance because
the God-ward movement has been checked, in their turn bring
upon that movement a still more effectual arrest. And thus, because man has shut out from his purview the end which God
contemplated as final for him—that of using the life which is his
own for the purpose of abandoning it to a life *not* his own—
both the power to recover the vision of that end, at any rate the
power to feel the glory and magnetism of the vision, and the
power to achieve the end itself, have been impaired or lost. And
all this, be it remembered, has become, through heredity and
all the intimate inter-relations of man with man, not a matter
of individuals or majorities, but of the race. In humanity—at
the stage in the long process of divinely-initiated cosmic development at which that process should, through humanity's conscious and deliberate agency, have been turned back upon its
Source—in humanity that process of cosmic development has
suffered suspense. The racial life-movement goes slowly, or goes
not at all, or goes in the wrong direction. That is humanity's
failure. Humanity has not moved out of itself into God; has
not used its selfhood in such wise as to empty itself of all save
what God, through a relation and a communion, voluntarily
entered upon from humanity's side, puts in; has not completed
the cycle and the circle as the eternal design ordained. And
God's "problem," in respect of a humanity which has thus
brought failure upon itself and in a sense upon Him, is to re-
quicken *in* it a new vision of the appointed end and to provide
for it a new possibility and power of achieving the appointed
end; to make humanity, centred as it is upon itself and suffering
all the moral invalidisms, the moral lamenesses, the moral in-
capacities for God-ward movement, which result from that
self-centring, both freshly desirous and freshly able to centre
itself *outside* of itself, in God, again; to bring about, or at least
to make possible, a resumption of the great cosmic march by
bringing about, or at least making possible, a resumption of

human personality's progress out of itself to God, to be held in God for ever. In brief, it is to re-create, or at least to make possible, for humanity a veritable *movement* of racial life whereby that which went forth from God in the earliest creative moment shall, through humanity's self-abandonment to God, come home once more.

The sin of mankind, that is, (taking the matter from another point of view) consists, not merely in isolated actions, not even in a moral condition whose elements are wrongly mixed or into whose substance alien elements have intruded: it is with a much more complicated and wrested situation than even these things would constitute that God has to deal. It is often asserted that one of the greatest needs of our time is a right sense of sin; that for lack of it our estimate of redemption's meaning and value becomes shrunken; and that for lack of it we fail to realize both how incompetent we are to establish our salvation for ourselves and how tremendous a demand our salvation must have made upon even such reserves of love and power as God has at His command. Certainly no faintest attempt to impugn this assertion is made here: on the contrary, the entire line of thought here being pursued requires the assertion to be emphasized tenfold. But the thing may be carried a step further on or back. Perhaps the advent of that profounder sense of sin which we need so much might be hastened if our intellectual conception of sin were corrected and brought up to truer level; for in the nature of things, a moral disaster which only looms small upon the mind is unlikely to sting sharply upon the sensitiveness of the conscience or make strong stir among the emotions of the heart; and it may be to some extent our small *ideas* of sin that make our sorrow and shame for it correspondingly small. It is really no matter for surprise if the average man— conscious as he is that even though he may not be a very white saint, he is not such a very black criminal after all—finds himself unable to weep those scalding tears which are said to be due from him for his sins or to feel such a heartbreak as he is told would in the sheer pain of it be something like commensurate with his faults. He has confessedly done some things which

he ought not to have done and left undone some other things
which he ought to have done; but the whole sum of them runs
into comparatively few figures when all is said. And the spaces
of his inner nature are confessedly tenanted by spirits not native
to heaven, spirits which not infrequently strive against the
better spirits and (the man's own will turning traitorously to
their side) finally prevail; but he cannot feel himself—and
the very existence of the inward strife bears witness that he is
right, since it bears witness that the better spirits as well as the
worse are there—to be *wholly* bad. It is no wonder if his sense
of sin—sin being conceived either with some shallowness as
act, or rather more profoundly as *condition*—remains at the
level of regret instead of rising to the height of soul-agonizing
pain. All that he does and all that he is of evil, taken at its
worst, does not seem to furnish material for such a very damn-
ing indictment; and yet he is called upon to feel as remorseful
as though he had wrecked a world! But the entire intellectual
conception of sin which lies behind all this is inadequate and
poor. Inability to feel a profound and searching sense of sin
results largely from failure to appreciate what sin is, not in
itself but in its ultimate implications and issues and in its effect
upon the eternal order; and if the mental sight pushes itself on
and on toward those further reaches, the sense of sin must
surely grow keener as sight grows clearer, and horror at sin
keep closer company with understanding of sin as this latter
opens out. All those lapses, positive and negative, of which the
sinner has been guilty—all that deterioration of moral quality
and character which he has allowed to creep in—all these
things, over and above what they were in themselves and over
and above the immediate guilt they brought, have marked
points at which the individual life has been checked in its movement out of itself into God or has even fastened itself to initiatives and sources other than God: they have, besides, through
the wrongly-directed impetus remaining from them after they
themselves were past, made the movement of the individual
life out of itself into God more difficult and slow, and must by
constant repetition bring that movement to utter stoppage in

the end; and thus, at the point where God's eternal purpose counted upon that individual sinner for its fulfilment, God's eternal purpose has come upon a blocking of its way. The failure of the one is really much more than the failure of the one. It carries within itself the proportionate failure of the whole; and the individual sinner may well be called upon to be as remorseful as though he had wrecked a world, for this is in effect what he has done, or at least what he has helped to do. For God, my individual failure to be what He wants me to be is part of a failure on a much larger scale, illustrating that larger failure, helping simultaneously both to constitute it and to make its scale larger still. And if the prevalent intellectual conception of sin were widened out along these indicated lines, the prevalent lack of the horror and remorse which sin ought to produce would surely pass away. He would be a hard man indeed who could remain unwrung in heart while realizing in mind that he had called a halt to *all* life's long circling march from its first home in the eternal God to God its last eternal home. It may well be on the recovery of a true *idea* of sin that the recovery of a true *sense* of sin in great measure depends. But however that may be, this *is* sin and sin *is* this. Through sin, the process of cosmic development has at and in humanity suffered suspense, because humanity's *movement of* itself *out of* itself suffers arrest. Through sin, the racial *life-movement* goes slowly, or goes not at all, or goes in the wrong direction. And God's "problem," read in the light of that tremendous fact, is to re-create, or at least to make possible, for humanity a veritable *movement* of racial life whereby that which went forth from God in the earliest creative moment shall, through humanity's self-abandonment to God, come home once more.

3

It is perhaps strange that the ideas which we have hitherto pressed—the idea of God's original purpose for humanity as involving a veritable movement of humanity's life out of itself to fasten itself to new creative sources in God and thus to become something other than it is, the idea of sin as involving that movement's arrest, the idea of redemption as involving that movement's re-start—that these ideas should be so frequently ignored when the doctrine of Atonement is being shaped. For one might well have expected that the dominance of evolutionary conceptions (since evolution is movement) would have turned the minds of men that way; and that under that dominance it would have appeared the natural thing to inquire, "What further change is to happen not merely *within* life, but *to* life? What further change is to happen not merely in the sense of consolidating or improving life *within its present constitution,* but in the sense of making life *in its totality* something different from what it was before, thus not only changing life itself, but pushing a stage higher on and up that entire system of things into which humanity's life has come as the hitherto last term?" One might well have supposed, in short, that the idea of some new stage in evolution, correspondent to such an emergence of new species as natural science speaks of —or correspondent, perhaps it would be better to say, to the initiation of a fresh march in that cosmic advance which philosophy pictures with larger and more daring surmise—would suggest itself as relevant here. And along that line of thought the ideas spoken of above might well have emerged. In point of fact, however, the very dominance of the evolutionary conception seems to have dulled the sense of a necessary movement of personality as a whole into some status quite other than that which it occupies now; and because personality, being what it is, is capable of evolution or growth *within itself,* both philosophic and theological thought have concentrated upon the development and perfecting of personality *as within its present constitution it is known* rather than upon the issue or the producing, from personality as it is known, of a personality unknown as yet.

Strange as this may at first appear, however, perhaps to closer thought it is not so strange. Possibly in the two following points some hint of explanation may be found as to why the evolutionary conception has hindered rather than helped an adequate apprehension of God's original purpose for man and of His "problem" in the salvation of a fallen world.

For one thing, we have become accustomed to apply evolution so largely to the past as to forget (concerning evolution in the larger cosmic sense, evolution not *within* man, but evolution of that entire system whereof man is the crown and climax so far) that evolution's last chapter is unwritten yet. Naturally and properly, the mind's first aim is taken to be the discovery of "the causes of things"; and the very fact that the present stage is the one to which all previous stages yield up their secret gives to the present one a plausible appearance of finality. That it is seed as well as flower is a fact which remains out of sight for those engaged in a busy digging for its ultimate roots planted long ago and a busy examination of the method by which its unfolding has come. The thinker of to-day, as he measures the distance backward and down to see from how low a point the whirling processes of time started and how vast a leap they had to compass before flinging him forth for their product "last and best," is apt to forget that he himself marks but a point which those processes want to pass on their way to produce a still further and loftier total order—albeit, of course, a total order whereof man, the hitherto "last and best," shall be an essential constituent part. The idea of evolution as history is so engrossing that the idea of evolution as prophecy knocks vainly at the mind's door. And we assume, instinctively and without any framing of the assumption in words, that evolution in the cosmic sense ceased to be operative on reaching the point whence, through movements and workings of the human mind, it could look back upon itself.

The other explanatory point is this. It is perhaps natural for us, being what we are, to confuse the conceptions of evolution and of growth; and because we are conscious of growth, or of the possibility of growth, within ourselves, we tend to become engrossed with it, and to view it as actually the last stage of, instead of a sort of parenthesis in, the evolutionary process as a whole. Thus the plausible appearance of finality in the present stage, previously noticed, becomes accentuated from another quarter. Self-conscious growth may easily forget the larger process whereof it forms a part: the fact that there is growth *within ourselves* occupies us so entirely that the idea of a growth *out of ourselves* fails to be suggested or at any rate to grip; and our business is taken as being merely the regulation of that internal self-development which we observe to be going on, the right adjustment of its elements, the preservation of it from deformity and from the intrusion of harmful things. Our conception of evolution loses its cosmic character because we can discern a sort of evolution acting itself out on the narrower and more enclosed stage of our own natures, and become absorbed therein. The processes which, since they begin and end within our own personality, we can watch and trace, make us turn away our thought from that vast evolutionary process in which personality as it is has appeared and in which something new—following upon and born out of personality as it is— ought now to appear. Or, as said before, the conceptions of growth and of evolution are confused. We forget that while growth is development *within* the moral organism (as indeed within any physical organism) evolution is the advance of the organism *to be something else and something higher*. And further, the fact (not to be in any wise denied, but rather to be emphatically and solemnly stressed) that all moral growth *within* personality is a factor in hastening or hindering the loftier evolution of personality—that every successive accentuation or diminution of moral quality, in short every movement in character as commonly understood, enables or disables manhood for that self-attachment to a ceaselessly recreative God which must constitute true evolution's next step upward and on—that fact becomes itself a drag rather than an inspiration. True it certainly is that every increase of good helps, and that every drop down degeneration's steep hinders, man's power of fixing himself in such an attitude as to find his life's source and initiative in God. But the very importance of each immediate moral change tends to keep us down to the conception of self-improvement, to fasten us in all the intensity of our thought and care upon the internal development we can mark and judge rather than upon that ultimate destiny of self-affiliation with God which internal development should assist us to fulfil; and thus, good though our watchfulness may be, the good becomes the enemy of the best. Precisely because an evolution, or a growth which we mistake for and term evolution, within personality can be discerned, and because this is charged with issues so solemn that our responsibility in regard to it may well appear tremendous indeed, do we forget that larger evolution which calls for personality to be—not merely in its internal quality and content, but in its essence, its basis, its constitutive idea, its creative source and spring—something different *in toto* from what it has been.

What it comes to, in the end, is that the evolutionary conception has hindered rather than helped an adequate apprehension of God's original purpose for man and His "problem" in the salvation of a fallen world, not because it has been emphasized too much, but because it has not been emphasized enough—at any rate, has not had its entire significance appreciated and drawn out. Press out the meaning of the evolutionary idea, and you must take it as prophetic as well as historic, that is, as supplying an imperative programme for what is to be as well as writing a descriptive programme of what has been. Press out the meaning of the evolutionary idea, and it takes you on from growth within yourself to a movement of the whole self upon and into a new condition. In other words, in the light of the evolutionary conception we are compelled to affirm that God's original purpose for man looked on to, and that God's remedial work upon a failing and fallen world must newly provide for, a movement of personality as a whole into a status quite other than that which it occupies now, a movement which shall carry it out of itself into God and hold it there, based upon Him, living from and out of Him, using its own life's power only to secure the rush upon and through it of a life not its own, for evermore.

Chapter III

CAN GOD FORGIVE AS MAN FORGIVES?

From the platform which we have now reached we may pass, with prospects of something like an adequate dealing with the matter, to the inquiry, "Cannot God merely ignore sin, if a change of mood and temper on the sinner's part makes it possible for Him so to do? Cannot God close the matter by simply forgiving as man forgives?" Some hint has already been given as to the point at which the superficially plausible suggestion breaks down; but the hint is worth somewhat more extended treatment. Plausible, undoubtedly, the suggestion is. But will it hold, when God's relations with a world gone astray are rightly viewed?

I

Let us recall the points already set down. God's original intention for man, we have seen, was that humanity's development should be something more than a sinless development *within humanity's own boundaries*—that it should rather be a development of humanity *out of itself,* causing humanity at length to abandon itself to a life not its own and to live, not from or by itself, but from and by God. Humanity has failed because that life-movement in and through which humanity should have been borne back into God has been checked—and this by humanity's own choice and fault. Through sin, the racial life-movement goes slowly, or goes not at all, or goes in wrong directions. And God's "problem," read in the light of that tremendous fact, is to recreate, or at least to make possible, for humanity a veritable movement of racial life whereby that which went forth from God in the earliest creative moment

38

shall, through humanity's self-abandonment to God, come home
once more. Humanity must somehow be made to move out of
itself into God, so that its life shall henceforth (as was from
the first intended) find its constant initiative in Him.

If these points be really grasped and accepted as valid, the
question whether God can meet the "problem" of redeeming
the world by forgiving as man forgives receives almost at
once an obvious reply, the reply being indeed suggested by the
very statement of the case. For clearly, a *movement,* retarded
or stopped or sent in a direction the reverse of the true, can
only be quickened or re-started or corrected by a veritable
dynamic, by the application to the impaired condition of an
actual *force.* Mere forgiveness, therefore, is immediately ruled
out as insufficient for the task which has to be performed. You
cannot, by gracious words or by sympathetic suggestions or by
the changing of frowns to smiles, set right a moral condition
which has wholly or partially lost the power of carrying itself
in a real development along its true and destined line. It is much
as though one should seek by smiling upon it to move an engine
whose fires have gone out. Yet something like this is in effect
all that forgiveness, if it stands alone, can offer. You cannot
impart a push or a pull to an arrested process by a transformation of the look with which you survey it. Yet this is in effect the
possibility which the idea of redemption by mere forgiveness
assumes.

All human analogies fail us here because they envisage a
situation entirely different from that with which, in dealing with
the relations between God and a sinful world, we are concerned.
Between man and man mere pardon may be enough. It is not
always so, as we shall presently see; but for the moment let the
statement pass. When a fellow-man transgresses against me or
I against a fellow-man, it is in very many instances simply an
isolated and local incident that is in question, and moreover, an
incident implying no more than a disturbance of *static* relationships. To deal with it is merely a matter of setting right the
immediate and local effect of an isolated action on one man's
part. My brother and I have fallen away from that right mutual

association (chiefly, of course, one of sympathy and love) which ought to subsist in order that we may both alike perform our part in the large and long process whereby humanity climbs into its true relation with God; and all that is required, as between myself and him, is that the broken or impaired relationship shall be restored. Between individuals there is involved no question of a movement and a goal: it is a question of re-establishing an equilibrium which has been shattered. Supposing the other to be the offender, he, by the injury done to me, has snapped a link from the chain of sympathy and affection which should have bound us: I, by any resentment I may have felt, have similarly snapped a link from my section of the chain. If now, by his repentance and my forgiveness, the severed links are re-united and the chain re-made complete, the former situation is restored and—as between the offender and myself—all is well. He and I are two constituent elements in a process whose beginning is far behind us, whose final result is far ahead, and whose ultimate issue depends in part on the maintenance of the appointed association between myself and him. At our reconciliation we take our places again as fitly framed together to fulfil our part in the mighty scheme. But in all this, ultimates —the ultimate issues of our temporary alienation as they touch the eternal order of things—have not been approached. Not the ultimate for the offender; for by his wrong-doing he has done something to himself as well as to me, and through himself to God. By whatever degree of moral and spiritual inferiority, in comparison with what he was before, he has brought upon himself, he has retarded, and created a possibility of further retarding, the God-ward sweep of humanity so far as it was intended to be carried along its path in and through him. Not the ultimate for me; for by my spirit of alienation, to whatever extent it has mastered me, I have done the same— have laid a detaining hand on the great advance and impaired my own power of keeping my place in the ranks. These ultimates have not, in my offer of pardon to the wrong-doer or in his acceptance of it, come into the reckoning at all. Nor is it necessary that they should. I have neither the direct responsibility

nor the power for dealing with them in the case of the wrong-
doer, nor he for dealing with them in mine. It is from sources
beyond either and both of us that the dealing with them must
come. All that is required, so far as our mutual relations are
concerned, is that we should be as we were before—that those
relations should once more become consonant with the place we
occupy in the great process which includes and involves us
both; and the bringing about of this re-established *status* is all
(though it is enough for its purpose) that forgiveness can do.

But between God and man the question stands quite differently. Here it is not merely (to repeat a phrase employed just
now) a matter of setting right the local and immediate effect of
an isolated act on man's part. God has to deal not only with sins
taken as it were one by one, and to blot out their stain in turn
from the pages whereon the history of the world is being inscribed. God's dealing has to be not so much with sins as with
the sinfulness which is altering the world's whole historic
course; or, to put it another way, not with the isolated acts of
sin which any particular man commits, but with the whole man
himself and with the sinfulness in him out of which the isolated
acts successively emerge. One may take it higher, and say that
God's dealing has to be, not only even with the sinfulness spoiling the whole man, but with the sinfulness spoiling the whole
race. And higher still one may and must take it, and affirm that
God's dealing has to be with the sinfulness spoiling the spiritual
movement of the whole race. Such dealing cannot be carried
through by the simple erasure of the immediate sin which is all
that mere forgiveness has to offer, by the erasure repeated and
repeated a million times to blot out a million sins. We are faced
with ultimates here. Forgiveness from God to man could only
do what is done by forgiveness from man to man—make things
once again, so far as *static* relations are concerned, just what
they were. There is no solution for God's "problem" of redemption along that line. In fact, it may be justly said that mere
erasure of sin in this high sphere would leave things worse than
they were before, since while it would sweep the *local* consequences of the immediate sin away (that is, in the sense previ-

ously indicated), the sinfulness out of which the immediate sin was born would remain in undisturbed possession of its seat, able to exercise an added dynamic power because with every exercise of that power it increases that power's reserves. To meet God's "problem," God must provide a new counter-dynamic to clash against and conquer and supersede the dynamic of sin which has gained so dominating an empire over the moral and spiritual movement of the world; and by simple forgive-ness no such dynamic can be supplied. To make across isolated acts of transgression some magic passes of pardon which bring the local and immediate relation between God and man back to its previous condition of sympathetic mutual kindliness, but which find that in that achievement they are brought up against the utmost limits of their power, is not to redeem.

2

Some cases there are, however, even as between man and man, in which simple pardon cannot suffice to eradicate the confusion wrought by wrong-doing and to send forth the wrong-doer, with the accusing slate wiped clean, free from further process. And since these cases indicate situations which ap-proach, however distantly, to the situation subsisting between man and God, they will repay a closer glance. Between one individual man and another forgiveness may be enough. But between man and *society* it is, by common consent, felt to be wholly insufficient. So deep does the feeling go that permission to pardon is, in the case of a crime against the social order, actually refused to the person most immediately concerned; and condonation by forgiveness is itself a punishable offence. Nor can an offence against the law, against social order, be merely blotted out of the record by the gracious waving of a flag of pardon on the judge's part and a promise on the offender's part that, if thus pardoned, he will not transgress again. Here, if we have not yet reached to dealing with veritable ultimates, we have reached at any rate to something more comprehensive than the relations between an individual and his fellow-men;

indeed it *is* an ultimate within the restricted field immediately under its survey. Of course, this ultimate, or quasi-ultimate, is itself a subordinate matter as regards the ultimate which is final and supreme; but it is nevertheless what it has just been termed. Or one may put it that the transgressor against law and the law he has broken constitute two intermediate ultimates bracketed together between the all-including ultimates of humanity and God. The effect upon the social order, the necessity of keeping every movement of its constituents on lines true and safe and advantageous for the community as a whole, have now to be faced. Here—in this wrong-doer's evil act—is the sign of a force at work in society capable sooner or later of impairing that health of the social system which must at all costs be preserved. That force of sinister threatening must at the very least be rendered harmless, or an effort must at the very least be made to render it so; and better still, of course, if a counter-force can be set in its place—better still, that is, if the law's dealing with the wrong-doer can be made not only deterrent, but reformatory as well. Once again, we come upon a *movement* and a *goal* and the regulation of the relationship between the two; and though we find the problem here to be on a much smaller scale than the one involved in God's "problem" of the redemption of the world, society's "problem," too, may be stated in the phrases just set down. And because the problem is of this order, it is recognized with practical unanimity that mere pardon is no solution for it at all. Did the law, having given needed admonition, follow this up by simply bidding the offender go free, nothing would have been done to damp down the dynamic influence of evil or to buttress the dynamic influence of good. Forgiveness, operating alone, would be like shutting one's eyes and pretending that because one cannot see an undesirable reality it is not there; and the law, with the ultimate on the social field in its charge, ordained to assist the forces that assist and to check the forces that retard the collective movement toward that ultimate, would but stultify itself did it so discharge, or rather parody, its appointed task.

Still more significant is it that precisely in proportion as we have actual direct personal responsibility for any one's moral and spiritual welfare does it become impossible to cancel a transgressor's account by writing "pardoned" in its margin and then permitting the matter to slide. The relations between members of a family and its head (to take one of the most obvious examples) cannot be so lightly ruled. A father on whom the sense of parental duty lies with adequate weight knows that he dare not, when his child has offended, always or often content himself with saying "I forgive." There may indeed be occasions when he considers that such mildness of medicine is all that the ill requires: the wrong may have been committed largely through ignorance; or the child may be, to the father's knowledge, of a conscience so sensitive that even the slight reproof implied in forgiveness can be relied upon to have permanent effect; or the wrong may be so trivial, and may stand as a sudden solitary breakdown at the end of such a long series of consistently praiseworthy deeds that whatever blackness lies upon it is relieved by the colours wherewith its contrasted antecedents tone down its ugly hue. But though a rare and slight transgression may be thus dealt with, the parent who takes his parenthood for a solemn trust cannot, when wrongs are repeated or when the act performed points to deep-seated flaws of character, be any longer so easily content. He must somehow bring a *counter-force* to bear upon—and if possible to continue working within—his child with a view to setting the *movement* of the child's character on a worthier track. The question of an actual formative or reformative discipline has from one angle or another to be faced. Perhaps by the infliction of penalty, perhaps by making it possible and compulsory for the offender to set himself under some influence which may act as a re-moulding power among the constituents of his inner self, perhaps by these and other things combined, but at any rate by some moral and spiritual medicine or surgery which will set the diseases and malformations of the child's inner nature right—thus and only thus will the parent who realizes the greatness of his charge feel himself cleared in the court of conscience from faithlessness to what the great charge demands. The basal fact of the position is that the parent stands, and knows himself to stand, as representative of the "ultimate" toward his child; the call of the moral and spiritual goal whereto his child should be stepping makes itself heard through him and will beat faintly or clearly on the child's hearing as he himself makes the echoes faint or clear; and he has to shape his treatment of delinquency as befits the representative character he bears. Till the child can see clearly enough and far enough to discern the "ultimate" with his own eyes, the parent, as the "ultimate's" high priest or ambassador endowed with plenary powers, must report his own vision of it and his own translation of its orders, and this in authoritative tones. Till the child can receive the influences of the "ultimate" at first-hand and submit himself to them without any intermediary to expound their nature and their aims, the parent must act on their behalf—disentangle them for the child's apprehension from influences whose origin lies elsewhere, focus their rays with as little refraction as may be upon the child's sensitive but more or less wayward soul, enforce their rights. And because, if he is faithful, he will so construe the obligations of his parental office, he cannot, when wrong-doing has come between himself as representative of the "ultimate" and the child whom through him the "ultimate" claims for its own, merely dismiss the wrong from the field with the simple phrase "It is forgiven." So far as the parent himself is only *personally* concerned, he might be satisfied with that— might indeed rejoice over so facile a wiping out of the score. But his trust imperatively forbids.

In the end therefore we are brought to this conclusion. The suggestion that God, in His dealing with sin, needs only to forgive as man forgives, breaks down in two vital ways. In cases where man does content himself with a mere dismissal of wrong, the situation is so utterly different from that prevailing between man and God that the inference from an easy pardon by man to an equally easy pardon by God is wholly irrelevant —has in fact no *locus standi* and can claim no right to be heard. And in cases where the situation does make some far-off approach to that holding between man and God, in these even

man does *not* deem simple pardon an adequate clearing up of
the confusion which wrong has produced; and once again the
inference fails, vitiated this time at its very base. In the first
set of cases, the analogy on which the suggestion is supposedly
founded does not exist: in the second, such analogy as does exist
proceeds, once it is put in the witness-box, to give evidence
against, rather than for, the very suggestion in whose interests
it was called. For whenever "ultimates" enter into the question,
whenever the question is one, not merely of restoring a *status
quo* which has lapsed, but of guiding or re-creating a moral and
spiritual *movement,* forgiveness is not enough. Then the demand for a veritable dynamic must be faced.

3

It may be asserted, however, as a final plea in favour of the
suggestion that God has but to forgive as man forgives, that
there *is* an actual dynamic in forgiveness, and that this dynamic
power has often been proved. We are constantly being referred
to cases wherein an offender has been so wrought upon by a
graciously-tendered pardon that the memory and inspiration
of it has afterwards prevented any repetition of his sin, and to
other cases, even more striking, wherein a character hitherto
irreclaimable from evil's grip has been to all appearance utterly
transformed by a kindness which under utmost stress of provo-
cation has refused to let itself be broken down into austerer
mood. In cases such as these, it is insisted, forgiveness has
become as a lode-star to keep the formerly erring bark on the
straight course—shall not God's forgiveness achieve a miracle
equally great? Pardon from man to man *does* frequently thus
act as a driving force in character—should not pardon from
God to man act in similar ways? Why, when flowing from a
different source, should the magic fail?

That such cases as those alleged do actually exist is not to be
denied. But the citation of them will not carry us far towards
the inference they are supposed to justify, even though we make
the unverifiable and surely grotesque assumption that the

change wrought by the dynamic of forgiveness is in these instances the equivalent of salvation in the full sense of the word. It must be remembered as a first point that before reliable inferences can be drawn in a matter like this the field whence the premises are gathered must be mapped out with ample breadth. And the careful observer on a sufficiently wide field finds that, even while he is setting down the cases alluded to one by one, his mind is simultaneously setting down another column of quite contrasted cases; and however high the total in the first column may grow, the total in the second at least keeps pace with it, nay, outstrips it before long. In the end, we have to admit that only for exceptional souls does mere forgiveness possess any appreciable dynamic power; and we cannot argue from what *may* happen in our dealing with exceptional souls to what *must* happen in God's dealings with the entire family of men. Put at the highest, the whole thing comes to no more than this, that there is a possibility, strong or weak according to the observer's estimate, of some dynamic influence emerging from the proffer of a pardon which is merely pardon and nothing more. Could God (one asks reverently but emphatically) be satisfied with the creation of such a bare possibility when He sets Himself to redeem a world? One remembers how many things, even within a single observer's range of vision and experience, impair or destroy the dynamic which forgiveness is said to provide; how for natures wherein evil is master any effect which forgiveness produces often proves to be but as the morning cloud and as the dew that passes early away; how, equally often, the proffered forgiveness finds such natures ironclad against it and, producing no effect at all, beats, futile as rain-drops against armour, upon the mail of obstinacy and contempt they wear. One remembers these things; and remembering them, one cannot credit mere pardon with possessing sufficient dynamic for God's restoration of man. The whole thing is on the human plane something in the way of an experiment which fails more often than it succeeds. And for that matter, it is not difficult to see why it must be so. For if we look more closely, we soon perceive that the dynamic supposedly resident in forgiveness is not in the fullest sense a dynamic at all; and to credit forgiveness with dynamic is really to put the term to very restricted, not to say semi-metaphorical, use. The dynamic of *influence* and *persuasion* is certainly there—and real enough so far as it goes. But there is nothing more than that; and this is "dynamic" only in a most limited degree. Influence and persuasion can touch a soul as it were from outside and may, if successful, penetrate far enough within it to waken dormant powers there and make them put themselves forth with greater strength; but to put *new* powers within the soul is beyond their reach. More than the dynamic of influence and persuasion forgiveness cannot provide. Could God satisfy Himself—satisfy either His authority or His grace—by adopting as His method of meeting the "problem" of redemption an experiment so uncertain in its issues? And could such a method of dealing with it have accomplished the half or the quarter of Christianity's proved results if there had been nothing more than an offer of pardon at work to set sin-ridden souls free from their slavery and to turn love of evil into passionate love of good? Can it be that to mere free forgiveness, which fails so sadly often in our range of experience, all this is due? To answer "yes" assuredly puts on credulity a strain it cannot bear. There must have been more than a mere forgiveness at work behind it all to account for these saints and martyrs, for these souls raised out of the horrible pit and the miry clay, for these Christian philanthropies, for all these moral and spiritual miracles that stud the over-arching sky of the centuries like myriads of scintillating stars. The suggested cause is so ludicrously inadequate to the admitted effect! But apart from this historical point, and going back to the inquiry whether God would be satisfied with bringing the dynamic of mere pardon to bear upon man, since it is a dynamic which fails so often, one may give yet another reply. One could believe that God would be so satisfied only if one believed also that in doing this God were exhausting all that even He could do. It is true, certainly, that even God's utmost output of redemptive agency may in the end fail against man's refusals: whatever interpretation we may take of the salvation which God has wrought out and offered in Christ, we have to admit that men have steeled themselves and may steel themselves still against its power. But one asks again, Could such a God as the God of the Christian faith be satisfied unless He had done for the world's redemption *all* that is in His power to do? The negative answer leaps immediately and decisively to one's lips. If it be possible for God to provide a "dynamic" in the full sense of the word—to fling among the evil forces which have usurped sway in human nature to its undoing a *counter-force* strong enough to annihilate their malevolent rule and to seat itself upon the recovered throne, and moreover a counter-stroke beyond all risk of failure if only it be accepted and allowed to do its work—then, we may reverently say, this is a thing which God *must* do. And to a God for Whom all things are possible save a denial of Himself, this is surely a possible thing. Let it be admitted that forgiveness from man to man sometimes reveals some measure of dynamic power. But the dynamic, because it is no more than a dynamic of influence and persuasion when all is said, is not enough to constitute the redemptive ministry and method of a God like the God we know.

One other consideration may be called up in reinforcement of what has been already adduced on this chapter's theme. When the mere gift of pardon for an offence works any measure of reformation upon the offender, it does so only because both the offended individual in offering the pardon and the offender in receiving it realize (more or less subconsciously, it may be, but none the less certainly) that the transaction has been as it were an *interim* one, and has been intended to help the offender back into touch with a greater dynamic than the gift of pardon itself can exert. If I in any real sense pardon one who has injured me—if I forgive him in any fashion that implies something more than a heedless waving off of his injury as a matter of no account—I in effect say to him, "I surrender whatever right I might claim to deal with offence or offender, and leave the issue of the whole thing to God's working upon you and to whatever response you may make. It is to Him, not to me, that you are

to look for an authoritative and effective dealing with the case."
Only if that impression is made by my offer of an act of oblivion,
and only if the offer is thus accepted, can there be any dynamic
in the offer at all. If the man who has injured me shows in the
after-time that my pardon has wrought some good work in
him, it can be only because he has caught that undertone in its
voice and has permitted the stronger power to which it has
referred him to perform something of its will. But if, when I
utter the word of pardon, I merely mean "It doesn't matter,"
or if the offender interprets it in that sense, pardon can have
no moral or spiritual effect at all. To this statement, surely,
experience cries out a loud assent. The pardon heedlessly proffered and heedlessly received can be but a mere breath upon
the offender's hardness, passing away almost in the moment of
its stirring and leaving scarce a memory of its passing behind.
Lightly come, it goes as lightly. Pardon has a measure of dynamic sometimes. Granted. But its dynamic only comes into
play in proportion as it flings the transgressor under a dynamic
mightier than its own, and in proportion as the transgressor
takes it so. It is in this, at the last resort, that the real dynamic
of pardon consists—in this transference of the wrong-doer to
an influence *not resident in the pardon itself*. We know, when
within our experience we have extended forgiveness to one who
has transgressed against us and any real moral change has been
wrought in him, that our forgiveness has done nothing more
than open a door through which he has passed into a sphere
where something over and above our forgiveness has taken up
the case. If this be so, then pardon from man to man, so far
from suggesting that pardon exhausts God's programme in
dealing with a sinner or his sinfulness, suggests precisely the
reverse. It is only against a larger background, wherein something more than pardon is discerned as being at work, that
pardon between man and man avails with any dynamic power.
If pardon from man to man has dynamic, the fact, when under
close scrutiny its implications are drawn forth, does but testify
to the necessity and reality of a dynamic greater still.

It is scarcely necessary to say—and yet, lest some under-current of doubt should stir in any reader's mind, perhaps it had better be said—that in all this there is no implied denial of the truth that God *does* pardon. Always, through the years of man's growing knowledge of God, He came to be more and more clearly seen as a God long-suffering and of tender mercy, abundant in compassion, ready to forgive; and that common-place of both Old and New Testaments remains and must re-main a commonplace of all thought upon the theme to-day. The contention is limited to this—that forgiveness in the human understanding and practice of it does not *exhaust* God's treat-ment of the sin of the world. What forgiveness, as from God to man, really means and involves will be considered at a later stage.

CHAPTER IV

THE LIFE-DYNAMIC IN CHRIST

We pass now from the formulation of God's "problem" in redemption, the topic which has hitherto occupied us, to His actual dealing with that problem in Christ. We pass, in other words, from the platform of more or less general considerations to that of historic fact; for it is—by common consent of at any rate all within the Christian boundaries—in Christ that God's solution of the "problem" has been given. We turn accordingly to the facts of Christ's ministry, inquiring how in that ministry, particularly (though this is an anticipation of what will be the more special subject of the next chapter) in the Cross and Resurrection which closed and crowned it, the new dynamic, which was to carry the life-movement of humanity onward and upward till humanity lost itself and yet found itself in God, came upon the world.

I

That Christ felt Himself to have brought such a dynamic is a fact which seizes more and more powerfully upon those who with sensitive attention read the records of His life. One realizes with ever-growing intensity and conviction, as scene after scene unfolds the story, that in all His dealing with individual cases Christ knew Himself to be at grips with a problem whereof the individual case was but an instance and a type; and the distress or sin of each soul He touched to heal or save was the embodiment of a power which was to be expelled, not only from that particular soul, but from its place in the process and progress and governance of the world as a whole. It was the usurpation of a cosmic force that Christ came to challenge and defeat. Necessarily, it was by treatment of individual men and women that in the first place—at any rate in the first place so far as human apprehension of enacted facts is concerned— the challenge had to be made and the victory won; but through the entire series of separate and special ministries the larger issue loomed up in Christ's consciousness as the background against which the issue of the immediate hour was fought out. The sinning and sin-sick soul was itself a prey, snatched and held and used by a sinister world-force for its own sinister pur- pose; and in the very act of dealing with the sinning and sin-sick soul Christ as it were reached over and beyond it to the tyran- nous power behind. Nay, one may go further. Merely by being what He was, and by being present on the historic stage, Christ threw down the challenge of a new cosmic force (yet of the primary and legitimate cosmic force whose function had been unlawfully usurped) before the cosmic force which was driving the world's life astray. There was that in Him, in the very essence of His life and Personality, which constituted a cease- less assertion of power against power—not merely of truth against falsehood, of ideals against degradation, but of *power* against *power*—on the cosmic field. It comes to seem not too high a flight of fancy, but a sober reading of fact, to say that there was always going forth from Him, even when no human eye perceived any sign of the struggle, a thrust against and an attack upon the battalions of the wrong marshalled behind and beyond the visible scene. His very being, His essential self-hood, was an offensive against sin, though no concrete manifestation of sin was at the moment being enacted on the human stage before Him. This high drama of spiritual battle went on, not only when in one episode or another it appeared on some plat- form within the sight of men, but also—perhaps most of all— when Christ was alone.

Admittedly, it is rather from the general impression made upon an open-minded reader of the Gospel accounts than from definite texts that all this is drawn. Yet there are recorded utterances enough of Christ's which, if scanned deeply enough, and still more if taken in combination, suggest it; and not a few which, if one goes back to them after the general impression has stamped itself upon the mind, seal and counter-sign the impression itself. The very directness and insistence with which Christ makes Himself the central figure of His mission implies a consciousness of being in the most intimate and literal sense at war with malignant powers; for that His mission was avowedly a revolutionary one, designed to correct and transform the existing order of things, is a fact lying so obviously on the surface that it can be questioned by none; and if it is His own Personality that He stresses as the source of the revolutionary change, this can only mean a claim that there resided in Him and issued from Him another power whereby the revolutionary change was to be wrought out and the malignant powers deposed. His person had, in Martensen's phrase, a "metaphysical and cosmical significance"; and that constant self-assertion of His, of which the greatest wonder is that one does not find it wonderful, shows that He Himself took it so. And if we seek for actual utterances to serve as sign-posts pointing along the same road, the search need not be long; nor will it yield scant results, though here one or two examples of what awaits the seeker will suffice. When the seventy disciples, returning from the heralds' journey on which He had sent them, joyfully announced that even the demons had become subject to them in His name, His mind leaped at once beyond their special and localized conflicts against evil to that larger conflict of His own within which theirs were so to say bracketed and which theirs as it were rehearsed, and said "I beheld Satan like lightning fall from heaven." When He declared that all things had been delivered to Him by His Father, the very sound of the words had in it the ring of a royal claim to be made good against a rival assertion of royal right. That He spoke of His "kingdom" as the aim of His mission—of His own kingdom, a kingdom wherein He was Himself to reign as sovereign, not merely a kingdom whose architect or builder He was to be—is again, in view of the fact that the world as it lay before His eyes was subject to evil's tyranny, an unmistakable proclamation of power matching itself against hostile power. But it is

unnecessary to multiply texts. The catena of them can be found
in many books that deal with Christ's self-expression, with the
majesty of the phrases wherein He embodied His claims, with
the calm assertions of lordship He made. All these utterances,
read in the light of the fact that they were put forth in face of
a world fallen prone beneath a far different rule, reveal that
Christ knew Himself to be the *de jure* Sovereign challenging
to mortal combat the *de facto* king. And, to come back to what
was previously said of the general impression made by the
whole of Christ's recorded life, one may well be content—
leaving texts to play a subordinate part, or using them chiefly
to endorse the verdict in which the general impression is embodied—that upon this general impression the matter shall be
based. From all that Christ said and did, from His preaching
and from His miracles, from His proclamations and from His
silences, from the very atmosphere which enfolded Him and in
which He lived and moved and had His being, Christ emerges
upon our vision as consciously holding within Himself the
power whereby the power in possession was to be overthrown.
In the long and large view, He had come to bring peace, true;
but He had a baptism of conflict to be baptized with ere, stepping forth from its swirling waters, He could hold out the gift
of peace in His triumphant hands; and until His enemies had
been made His footstool, He was to be the Christ militant,
bringing not peace but a sword. In Him the new dynamic came
to the world, to wrestle with and expel and supplant the dynamic
whereby the world had hitherto been drawn or driven; and this
dynamic, once its battle was over and its victory won, was to
turn the life-movement of humanity God-ward again.

Nor was it within the limits of Christ's earthly life that the
conflict was to be confined. Far beyond those limits He foresees
the war carried; and always with Himself still as the protag-
onist on the side of the new order, and with Himself as the
victor who deals the final stroke. The fight of the new dynamic
against the old was to be for all time under His personal charge.
He enters the world's life not to make a passing visit and then
to go, but to grasp the historic movement and to keep it in His

grasp; or if He disappears under the temporarily engulfing shadows of the Cross, He does so only to return and to abide. Of His death He spoke, but of the resurrection that was to follow it too; and of this last, not so much as of an evidential miracle as of a passage through which He passed from one phase to another in a course uninterrupted by what had seemed so sadly to cut it short. If for a moment death was to rend from Him His kingly robes and shut Him fast within its prison-doors, He would, almost while that door was closing, win free through another door whereof He held the key, and emerge yet more royally robed, a King whose throne and sceptre were established for evermore. Through many of His utterances—through many of them even for a superficial reader, and through many more for any reader who digs beneath the first layer of sugges- tion—there rings the assurance that with His entrance on the scene all the past is done with and a new and lasting chapter opened which all the future is to carry on and complete under His own supreme authority. But here again, though texts in abundant measure can be found, it is the cumulative impression of the record that tells. Christ's glance sweeps on to some great consummation of all things, and over this He presides; and meanwhile He is there, central and regnant in the midst of the entire historic process till the panorama of the ages closes down. His earthly life was no interlude. He did not come merely to lay down a policy, to plan a campaign, to supply arms for soldiers enlisted in His cause, to win the first tremendous clash and leave those whom He inspired to go on from victory unto victory. From first to last the battle would be His own. One may venture to put it that Christ saw Himself through all the looming ages, as surely as when on the high mountain of temptation He bade Satan go hence, engaged in single combat with the spirit which had enslaved and was devastating the world. It was in Him that the new dynamic had landed on the shores of time: it was in Him and through Him that the new dynamic was to be opera- tive till time should be no more.

2

What then is the new dynamic which Christ brings to help forward man's life-movement toward and into God?

He brings the veritable creative life of God himself, afresh and from a new direction, to the plane and into the range of man; and His mission is to be the Creator and Sustainer of a new manhood, first for every individual and ultimately for the race. The new dynamic is the *creative* life (the italicized word is crucial) of Christ Himself, giving birth out of Himself to a new life for man which is to supplant the life man possesses and to re-make man through the whole range of what he is. In so far as man allows this creative power to recreate him and to maintain the newly-created life in him, the dynamic accomplishes its destined work, and God's plan for mankind recovers its lost sovereignty once more.

It may be said that this is in one form or another a commonplace. So far as mere word-practice is concerned, it may be; but it is questionable whether the conception of the actual *creative* power of Christ is not sublimated in ordinary usage till its essence dissolves in vapour. Christ is not the supreme Reformer of human nature or of the soul. He is not the physician who heals this and that infected patch by medicines made up to sounder formulae than those which other physicians have prescribed. He is not the re-builder of waste places, using the old foundations and the old materials so far as possible and supplying satisfactory substitutes for the corroded timbers and the storm-worn stones. Of course we may employ all these terms, draw all these parallels and many others, and may do so quite legitimately, so long as we recollect that they fall far short of the mark and that Christ is all these things and does all they imply only because He is and does much more. "Life" must be taken—as Christ Himself took it in much that He said and in all that He implied—for the key-word of Christ's mission; and if it be so taken, it is obvious at once that all the suggested parallels are but pale shadows cast by the full-orbed truth. Not even miniatures of the complete idea can they properly be called; for a miniature may reproduce all the features of a large-scale portrait within the circle of its tiny disc; while these parallels or analogies omit the most essential trait. To give life means, not reform or repair, but creation; and creation is the prerogative of God alone. In Christ therefore the very creative life of God steps forth on the human platform to create a new manhood which, by man's appropriation of it, is to be substituted for the old. In and through His Son, God creates, actually *creates,* and thereafter by ceaseless emerging of His life-giving power sustains, a new life, which means a new manhood and a new nature, for man's taking; just as it was in and through His Son (though this particular theological reference needs at the moment no more than a side-glance) that He created the world, with the earlier manhood, then unspoilt, as the supreme issue of the creative work. Christ, in His ministry, comes to repeat the act which God put forth when He made man long ago. Christ's work is to re-make man in His own image—if one may dare the high expression, out of His own substance; and this means, if one may venture more daringly yet, in God's image and out of God's substance, since Christ's creative life and power are God's. We may put it that Christ came to create and to maintain a new *personality,* first in each individual man and then, by ceaseless repetitions of that same re-creative act, in the entire family of mankind—a personality in which nothing of the former constituents of personality shall be left except the will whereby the old personality attaches itself for its own self-loss to the new, and in which even this final remnant of the old personality becomes gradually so penetrated by the re-creative power flowing from Christ that it in its turn becomes Christ's own. Christ's work in man's redemption—which means the restoration of man's life-movement God-ward, and by implication, speaking cosmically, the restoration of the whole world's life-movement to its originally-ordained track—is to transmit perpetually to man the life of God Himself in such wise that the newly-created life shall spread from centre to circumference of degenerate manhood till all the former things in that degenerate manhood have passed away and all things have become new, till Christ is all and in all, and till it is no longer man that lives but God through Christ that lives in him.

Emphasis must however be laid on one or two phrases already used, in order that the entire conception may be grasped and held. Christ came, it has been said, to be the Creator and *Sustainer* of a new manhood; and it was His appointed mission, it has been said, to impart and *to keep in being,* out of His own unfailing resources, a new humanity on the cosmic and historic stage. The conception of Christ as Life-giver is not adequately framed unless it be taken as involving the continuity and permanence of Christ's creative ministry in each individual man. This, moreover, goes further than the elementary truism that because the first work of re-creation is yet incomplete Christ's work in mankind is not yet wrought out to its end. *That* continuity of His life-giving ministry is a necessity obvious enough, for where in human history can one find an example of a human life so entirely abandoned to the influence of Christ's re-creative life that the old has been irrecoverably swallowed up in the new? It would perhaps be an arrogant stretch of boldness to affirm categorically that no such life has ever been; for the affirmation would imply a knowledge of men, from the highest to the least, through all ranks and classes, through countless nations and peoples and tongues, to which no one can lay claim. But it is a safe assertion that none such reveal themselves on the stretches of road which history's glance can scan. According to universal experience and confession, from Paul onwards, the need for continuity of Christ's *re-creative* ministry is obvious enough, since out of Christ's re-creative life not even the Christliest of His disciples are as yet wholly re-born. But the conception of Christ as the Sustainer of a new manhood goes further and deeper than that. It was not only His *re-creative* ministry that was to be maintained while the ages passed on, but His *creative* ministry too: were the re-creative ministry carried through to perfection in any individual man, Christ's creative life was to be still, in that same man, the source whence moment by moment the new life continued to flow in. The

Christ who by His self-communication was to *re-make* man was thereafter, by that same self-communication, to continue the *making* of man by a series of acts *ejusdem generis,* even when once the re-making should be done. The ultimate programme was not that Christ should, by a supreme miracle enacted once for all, pour into humanity so abundant a baptism of new life that humanity would thenceforward possess within itself a reservoir from which, fearless of any return of drought, it could confidently continue to draw: it was rather that Christ was to be Himself the fountain out of which the never-failing waters should spring. What Christ did in His re-creative ministry, however long that might be in reaching its consummation, was to be no provisional act, destined to fill a gap till man had passed from an impaired to a fully repaired condition, and to be suspended then: it was rather, though certainly an act performed under hindrances and limited by barriers of human reluctance and resistance against which the perfect exercise of its power was checked, to be nevertheless an act prophetic of its own continuance and enlargement when the barriers should have been broken down. The new dynamic was to be the very throb and thrill of Christ's own life controlling, or rather enveloping and energizing in, humanity's life-movement at every forward step. And the new dynamic would be doing its perfect work only when humanity, having by an initial act of will attached itself to Christ for its *re-making,* and with that re-making perfected at last, should by an unintermitted exercise of will keep itself moment by moment in that same Christ-ward attachment for its ever-renewed *making,* and when it should thus be out of Christ's creative life that humanity was being ceaselessly re-born.

All this, it must be admitted, is an attempt to say the unsayable. The conception of the re-creative and perpetually creative Christ lies in a region so lofty that human speech falters and faints into helplessness when it tries to compress the conception, without impairing the transcendent and unique grandeur of it, within its own too narrow bounds.

The word that climbs the nighest to seizure of the Highest
  Falls down torn-winged from its soaring, trembles back a dying prayer.

Nor does metaphor bring anything but very halting help: indeed—since so fundamental an act as that of creation can have no real analogues in human knowledge or experience—any metaphor must in this case be an attempt to illustrate the conception, not merely by something intrinsically less than, but by something bearing an entirely delusive similarity to, the thing illustrated, and consequently to lose grip of the conception in the very act of flinging out a hand to take hold. In the last resort, after all, one can only accept the bare statement of the idea, and then brood over it till the mind's embrace matches itself as nearly as may be to its length and breadth and depth and height. It is possible to miss the true meaning of some statements by taking them too literally; but with fundamental statements such as the one in question it is possible to attain their true meaning only by daring to take them literally enough. Christ as Re-creator and thereafter perpetual Creator of a new manhood—only in some such language, taken at its face value, can the idea be accurately and fully framed. Perhaps, if we must have a single word, "vitalism," as descriptive of Christ's dynamic ministry to man, will serve the best.[1] But one way or another, we must grasp the fact that it is a veritable *life-dynamic* that Christ brings.

Here again, it is the cumulative impression of Christ's recorded life, rather than isolated texts, which drives us to the conclusion that in the depths of Christ's being this consciousness of possessing the actual creative life of God found place; for the impression, when made to yield up its full content, is that of a Personality seeking to transfer itself to or to embrace the personality of man; and this is but to say in other words that it is

[1] Some hesitation in using the form results from its pre-engagement for the biological theories of Driesch and others. It is used here, of course, in an entirely different sense. Its employment in connection with Eucken's philosophy is more closely related with its employment here, but the difference will be evident to any student.

one of creative life passing forth from itself to create. And yet
here again, if we go back to many of Christ's recorded utterances, particularly to those in which He so emphatically and yet
so naturally asserts *Himself,* and if we use for the key to our
interpretation of them the idea that it was by the consciousness
of God's creative life in possession of Him they were inspired,
we find that the key fits and the door is not merely set ajar but
flung wide. What precisely do we mean when we say that Christ
held His own Personality to be the essential thing in His Gospel, and that He thus exalted it in a sense in which no other
founder of any religion has ever exalted his own personality to
the supreme place? Do we mean that He claimed to have
larger knowledge of God than even the greatest of His fore
runners had possessed? Certainly we mean that much. But if
this were put before us as an exhaustive rendering of our impression's meaning, we should immediately demur, feeling that
this explanation of Christ's self-assertion and its impression
upon us leaves something still untranslated, some deposit within
our minds unliquidated still. Do we mean that Christ proclaimed Himself as One who laid down lines of right conduct
which superseded all those laid down before, whose word on
such themes washed out and cancelled all that had been said
by ethical teachers of an older time? Certainly we mean that
much. But that rendering of our impression, no less than the
former, is realized at once to be only partial and fragmentary,
leaving for us, after its proffered settlement of the account, a
very substantial balance of the impression unreferred to its
proper and sufficient source. Do we mean that Christ required
from His followers an obedience absolute and unquestioning,
were it even unto death, and that they must for His sake count
all the world well lost? Certainly, under the remembrance of
many things He uttered, we cannot mean *less* than that. But
do we not mean *more?* Surely. We know that even this does not
exhaust our impression's contents: there lurks still in it the
murmur of inarticulate voices with something more they are
straining to say. We can only do justice to the impression
Christ's self-assertion makes when we declare it to signify

something like this—it implies that Christ asserted the presence within Himself of something which waited to emerge, as an emanation from the very depths of His being (though again words fail), to change the human soul and make it free of an entirely new range of life. It was not merely the greatness of His Personality *per se* that Christ asserted, but the greatness of His Personality *as able out of itself to make other personalities great*. For the most outstanding declarations Christ made about Himself—to turn now to some of those utterances in which that self-assertion of His finds voice—were not "I know," "I teach," "I command." Such declarations as these do indeed stand in His speech plentifully enough; but for arresting wondrousness and sublimity of daring there are others to which even these must yield; and it is these others that linger in our memories and, when imperfect renderings of our inmost impression are tendered for our acceptance, imperatively pronounce their rejection "Not enough!" "I *am*" is the index-phrase—at any rate the index-idea—for Christ's supreme statements about Himself; certainly the index-idea even when the phrase itself is absent. And on some of the Gospel pages the actual phrase leaps to the eye often enough. "I am the Door." "I am the Bread of Life." "I am the Light of the world." "I am the Living Water." So the phrase clamours to be heard. So the ceaseless chimes ring their peal; always having for the basal note whereon the entire superstructure of the music is built the note which sends the idea of *self-communication* echoing round the chambers of the listener's mind. For the very metaphors imply it. Christ's assertion of Himself as the Door tells of entrance of personality into Personality, of self-communication of Christ to man, though the process is viewed from the side of man's entrance into Christ rather than from that of Christ's entrance into man. Christ's assertion of Himself as the Bread of Life—since bread gives no sustenance save as it enters into the very fibre and substance of him on whose table it is placed—implies the very passing of Christ into man, the very receiving of Christ by man, if Christ's appointed ministry is to be fulfilled. Christ's assertion of Himself as the Light of the World can imply noth-

ing less than the very penetration of man's being by Christ's, as
light penetrates through and communicates itself to the dark-
ened room when the obstructing shutters are drawn back. And
it is always "I *am*"—not "I point you to the Door," "I kindle
the Light" "I provide you with the Living Bread and the Living
Water," but "I *am* all these." A Personality seeking to transfer
itself to, to embrace within itself, human personalities which
are willing to bow themselves to receive it—we cannot, unless
we take each metaphor to be so extravagant a representation
of the underlying truth as to be well-nigh a caricature, drape any
dress of inferior meaning round utterances such as these.
Equally clearly does the same idea of self-communication
emerge from the declaration "I am the Vine, ye are the
branches." [2] "Ye are the branches"—"your life is derivative,
drawn from Me Who am its source and spring." True, it is
from the Fourth Gospel that all these instances are gathered.
But if in any reader's mind that fact causes the spirit of questioning or of actual criticism to raise its head, let it be remembered that outside the Fourth Gospel the record teems with
utterances in which "I am" is still the index-idea even though
the phrase itself be absent. Their reverberating echoes bring to
us, as it were gathering the words from the speaker if not from
the actual words He spoke, that same "I am." What, when
we dip deeply enough into the profound ocean of "selfhood"
on which it is a passing wave, is the meaning of Christ's promise of rest, coupled as it is with "Come unto me" as the ordained
condition of receiving the gift? The "coming" must indicate
more than the mere physical approach, for that the hearers
had already performed. And the giving of rest—must not the
phrase be whittled down to signify mere instruction for the
winning of rest (an unsatisfying translation of it, surely!) unless we read it in the larger sense of a Personality bestowing

---

[2] One's mind goes back to God's reproach against His people, "Yet I had
planted thee a noble vine, wholly a right seed; how then art thou turned into the
degenerate plant of a strange vine unto me?" (Jer. ii. 21.) Was it in Christ's
mind? He seems to say, "You cannot yourselves be the vine. It is too great a
part for you to play. But I will be the vine. You can just be the branches, with
nothing to do but to take your life from Me."

something out of its own fulness upon a personality it enfolds?
"It is because I am what I am, and can give Myself, that you
shall find rest in Me." Does any lesser meaning fit? Even
utterances which appear at first to run on quite another line of
significance curve back to join the line running out from the
direct "I am" if we follow them far enough. "Whosoever shall
confess me before men, him will I confess before my Father
which is in heaven." Is it simply a pledge that faithfulness to
Christ in face of scorn and danger will be favourably reported
by Christ to His Father, and the faithful one be as it were
recommended for his merited reward? Surely such an interpretation is altogether too meagre, too pedestrian, on too low a
plane; and besides, on such a reading the parallelism of the
saying is left with nothing more than blunted edges. Is there
not a far profounder suggestion—a suggestion that he who has
so related himself with Christ as to become one with Him will
be seen and recognized in that oneness by the God with Whom
Christ Himself is one? How else can a "confession" of man *by*
Christ before God be satisfactorily correlated with a confession *of* Christ by man before men? Or pass to another word.
"He that receiveth you, receiveth me, and he that receiveth me
receiveth Him that sent me." Does it not, when deeply scanned,
indicate the veritable transmission of something through a
chain of personalities which runs down from God through
Christ to His disciples, and from the disciples—these becoming
in measure the transmitters of what they have received—to the
later disciples whom the earlier ones might win? It is possible,
no doubt, to read all these and many other utterances of
Christ's as it were through minimizing spectacles and to find
far shallower meanings in them. But contentment with superficial interpretations can be only short-lived for serious minds.
Of the last-quoted utterance Dr. Sanday observes: "These
simple-looking sayings are not so simple as they seem. . . .
The words are almost child-like in their simplicity, and yet they
lead up to the highest heights and down to the deepest depths.
No doubt we may rationalize it all away, if we please. We may
shut out the mystery from our minds. But we shall not keep it

out for long." [3] No, not for long. All the minimizing interpretations—the elementary interpretations, so to call them
—leave in us, as was previously said, a wholly "unexplained
residuum" of the impression the sayings make. Moreover, it is
under the *cumulative* effect of these sayings that this sense of
an "unexplained residuum" grows irresistibly poignant. We
may read one of them, and perhaps another, without feeling the
prick of it; but with an enlarging number of them presenting
themselves at our hearing's gate and knocking for admission,
the mind's pulses, stirred to more sensitive wonder and surprise, set us on an insistent quest for the deeper meanings whose
murmurs are caught beneath the superficial sounds we hear;
till at last that suggestion of a self-communicating Personality
disentangles itself from the whispers hitherto formless and
vague. And if, the suggestion having thus come to birth, we
go back to this utterance and that and use the suggestion for
the interpreting key, we find that the key fits all the doors. Go
back to some of the Fourth Gospel's most frequently quoted
and most inadequately comprehended passages, taken from the
prayer in which Christ pours forth to His Father His last tender and yet passionate aspirations for those He is about to
leave. "Holy Father, keep them in Thy name which Thou hast
given me, that they may be one, even as we are"; followed a
little later by a still deeper-reaching utterance, "That they
may all be one; even as Thou, Father, art in me, and I in Thee,
that they also may be in us"; and then by this profoundest
word, "And the glory which Thou hast given me I have given
unto them; that they may be one, even as we are one; I in them,
and Thou in me, that they may be perfected into one." It is as
bearing upon what is termed the "union of the Churches" (certainly an important matter enough: nothing said here is meant
to put its importance in question) that these utterances are
almost unanimously taken. But is not this to scale them, and the
whole range of thought to which they are native, down to a
standard far too low? That Christ's disciples are to be *in* both

[3] *The Criticism of the Fourth Gospel,* p. 225. It is not meant that Dr. Sanday
finds in the quoted passage the meaning suggested for it here.

the Father and the Son in the same sense as that in which the Son is *in* the Father and the Father *in* the Son—does the idea of breaking down the barriers which divide ecclesiastical organizations from one another fill up that outline with a sufficiently ample content? Can the "glory" of such unity as this be said to match the "glory" of that "oneness" with the Father which the Son, before the world was, received as His Father's gift? Surely the common interpretation of these words is "as moonlight unto sunlight and as water unto wine." Is not the transcendent conception rather that of a veritable *life* derived from the Father by Christ and handed on by Christ to His disciples—the Father, Christ, and man being thus linked together by a life-tide which starts from the first as its source, sweeps through the second as its intermediate channel, and finally beats upon humanity to fertilize humanity's otherwise waste and barren shores? Take the idea of a self-communicating Personality as the key wherewith to unlock the door behind which the ultimate meaning of such words as these lies hidden; and as soon as you test its efficacy, the door swings back, and there on the threshold the ultimate meaning of the words stands waiting to make its unreluctant confession, "Found at last!" The key fits. And so with all those utterances of Christ's, in other Gospels than the Fourth, at which we have glanced, and with many more; it is at the same "Open Sesame" that all the doors turn back their leaves.

Finally, in connection with the "unexplained residuum" of impression left within us by the easier interpretations of Christ's words of self-assertion, what of the sense of timelessness that broods over them all? Apart from His direct declaration to His disciples that as they discharged their missionary task He would be with them to the end of the world, we are conscious that, whenever He spoke His profoundest words about Himself, the years and the decades and the centuries vanished and that, rising sheer above them as they dissolved, there was still the changeless "I *am*." Christ held His own Personality to be the essential element in His Gospel, not only for the brief period of His earthly ministry, but for as long as the world should be. For us, this means that Christ is *now*—as indeed all profound Christian experience asserts and finds Him in some sense to be—the present and vitalizing force. And this means in its turn Christ's self-communication to us to-day. The truth that He is still all in all cannot, without emasculating it, be made to mean only that while we seek to set ourselves under the influence which issued from His Personality long years ago, He is with us in sympathy, in encouragement, in inspiration. That would *not* make His present Personality all in all, as an "unexplained residuum" of impression, restlessly haunting the mind, could not fail to declare. For it would not be actually His own Personality in its *direct action* that would be the supreme element in His ministry to us men of to-day, if that were all the permanence of His spiritual lordship meant: that would be no more than the Christ that *is* assisting us to find the Christ that *was;* and Christ's Personality remembered, or comprehended, or made vivid to the imagination—even though it were Christ's own holy magic that raised us to such dazzling heights—does not mean the Christ of Palestine perpetuating His ministry in the twentieth-century world. It means only a later Christ pointing us back to an earlier; and Christ contemplated no such programme as one Christ pointing us back to another, even though the two Christs were one. Christ's Personality as the supreme element in Christ's Gospel *now* can mean nothing less than the self-communication of Christ to us daily and hourly, anywhere and everywhere within the furthest geographical limits our expanding knowledge may discover and our wandering feet may range—a self-communication continuous in the hours of silent meditation and in the hours of strenuous toil, and no more uninterrupted in the quiet of worship than amid the din of the city's streets. And so we return to the idea with which we began—that according to the testimony of Christ's own consciousness there was in Him a veritable creative life pressing forth to create out of Himself a veritable new life in man. It is this that many of His direct utterances proclaim: it is this that satisfies the "unexplained residuum" of impression left by many of His indirect utterances after half-interpretations have done the best that they can do.

Christ brings the veritable creative life of God Himself, afresh and from a new direction, to the human plane and into the range of man; and His mission is to be the Creator and Sustainer of a new manhood, first for every individual and ultimately for the race, thus restoring humanity's life-movement to its originally-appointed Godward track.

3

It is by taking the doctrine of Christ's true Deity as including (not of course as exhausted by) the idea that He thus brought the dynamic of God's creative life to the world for the re-creation of man—it is thus that the doctrine is most emphatically demanded, justified, and brought into intimate connection with Christ's redemptive work. It is the last of these phrases that is worth noting above the rest; for the assertion that the doctrine of Christ's Deity is *demanded* and *justified* by His possession of God's creative power is self-evident as soon as stated, since only God can create, and may therefore be left to win assent by its own intrinsic force. But it is worth while to see how, if we construe Christ's absolute Deity as implying His divine creativeness, the doctrine becomes of immediate practical import when the soul is faced by the inquiry "What must I do to be saved?" For any doctrine, if it is to maintain a permanent place in the circle of doctrines to which men yield anything more than a nominal assent, must be capable of being viewed in organic connection with the development of right relations between man and God. It must show a definite value for practical religious purposes if it is to keep its ground. Failing that, the doctrine remains a mere excrescence—fated, like the excrescences of nature, to dry up and disappear at last. And for much current religiousness it is such an excrescence that the doctrine of Christ's unique Divinity has become, or is on the way to become. It must be admitted that to not a few the doctrine, while not questioned nor (still less) denied, remains out of cognizable relation to the method whereby man sets himself in line with Christ's redeeming power; and by consequence it comes to be not much more than nominally held. It is not unfair to say that many who would not acknowledge the Unitarian name have in reality little or nothing more than the Unitarian Christ.[4] And the tendency to drop into a mere nominal holding of the doctrine is indeed intelligible enough. For as the cruder credal statements in which the ideas of atonement or redemption were formerly clothed lost their hold, and nothing very clear-cut took their place, the imperative call for a Christ who should be very God of very God grew fainter. Those earlier statements at any rate demanded a Christ in the strictest sense divine, inasmuch as in one way or another they represented Christ (of course quite rightly) as doing something for man which man could not do for himself, and which therefore God must do. But with the old statements question-marked as to their validity, or at any rate as to their true meaning, and with the consequent gathering vagueness as to what redemption really was, the demand for such a Christ became less insistent by far. The answer to that central and searching inquiry *"Cur Deus Homo?"*—the answer which, as Anselm long ago held and as the true instinct of profound thinkers has always confirmed him in holding, can only be found in the establishment of an organic and vital connection between Christ's nature and Christ's redeeming work—failed now to write itself on the screen where it had stood out in such brightly-illuminated lettering before. There was not enough definiteness in the conception of what Christ accomplished for man to necessitate the ascription to Him of Deity's fulness; and with the doctrine no longer imperatively required, it passed to the rear of the mind's field of survey, and, though still catalogued in the list

---

[4] A scholarly and devout Unitarian friend once asked me whether I really thought the question of Christ's Deity worth debating. He said in effect, "What difference does it make? I get as much out of my human Christ as the non-Unitarians get out of their divine Christ." I was astounded for the moment—then I realized how sadly far my friend was right. And certainly he himself, with his imperfectly-conceived Christ (as I must hold), might well put many non-Unitarians to the blush. But the pity of it!

of the articles to which the mind yielded its "Amen," was capital no more. The tendency is natural and intelligible enough.

In what way, other than by speaking of Christ as possessing within Himself the creative life of God, can we reconstitute the lost connection between the divineness we ascribe to Him and His redemptive work? Shall we say, for example, that He is the supreme revelation of God? Beyond all doubt He is that. But does that, taken by itself, help us very far? Nay, does it accomplish even so much as to *demand* or *justify* faith in Christ's full Deity? Scarcely, it would appear. Of course, if the phrase signified that Christ set clear before the eyes of men *all* that God is, then *cadit quaestio:* to say that would be only to say in other words that Christ *is* God; but only by suppressing or refusing to see the fact that the phrase does *not* mean this is it possible to find in it sufficient guard and guarantee for Christ's veritable Deity. For what can a revelation of God mean to the world as we know it except a manifestation of God's moral attributes, so far as man's mind can apprehend and man's bleared and limited vision can behold them, in their unalloyed purity? But the indicated limitations in the definition—essential ones, surely—are sufficient to prevent the *inevitable* implication of full Deity in the Person so defined. The full Deity may indeed be in Him, but the warrant for affirming its presence is not given in our data. Essential the limitations assuredly are. Could man take in the *whole* revelation of God's moral attributes, or fail to be smitten into stupefying bewilderment of soul and spirit, if it were given in all its length and breadth and depth and height? How should man, whose native sphere is dark and whose mind is dim, bear the paralysing glory of that uncreated beam? Supreme as may be the revelation of God which Christ brings, it cannot be a revelation exhaustive of what God in His essential perfection is. Or, if it were, man could not know it to be such. There must still remain in the depths of the divine nature immeasurable reserves, vast tracts (one has to employ terms absurd in their inadequacy) of unexplored territory, qualities and attributes which man could not recognize though they looked out on him through the parted

veil behind which God dwells, and for which the world's accumulated vocabularies could find no name. Nay, even such divine
attributes as human comprehension can in measure grasp, those
which enter into common human experience—love, faithfulness, and the like—must mean far more in God than they can
mean in or to man; must, as apprehended by man, be mere
miniatures of something greater, pale reflections of what glows
with infinitely heightened colours in God Himself. You cannot
say that such a partial revelation as man is able to receive *necessarily* implies the Deity of the Christ in and through whom it is
given. God He may be, but the inference that He is so, if you
seek to make it from the premise that He is God's supreme
revelation, requires a longer stretch than the arm of your logic
can cover from the platform on which you have taken your
stand. It is at least conceivable that a revelation of God,
supreme in so far that it fills the circle of man's comprehension
from centre to circumference, complete in the sense that it offers
in its out-stretched hand everything that the out-stretched hand
of man can grasp, but partial in the sense that it leaves much
hidden in the unexplored background of God's infinitude still,
might be provided by something else and something less than
an incarnation of God Himself. In fact, it may be said without
irreverence or presumption that such a revelation, transmitted
through a specially-endowed human medium, would probably
exercise a more powerful appeal. To say that Christ *reveals*
God is not to say that Christ *is* God, unless we are prepared to
declare, "We know all that God is, and looking on Christ, we
see that all of it is there." It may even be said that the inference
from the supremacy of Christ's revelation to Christ's Deity
would be valid only if we possessed a previous knowledge of
God by which the revelation could be checked; the revelation
being thus robbed of its highest worth, since it would be, not
an imparting of knowledge, but merely a confirmation of what
we knew before. When, therefore, we seek to establish an
organic relation between the Deity of Christ and His redemptive work, and begin by construing Him as very God of very
God because He is the supreme revelation of the Divine, we

find that at the very initial stage of our effort we are brought up
short; for of the two correlates whose mutual adjustability we
want to demonstrate we cannot set even the first steadfastly on
its base. But even if we succeeded in doing that much, we could
not complete our scheme. Given a Christ who is divine because
He is God's supreme revelation, there is no direct passage from
the idea of revelation to that of redemption: redemption is not
given in revelation as an essential part of its constituent essence
nor implied in it as—shall we say?—heat is implied in fire or
cold in ice. Revelation imparts *knowledge* alone. As the Revealer of God, Christ doubtless could and would proclaim God's
way of salvation, but would not necessarily be Himself the
Saviour: indeed, *quâ* mere Revealer, He could not be. The imparting of knowledge is not the gift of a dynamic power. What
is wanted is a redemption that is a *dynamic:* what is given is,
ex hypothesi, a Christ who *reveals* God; but you cannot make
what is given minister, as by a natural outcome from its own
innermost essence, to the need, nor make the need lean back
upon what is given with a certainty that it will be supplied.
Start from a Christ who perfectly reveals God, and, if that is
all you can say about Him, you cannot infer a dynamic redemption given in Him: start from a dynamic redemption given in
Him, and you cannot justify your belief in it by merely affirming
that He is the supreme revelation of God. Either way, the wing
on which you hoped to make your passage droops and fails you
before your flight is done.

Can we make another attempt, from another direction, at
establishing the desired organic relationship between Christ's
divine Personality and His redeeming work? Shall we put it
that Christ is the ideal and representative man, the full exem-
plification of what man was meant to be and of what man may
become? It has often been so put in recent decades; though the
reminder must again be given that it is not a definite Unitarianism we are speaking.[5] From the side of those who cling fast to

[5] Nor are we concerned here with the idea that Christ is the "representative"
man in the sense of being the "Federal Head of the race." This idea will come
into our view later on. (See Chapter VI, §§ 3, 4.)

some altogether special divine quality in Christ, who indeed wish to conserve the conception of Christ's coming as in some real sense signalizing the advent of a veritable Incarnation, the idea of Christ as the ideal of humanity is presented in two different ways. Sometimes He is spoken of as though in His Person the forces at work in the nature of ordinary men were suddenly interpenetrated and strengthened by a fresh invasion of divine energy, with the result that they leaped forward to produce a sort of advance proof of the picture humanity was to make when its destiny was fulfilled. And the reasoning runs something like this—that precisely because Christ is the ideal *man,* and because only through a special emergence of *divine* power could the ideal *man* emerge at the particular point of the historic process when Christ appeared on earth, therefore He must be *more* than man, must in fact be *divine.* Sometimes Christ is spoken of, still as showing the pattern of perfected humanity, and doing this by manifesting a special embodiment of the divine nature and life; but that embodiment—one might almost say the process whereby it is wrought out—is *itself* taken, on this second view, as representative of man's consummated moral and spiritual growth; and as God became incarnate in Christ, so will He at the long last become in greater or less degree incarnate in us. The actual *process* of the incarnation is increasingly to repeat itself in the experience of man. In some such ways as these it is sought to preserve a Christ who is in the full sense divine and at the same time the Redeemer of men, and who is the second because He is the first. Do they succeed? Scarcely, it would appear. By neither of the two formulae descriptive of Christ's Personality on its divine side is His *absolute* Deity demanded or justified. There is a check at the very outset similar to that which operated when we tested the description of Him as the supreme revelation of God. If Christ was the perfect man suddenly displayed upon the historic stage in consequence of a miraculous interposition or interpenetration by God in the midst of the historic process, that does not make Him *essentially* an embodiment of God. The result of a special divine energizing it undoubtedly

makes Him; and one might perceive the divine activity within
Him so transfiguring Him as to remove Him even further from
the ordinary categories of humanity than a merely human perfection would carry Him; but this will hardly suffice to make
Him one before whom we would bow and say "My Lord and
my God." And if, accordant with the second reading of the
matter, Christ's incarnation be a prophecy or rehearsal of an
incarnation to be repeated in all humanity, it becomes still less
possible to term Him, merely on that ground, God manifest in
the flesh; else stern logic at once bids us "stand and deliver" to
the inevitable inference that man is to become God. *Something* of
God, it is true, He must have manifested on the given presupposition. But very God of very God—God in the whole range of
His essential Being brought down to finite levels and veiling
His glory there—the presupposition cannot bear the weight of
so transcendent a corollary as that. And further, to make any
organic connection from an ideal man to a Saviour is as impossible as to make a similar connection to the same desired cor-
relate from a perfect revelation of God. How could even an ideal
man, however vividly the ground-stuff of His humanity were
shot through by gleaming threads of gold which the special
divine agency at work in its production might draw through it,
become, *quâ* an ideal man, redemptive in any truly dynamic
fashion? What would be the *rationale* of the process? What
force—unless you restrict the term to the qualified meanings of
inspiration and stimulus—lies potential in the most clearly-
visioned ideal? True, the traveller's goal, discerned looming on
the sky-line, may lend wings to his feet and re-quicken his dying
pulses; but not if the ascent to the goal be too far and too steep;
and from the common man to the ideal man in Christ is an
ascent far and steep indeed. In fact, the analogy fails. For the
common man, gazing upon the ideal man in Christ, must rather
be compared to the mariner, stranded on some desert spot,
marking on his map the place where lies his home, and mourning
because no sail will ever carry him over the thousand leagues of
intervening sea. How can the "ideal man," as such; redeem? It
is difficult to find a reply to the inquiry. Once again, we are

forced to the conclusion that if the attempt be made, while avoiding the ascription of God's actual creative power to Christ, to keep Him as an incarnation of God and to run lines of organic connection from Him to His redeeming work, the attempt breaks down.

From an *impasse* such as this we are delivered if we take one of the essential points in Christ's Deity to be His possession of God's creative power, and His advent as being His bringing of that creative power to the human plane in order to exert it in communicating a new life and a new life-movement in substitution for the impaired life and the strayed life-movement into which humanity had dropped. For only God can create: Christ's work is re-creation: it is therefore a veritably divine work He performs, and it can only be out of Deity in Him that the work can come. It is not suggested that to find the two ideas so fitly framed together is a positive proof of either. But it does at least offer credentials on behalf of both. Each idea slides smoothly into the other as a key slides without friction into the lock for which it was made; and the correspondence of the two ideas goes some way to show that both play a real part in some larger system of truth to which they both belong. A vainly-imagined idea most frequently floats like a wandering star across the mental firmament, declining to confess affinity with other ideas (whether these be themselves valid or only vain imaginations too)—most frequently, indeed, shows a set refusal to acknowledge any other idea as its true mate. But two ideas which run readily to meet one another and to embrace have passed at any rate the first and not the least important test. They have established, at a *minimum,* a claim to such respect as further examination may imply. And so here. It is something gained to perceive that if we take Christ as bringing the veritable creative life of God to the human plane, and as being the Creator and Sustainer of a new manhood, first for every individual and ultimately for the race, and as thus restoring humanity's life-movement to its originally-appointed Godward track, we have constructed an organic and vital connec-

tion between Christ's essential Deity, in the fullest sense, and
His work in the redemption of man.

We take Christ, then, to be this. And we take Him to be this
for all time. But how is such a possibility of being "born again"
as this implies to be perpetually set within man's reach as the
ages proceed? How may man feel assured that it exists? How
can the Christ who once made His historic appearance on an
earthly stage so limited and temporary, be the re-creative
Christ for always and for all mankind? There within the con-
fines of a country which fills but a small space on the map He
enacted a ministry which endured at most no more than a few
months or years. How shall He be the world's perpetual Saviour? The Cross and the Resurrection give the reply.

CHAPTER V

CROSS AND RESURRECTION

By the Cross and the Resurrection the local Christ becomes the universal Christ, the Christ of a swiftly-transacted earthly ministry becomes the Christ for the world's entire after-time, let that stretch far forward as it may. There is of course more than this to be said of both His death and His rising; but this is the idea within which all else is enclosed and out of which consequently all else springs. And let it be emphasized at once, and borne in memory throughout, that Cross and Resurrection must be taken *together* if the significance of either is to be grasped. To isolate the Cross from the subsequent reversal of its tragedy, and to treat the first as if that alone constituted the supreme event in which Christ became the world's Redeemer, while looking upon the second as being not much more than a miracle whereby Christ's title and competence (if the poor word may pass) to have performed the redemptive work are proved, is to separate two halves of one double-sided entity and by the severance to blur the contour and lose the true vision of the whole. Yet this is in effect the line on which much discussion of the theme proceeds. It is like dividing a jewel in two. Each segment of it may indeed remain wonderful enough in itself, but the more excellent glory of the perfect gem is not thus yielded to one's gazing eyes. Cross and Resurrection taken *together* make the life-dynamic in Christ available for all the ages and for all the world. They are not so much two successive events as two constituent elements in one transcendent event. Christ, because He died *and* because He rose again, lives here and everywhere—will be living everywhere while the ages run— and will therefore be everywhere and always what He was when He lived on earth, the Christ who brings the veritable

life of God to the human plane and communicates it ceaselessly
to all the generations of mankind. Through the tragedy and
the triumph, taken *together*, He stands out as the Lord of
life, as Jesus Christ the same yesterday and to-day and for ever.

It should be noted, before we pass on to consideration of the
idea immediately in hand, that just as on the lines followed in
the previous chapter we traced an organic and vital connection
from Christ's perfect Deity to the life-dynamic He puts forth,
so, on the line we propose to follow here, we trace an organic
and vital connection from Christ as possessor of the life-
dynamic to the Christ who died and rose again, and thus add a
third link to a growing chain of thought. It is only in a Christ
who is very God of very God that a life-dynamic can reside : it
is by Christ's dying and rising that the life-dynamic becomes
and is proved universal and enduring. So to our search for some
unified view of God's dealing with the "problem" of the world's
redemption three contributing factors are yielded, each one
both giving and gaining added strength by its intimate harmony
and correspondence with the rest.

I

Voices have sometimes been raised to ask whether the redemption of the world could not have been accomplished without the tragedy of Calvary. The question, if intended to start
us on research into all the alternative methods of redemption
(supposing that there were such) from which God might have
selected some other method than that which His wisdom chose,
must lie under suspicion as being perhaps the off-spring of idle,
not to say irreverent, curiosity, and as being in any case useless,
since it is one to which only God Himself could give the reply.
Any attempt to answer it is in effect to claim omniscience as our
own; for only omniscience can discern all the possibilities which
omnipotence has at command. Yet the same question in a more
narrowly conceived form and with more restricted scope is
natural, and may be reverent enough—may in fact be prompted
by adoring reverence itself. Given the fact of Christ's coming

to our earth, was it an absolute necessity that in order to become the world's Redeemer His earthly course should have terminated thus? The agony, the shame, the bloody sweat—*must* these things have been? What and where was the dire compulsion that could not be baulked of its prey? The stark horror of the thing—of such a life so ending, of such a Christ delivered into the hands of wicked men to be crucified and slain—wrings the tremulous question not only from one's lips, but from one's half-broken heart. Somehow it seems as if even the salvation of the world were not a matter great enough to demand such a sacrifice as this. So sometimes the feeling, inarticulate perhaps but real and passionate, beats up; springing, it may be, if one dug down to its roots, from a still deeper feeling that the salvation of a world so far fallen was scarcely a matter great enough even to *justify* such a sacrifice as this. Was it really only at a price so high—the price of His own blood shed by scourge and nails and spear—that even Christ could purchase His heritage of a redeemed mankind? How and why should He, the incarnate Son of God, be bound by the chains of a necessity so dire? Why should He, very God of very God, have to acknowledge and bow beneath the imperative of a *"must"* like this? It is not idle curiosity, but a conscience stirred to aching sensitiveness before the balm provided to ease it, and a humility which hardly dares to stretch out a trembling hand for the proffered gift, and a wonder almost turned to dizziness at the love which valued man so high, that will in hours of the spirit's tensest quickening give birth to questions such as these. *"Amor meus cruciatus est!"* Why must it have been? Even while lost in wonder, love, and praise, the heart repeats its "Why?"

Yet, though in uttering the words one steps upon ground so holy that one almost hears a voice from heaven bidding one be silent, and though one must at least speak with bated breath, one may dare to say that if the Christ who has life in Himself is to be the Life-Giver to man for ever, He *must* die. For if He is to be the ever-living Christ, a Real Presence in the world till time shall end, He must prove Himself to be the conqueror of death; and He can only do this (dimly the truth of it looms outlined through our wonder and our tears) by submitting Himself to death first and then snatching its victory from its hands. Whether or no we should or could have come to an antecedent realization of that is beside the mark. With the historic facts before us, we can at least venture to affirm, "This was God's ordained way," and then, recognizing humbly what may be called the entire fitness of the way ordained, go on to add, "How else *could* the Christ of Palestine have become the Christ of the world?" There is no presumption in that. Verily it behoved the Christ to suffer. Had He held death at arm's length when it threatened, and were He still present on earth in human form, how could He thus be brought into that close contact with all nations and kindreds and peoples and tongues which the world's Life-Giver must establish? He would still be the local Christ, sending His messages it may be across lands and seas to the earth's furthest bounds, but not known for the everywhere-present Christ who gives *Himself*. Or had death come to Him bringing no other weapon than that unseen sword wherewith it lays all men low, and had He bowed Himself to that weapon's milder stroke—ay, even had He thereafter burst the gates of the grave and revisited the scenes He had left—how should the voices of mockery or doubt have been adequately silenced when they said (as in face of proved historic realities not a few voices have actually said) that He did not die at all? But that uplifted Cross, with its testimony of the shattered frame it bore and of the heart that broke upon it, and that empty sepulchre with the witness it offers to the vanity of death's transient triumph—these, *taken together,* give the Christ of Palestine to the whole world; for if the first speaks manifestly of One who not only tasted death, but drank its bitter cup to the dregs, the second tells equally manifestly of One who is alive for evermore. Henceforth the limitations of time and space cease to come into the reckoning of Christ's redeeming ministry: what He was for the land He trod He is certified as being for earth's remotest ends and time's remotest year; and the tragedy and the triumph stand as proof that He did not surrender His earthly and local ministry in order to take up a ministry of universal application and scope. And once again it may be reverently asked, "How else could this be?" It was expedient that He should go away, and should go through a door so rudely flung open before the gaze of men; expedient too that the going should be followed by a return so patent; for thus the world may know that He has not gone, but still abides. We stand before His Cross; and remembering that He is to be the Creator and Sustainer of a new-made race, the veritable Life-Giver to mankind—remembering besides that we may pass at once to His empty tomb and say, "He is not here; He is risen"—we repeat for His praise and glory the words which mocking passers-by at Calvary spat at Him for His scorn and shame, "He saved others: Himself He *cannot* save."

2

Christ took His death as inevitable and His Resurrection as sure; and He took both as essential for the discharge of the mission given into His hands. Whether He occupied this standpoint from the outset of His ministry, or whether He reached it by a road which led Him through a growing consciousness of probability till probability took the clear outline of certainty at last, we need not here pause to inquire. There is ample testimony that, if He made such a passage, He made it swiftly and soon. Certainly His ministry had not been exercised long when the coming events of the Passion and the Resurrection cast their shadows across His soul. Inevitable and essential He assuredly held both Cross and Resurrection to be. But they were inevitable and essential for His thought only because they constituted the inevitable and essential prologue to the continued work which waited for Him beyond them both: they were central, not terminal, deriving their inevitable and essential character from their place between what was then happening antecedently to them and what was after them still to be—the Cross being destined to take Him from the narrow world in which His work was then being done, and the Resurrection being appointed to give Him back to the whole world again, clothed with power to repeat that earthly work on the universal scale. And any reading of Christ's mind which does not give due weight to *both* these factors—on the one hand any reading which does not recognize that Christ saw and felt the Cross and the Resurrection to constitute something absolutely vital to His work, something which by its unescapable imperativeness "straitened" Him till He had passed through the deep waters of its baptism, and on the other hand any reading which makes Cross and Resurrection *in themselves* the terminal and final element in the redemptive process, forgetting the "long look" which, as we have previously seen, Christ threw forward into the far vista broadening out from them as its starting-point—any such reading fails, I think, to see deeply enough into Christ's mind and heart.

"Inevitable" is, to be sure, scarcely a word of sufficient accuracy to be used without some qualification in connection with Christ's view of His own death. For He laid down His life, did not have it torn from Him by a force He could not resist. This is of course involved in His Deity. It was impossible that the divine life in Him—the very creative life of God—should yield itself to defeat except at its own unconstrained choice. But to realize this is only to realize also, and with added intensity, how essential Christ held His death to be. He deliberately faced the cruelties of men, and let them have their way and will with Him, because His timeless and world-wide mission could not otherwise be fulfilled. The legions of angels who would have rallied to Christ's battle-standard had He chosen to unfurl it heard no signal-call. Inevitable in the sense of being a fate from whose clutch He could not free Himself, Christ's death was not: inevitable in the sense of being something which He must pass through if His work was to be done, He most assuredly took it to be. Death could say no "must" to Him; but "I must" He, for the furtherance of His redemptive purposes, chose to say. From that anticipation of the end which came upon Him so early in His career, up to that "It is finished" which seemed to the unknowing on-lookers a proof that death's triumph was complete, death had no dominion over Him save such semblance of dominion as He permitted it—or we may dare to say willed it—to assume. This is not, of course, to lend any countenance to Renan's fancy-picture of a Christ who had at the close of His life become a disillusioned would-be Messiah, realizing that "it was time for death to come and unloose the knot of a situation of extremest tension and relieve Him from the impossibilities of a path without issue." Such a suggestion is merely an extravaganza of surmise and hardly merits even contradiction, so manifestly absurd is it to any open-minded reader of the Gospel story.[1] If there is anything that impresses us in the record of those final weeks and days, this impression certainly persists—that of the utter serenity of Christ's soul as He set His face to go to Jerusalem and of His unruffled self-possession through all the scenes of the tragedy enacted there. And not only through those final weeks and days, but always while His ministry went on, Christ met death's gaze with the same tranquil mastery looking back from His own. This is not said in forgetfulness of Gethsemane or of those hours when Christ's "soul was troubled" under the anticipation of the impending Cross. But these things only indicate that as He looked forward to the experience of death Christ foresaw certain elements in it from which He, *because He was what He was,* shrank back in sensitive pain—a point to which we shall presently return. It was something special *within* death that lay heavily upon Him sometimes: over death *itself* Christ always calmly realized His entire lordship: in that respect, the terms "utter serenity" and "unruffled self-possession" and "tranquil mastery" unquestionably hold good. He chose to die, true; but only because in the very act of dying He would make death His unwilling ally. For that reason, and for that reason alone, it should win its seeming victory. He turned its sentence into an invitation it pleased Him to accept. At the beginning, Christ could have refused to drink the cup. At the end, He could still have refused to drink it. But freely choosing, He said His great "I must," and drained it to the dregs.

---

[1] An allusion was once made by an American scholar, in an interview with Dorner, to Renan. Dorner's only reply, the visitor relates, was a shrug of the shoulders, a wave of the hand, and the concise comment, *"Das ist Nichts."*

But equally essential with death in Christ's thought was His Resurrection. The two were as twin stars in His sky. It has often been noticed that with what may be termed His more formal and official announcements of the first an announcement of the second was linked.[2] Of course Christ made other allusions to His death with which no companion-allusion to His Resurrection was joined; as, for example, when He spoke of Himself as having come to give His life a ransom for many. But these allusions were made in a context of circumstances which rendered a further allusion to His rising unnecessary, which would indeed have rendered such an allusion redundant and would have caused it by its redundance to spoil the point of the lesson the Teacher had immediately in view. When it was a matter of giving some account of His mission in the length and breadth and depth and height of it, then Cross and Resurrection stood out in Christ's statements as two constituent elements of an indissoluble unity. The fact stands as proof—it is not too strong a word—not only that Christ took death and Resurrection as one whole, but, inasmuch as Resurrection is in itself and by its very nature a new beginning, that He, taking them *together,* looked beyond them *both.* The long look which Christ took over the entire historic process of the future—Himself central and regnant in the midst of it—till the panorama of the ages should close down! The long look! And the fulfilment of its expectation and its prophecy was to be made possible and to be proved possible to the world by His rising from the dead; and in order to rise from the dead He must first submit Himself to death! A few years on earth; a transient descent into the valley of the shadow of death; a swift and splendid emergence on the mountain-top of Resurrection with death's disappointed shadows drifting away foiled and shattered from beneath His feet back to their dark haunts below; a far-stretching, yea an endless, ministry thereafter while the world should endure— so, if the line of thinking we here follow be valid, did Christ behold the sequent factors of His redemptive work framed together into one perfect whole. Christ held Cross and Resur-

2 Mark viii. 31; ix. 31; x. 32–34.

rection, taken *together,* to be inevitable and essential for the sake of what lay beyond them both.

3

One remembers, of course, that this is not the customary reading of the matter. Thinking on the subject of the Atonement has almost invariably taken Christ's death to be not merely *essential* to His redemptive work, but the very totality of it. It *was* the Atonement. It is not to be viewed as the opening section of a volume to which many a chapter had yet to be added, but as the completed book which needs but to have its seals broken and its pages read by those who would learn redemption's secret. So the usual conception affirms. Yet if one were not so accustomed to hear that conception stated and pressed, or rather taken for granted, that one becomes unobservant of its flaw—its exaggeration of emphasis upon one admittedly essential thing to the exclusion of much else equally essential, and, it may be added, its reading of the New Testament Scriptures with the accents similarly disordered—one would surely find that conception open to doubt. One question at least cannot fail to leap to the mind of every one who with unbiased movement of thought puts the conception to the test. If what so many theories of atonement under varying forms of phraseology declare to be true, holds good—if Christ by His death, and by His death *alone,* made satisfaction to God, or reconciled God's justice and God's grace, or made it possible for God to let His heat of anger die, or set man free from sin's penalties by Himself enduring them—if, doing these things at Calvary, He left nothing else to be done—if Christ's Cross be, not merely *essential* to His redeeming work, but the beginning, middle, and end of it—why did Christ Himself say no word to establish that truth once for all? That He came to die for men, He affirmed again and again. But He did not say that His submission to death was *in itself* the all-inclusive saving act, round which all else was gathered as accessory—important indeed, but accessory none the less. The theories spoken of are in fact doctrinal explanations of an event which has previously been isolated from other events as Christ Himself never isolated it, and explanations probably rendered more difficult and complicated by the isolation into which the event has been forced. Had Christ, in foretelling His death, intended that it should be taken out of all context, and its significance thus puzzled out without reference to aught else that might throw light upon its mystery, would He not have said so? If His death were in itself the perfect work, why should He thus have kept that truth in reserve as a hidden secret for which future ages must dig and delve with such anxious strain?

The question has not gone unraised (though usually in the stronger form "Why did not Christ *explain* the Cross?"), and some attempt at reply has been made. I confess however that the attempted replies appear to me to fall far short of success. They are commonly set to some such words as these—that Christ came less to preach the Gospel than to provide, by His life and particularly by His death, that there should be a Gospel to preach (a phrase whose slightly epigrammatic flavour may give it an impression of plausibility at first); or, which comes to much the same thing, that Christ could not set forth the real meaning of His death before He actually died, and must necessarily leave His apostles and evangelists to declare its significance after it became an accomplished fact.[3] If these explanations of Christ's silence are found convincing, there is no more to be said, and one must leave it at that. But for me they do no more than cause a further question to raise its head. *Why* could not Christ explain the significance of His own death before He actually died, or at least have openly allotted to it its alleged rightful place as the one event by which the whole of His redemptive work was to be achieved? He went so far as to

---

[3] "The real truth is that while He came to preach the gospel, His chief object in coming was that there might be a gospel to preach."—Dale, *The Atonement* (tenth edition), p. 46. Similarly, though more baldly, Dr. Stalker remarks (*Life of St. Paul*, p. 15): "There was one great subject which Christ had to leave unexplained—His own death. He could not explain it before it had taken place." The quiet assumption with which the statement is made, as if its truth were a matter of course, is rather provocative of a quick "Why ever could He not?" by way of reply.

proclaim it essential and inevitable. There is no dispute about that. Why should He not have gone further and proclaimed it as in *itself* constituting the Atonement, if it did so? If there were a restriction, imposed or self-imposed, set upon His lips, in virtue of which He might announce His impending death but might not announce that in and through that death the perfect work was to be done, in what way could that help His Gospel's cause? On the face of it, it would seem a hindrance rather than a help. For, be it noted, the *crux* of the difficulty is not only that Christ avoided any *explanation* of an Atonement which was to be perfectly wrought out at the Cross (the stronger form of the question, as indicated previously), but that He did not even assert that it was to be made. On the assumption that the *whole* atoning process was to be accomplished by the Cross, we should at least have been set by Christ's authoritative declaration to that effect (even though He had gone no further) precisely where we are now, only without room for any doubt as to the assumption's validity to creep in; and though the question "Why did He not make the *rationale* of the Atonement clear?" might still have pressed, the yet more fretfully haunting question "Why did He keep silence as to the *fact?*" would never have risen from its sleep. We might still have been wondering over and searching into the *method* whereby the Cross redeems; but we should not have been doing so under an additional burden of uncertainty whether our insistence on the Cross as the exclusively effective factor in redemption be not mistaken. Against all this no gain, derived from the seal which Christ is supposed to have set upon His lips, can, so far as I see, be pleaded. To invite discipleship, and yet to leave unkindled the lamp over the very door by which the disciple must enter, would surely be a strange procedure for the Saviour of the world. There can scarcely be so much of reserve, anything so esoteric, in the cardinal tenet of a Gospel designed for the redemption of mankind. To say that Christ withheld all assertion of the most out-standing fact in what was afterwards to be His message to the world, is surely to say that He gratuitously threw difficulties across the progress of His own cause; that while summoning men to "come to Him," He maintained on an all-important point a reserve which made it harder for them to find the way; and that while calling for faith, He left unrevealed the one truth whereon faith was after its responsive flight to settle down with folded wings in rest.

Equally difficult of explanation with Christ's own silence, on the assumption that Christ's death *taken alone* embodies the whole method and process of redemption and that on His death *taken alone* saving faith must rely, is the fact that the very earliest Christian preaching recorded for us does not so declare. The apostle Peter, with all the first ardour of his commission kindling his soul, on fire to disburden himself of his great message, seizing eagerly on a unique opportunity of doing so before a congregation of "Jews, devout men from every nation under heaven" gathered together for the Pentecostal feast, takes quite another line; nor in subsequent discourses— those to the crowd at the Temple gate or to Cornelius and his assembled guests, for example—does he repair the omission, if omission it was. As a matter of fact, it is on the Resurrection rather than on the death of Christ that the emphasis steadily falls. "Whom God raised up, having loosed the pangs of death; because it was not possible that He should be holden of it"— "this Jesus did God raise up"—"whom God raised from the dead, whereof we are witnesses"—"Him God raised up the third day"—the idea recurs like the echoing refrain of a poem at every stanza's end. Paul's early missionary preaching shows an insistence on the Resurrection as marked as Peter's own. At Antioch in Pisidia it is on this that he lays his utmost stress: at Athens it is about "Jesus and the resurrection" that he talks with the philosophers in the market-place, and to this same theme his sermon on the Areopagus deliberately leads up. Later on, in presence of Agrippa and Festus, Paul strikes the same strident Resurrection-note. Resurrection, not death, is the topic on which all the emphasis is thrown. It is true that in Paul's epistles the death of Christ advances into a prominence his preaching did not yield to it, and of this and of the reason for it something will be said by-and-by.[4] But of the apostle's early missionary preaching (in which, if anywhere, we should on the "orthodox" theory expect the Cross to be predominant) what has been said holds good. For this apostolic silence, as for the silence of Christ Himself concerning the supposed all-inclusive efficacy of Christ's death in redemption, explanations have been found, or at any rate sought—sought, I cannot help thinking with as little success. Dr. Dale's explanation in regard to Peter (it covers Peter's case only, and whatever may be its success in regard to Peter's preaching, it is obviously inapplicable to Paul [5]) is perhaps as strong as any. He holds that Peter's principal aim in these early discourses was not to declare the secret of salvation, but to convince the Jewish people that in crucifying Christ they had committed an appalling crime of whose enormity they must immediately repent; that this was the "one solitary aspect under which for the time being it was

[4] Chapter VII, § 5.

[5] At a later stage in his argument Dr. Dale, while admitting that in the discourse at Antioch "nothing is said about the relation of our Lord's death to the forgiveness of sins and justification," attempts to deduce from Paul's language in the first Epistle to the Corinthians that the apostle's preaching at Corinth had insisted upon the point. (*Op. cit.,* pp. 200 ff.) Paul reminds the Corinthians that he had known nothing among them "save Jesus Christ and Him crucified." But this is far from a statement that the Cross had been set in the forefront as the *exclusive* ground and means of redemption. Leaving out of account what will be said in Chapter VII, § 5 of this book as to the reason for the prominence given to the death of Christ in the New Testament Epistles (written, as will be stressed, not to non-Christians nor for purposes of evangelization, but to established Christian Churches), it must be remembered that Paul had a very special object in view in the cited passage. He wished to contrast his message with that of others. They used "excellency of speech or of wisdom." He was content to preach what seemed "to the Jews a stumbling-block and to the Greeks foolishness." More than content, indeed; for he glories in the apparent "foolishness" of his message and makes the most of it. He almost aims at making it appear as extreme as he can. Insistence on the Cross and its place in his gospel was the obvious line for him to take. And his statement that he had preached it at Corinth presents no difficulty from the standpoint of these pages. Of course he had, for insistence on the risen and living Christ necessarily *implies* the Cross. For that matter, if one chooses to make much of the order of words, one might point out that the very phrase "Jesus Christ and Him crucified" rather favours the contention that it was *not* as crucified that Christ had been primarily preached, but as living, and as crucified only by implication. In any case, we certainly cannot—particularly with the Antioch discourse and the others before our eyes—infer from the Corinthian passage that Paul had represented Christ's death as holding the *one* and *all-inclusive* secret of redemption.

indispensably necessary that they should regard the death of Christ"; and that "to have spoken of the expiatory power of His Sacrifice to those who had been guilty of that supreme offence, or who had condoned it, would have been useless"— "worse than useless," Dr. Dale goes so far as to say,[6] though he does not offer any justification of the severer verdict. I can only repeat what was said in respect of the silence of Christ, that if this explanation of Peter's silence be found convincing, the matter must be left there, but that for my own part I find the difficulty unrelieved. It may be admitted without hesitation that one of Peter's objects was to lash conscience in his hearers from slumber into storm. But it is not on this that the real emphasis falls. Always it is "this Jesus whom ye slew is risen again, and lives for evermore" to which Peter returns. He begins, as it were, a new paragraph of his speech: straightway, wherever he begins, he catches at the end of it a glimpse of the great Resurrection truth: immediately he rushes on with accelerating speed in haste to be there: then, his swift course accomplished, he lifts the trumpet to his lips and blows the Resurrection blast. One notes—what may be a small point, but nevertheless not a wholly insignificant one—that in one place he tells his audience how the Christ whom they slew had been "delivered by the determinate counsel and foreknowledge of God"; a statement which he would surely have recognized as likely to weaken rather than forward his case with his listeners had he been completely engrossed in stirring them to a sense of the enormity of their fault. They might well put in the demurrer (and Peter could hardly fail so to bethink himself), "If it was by God's counsel and foreknowledge that this thing was done, is not the blackness of our sin toned down to a far lighter shade, and are we not at any rate in part absolved?" But the real counter-fact against the offered explanation is this. Peter *does* actually associate the Christ whom he summons his hearers to look upon with salvation and the remission of sins, and this in all the three discourses named, while yet nowhere indicating that the death of Christ is the one and only point on which

[6] *Op. cit.,* p. 113.

saving faith is to focus its rays. "Repent ye, and be baptised every one of you in the name of Jesus Christ unto the remission of sins." "Turn again, that your sins may be blotted out." "Neither is there any other name under heaven, that is given among men, whereby we must be saved"—a sufficient proof, this last utterance, that the question of salvation was tolerably prominent in Peter's mind. "Through His name every one that believeth on Him shall receive the remission of sins." And once again, and most emphatically, *"Him did God exalt with His right hand to be a Prince and a Saviour for to give repentance to Israel, and remission of sins."* It is the risen and exalted Christ then, not—at any rate not exclusively—the dying Christ, from whom salvation is derived! And it was by acceptance of preaching like this, in which no word about Christ's death being the sole channel of salvation occurs, that three thousand people were admitted to Church fellowship and to "breaking of bread" on that Pentecostal day! It should in fairness be said that these passages are fully present to Dr. Dale's mind, and that he quotes some of them. But his comment is to this effect—"these statements do not necessarily imply that by His death the Lord Jesus Christ had atoned for human sin, but they imply that the relation between Him and the remission of sins is absolutely unique." [7] And the comment is made in apparent forgetfulness of the fact that it flings ruthlessly overboard what has previously been said as to Peter's chief aim. With the comment itself there need be no disagreement: certainly there is none in my own mind. But Peter, then—it inexorably follows—was after all *not* exclusively occupied with bringing home to his hearers a sense of the heinousness of their crime: but, travelling quite beyond the limits within which such a purpose would have restricted him, spoke of how, when that haunting consciousness of guilt had gripped them, its strangling coils might be unwound. Indeed, he stood, and asked his hearers to stand with him, upon the idea of their crime only in order to employ it as a platform whence he might leap, and ask them to leap with him, to the idea of their salvation. So we find ourselves suddenly face

[7] *Op. cit.,* p. 118.

to face with the original problem once more. Dr. Dale's reading of the situation appears to turn sharply back upon itself at
its end and destroy its own beginning: at the very least, it makes
more insistent at its close the very question it started out to
solve. If Peter *did* thus speak of salvation, and if the death of
Christ is the *sole* factor upon which salvation depends, why did
not a syllable to that effect pass Peter's lips? To me, indeed (on
the hypothesis that in Christ's death *taken alone* the secret of
redemption lies), the reasons adduced both for Christ's own
silence and the silence of this early apostolic preaching yield,
even when pressed to their utmost and allowed their largest
possible value, extenuations rather than justifications—appropriate enough perhaps as excuses if it were admitted that
omission of the vital point had occurred through error or forgetfulness, but far from convincing when it is claimed that the
omission was deliberately made. And I cannot but be doubtful,
finding in the proffered explanations what sounds to me so
apologetic a ring, whether the ultimate hypothesis which necessitated them is not itself unsound.

But we are told, by way of justifying insistence on Christ's
death as embodying the entire redemptive process (and of
justifying also the various theories of atonement which follow
it), that this insistence must in the first place have grown out of
the experience of the Church, inasmuch as when present-day
experience puts it to the test, it still proves its efficacy for producing a sense of reconciliation with God. And certain facts
undoubtedly yield apparent support to the contention. Multitudes have trusted themselves to the atoning work said to have
been completely wrought out at the Cross—have, in the language of revivalism and of that preaching which claims to be
superlatively evangelical, "clung to the Cross" for salvation—
and have so found peace. Of the fact there can be no denial or
even doubt. Whether in reality many of those thus summoned
to bear their witness have not unconsciously done more than
their supposed programme contains, and whether the ultimate
source of their peace has not therefore been imperfectly discerned, is a point which will come up later on. For the moment

the statement, as just given, may be allowed to pass. Nor would one wish or dare to say a single word of question against the genuineness of the experience thus described or of the depth and worth—so far as it goes—of the peace it claims to enjoy. But whether the programme thus laid down as authoritative, with the isolation of the Cross from all other possible redemptive factors that is implied in it (and this, be it remembered, is the *crux* of the matter), was originally born out of the Church's experience of salvation, and whether a richer and fuller experience of salvation might not emerge to-day, even for those to whom the prescribed programme has yielded so much, if other factors were reckoned in—such questions as these cannot be held put beyond need of further examination even by facts so well attested as those just named. At any rate, in view of what we have noted concerning Christ's own silence and the silence of the earliest evangelistic preaching on what is held to be so firmly fixed and sure, such questions merit a closer scrutiny; and directly the closer scrutiny is begun, certain considerations immediately slip out of their hiding-places demanding somewhat imperiously to be heard.

For one thing, if we travel back through history's long corridor, we find that while for centuries past the death of Christ has been stressed as the all-important factor in the redemptive process, the stress gets less and less pronounced when we are once past the scholastic era, sinks into increasingly-marked faintness as we retrace our steps yet further, and dies wholly when we reach the earliest age. There can be no controversy as to the fact. The first Christians made no such isolation of Christ's Cross from all the other elements of His work as that which it became customary to make later on, and which has now been made for so long that Christian thought takes it practically for granted. His death was indeed a fact of first order of importance to the Christians of those far-off years, woven into the very warp and woof of the redemptive scheme. *Essential* to redemption, it assuredly was. But it was only as one star shining brilliantly in a constellation of many other stars all equally bright; and Christ as risen, glorified, ever-living, ever-present,

counted for as much to them as the Christ who died. Still less
was the Cross so exclusively out-standing in their eyes that they
felt compelled to frame theories about the way in which by its
own special virtue it rectified man's relations with God, or to
make acceptance of any particular theory a *sine quâ non* of saving faith. *Their* experience, at any rate, gave birth to no such
view of Christ's death as we are told experience has produced.
"Christ's death"—so one scholar sums the matter up—"in
ancient Christian theology did not pervade by any means so
much space as it has done for several centuries past, but it was
regarded as a single incident—of transcendent importance and
value indeed, but still only a single incident—in the great chain
of events from the Incarnation to the Ascension." [8] And another competent scholar shows by a careful examination of the
relevant literature of the first three centuries that it contains no
trace whatever of the theories promulgated by the sixteenth-
century Reformers: indeed, stretching his outlook far beyond
the first three centuries, he affirms that the "Lutheran view of
the Atonement . . . is a complete innovation on that previously held in all its essential points." [9] It was not till the
theology of the Latin Church had become dominant, and its
strong contrast at many points with that of the Greek Church
heavily accentuated, that exclusive emphasis upon the Cross
became established as the rule. Any impartial survey of the
history of thought must confirm the statement. "One result of
the legal attitude in the Latin Church was that the whole stress
of its thought was thrown upon the death of Christ, and not
upon His Incarnation. The Atonement was looked upon as
almost accidental, certainly no necessary part of the Divine
Nature, as distinct from the duty of a Divine Law-giver. Regarded thus under the category chiefly of satisfaction, it was
almost limited to the Cross, to which the Incarnation was but
ancillary." [10] It was not out of the early Church's experience of

[8] R. F. Littledale in *The Atonement: a Clerical Symposium*, edited by F.
Hastings, p. 9.
[9] H. J. Oxenham, *The Catholic Doctrine of the Atonement*. See Chapters I–IV.
The quotation given is from p. 120.
[10] Principal Workman, *Christian Thought to the Reformation*, p. 94.

salvation that exclusive insistence on Christ's death comprising His complete redemptive work emerged. And we go on to note the equally significant fact that when at last it did emerge, the redemptive work received so many explanations, various and often contradictory, that it would be an impossible task indeed to select any particular one with indisputable claim to such a parentage. The long procession of them passes—the death of Christ as a ransom paid to the devil, the death of Christ as payment of a debt due to God, the death of Christ as a satisfaction to the demands of divine justice, the death of Christ as the bearing by Him of the penalty which without Him man must have endured, governmental theories, "acceptilation" theories,[11] and the rest—they pass in kaleidoscopic shapes and colours from their beginning in by-gone centuries till to-day. There is in fact no explanation that can be termed "orthodox" in the sense of having formed part of the Catholic faith the ages down: there have been explanations many and counter-explanations many, whole arrow-flights of them speeding across the theological sky as it broadened out concurrently with the expanding years. Can it be maintained that an idea born out of experience would be born in a shape so nebulous as to be capable of wearing such a variety of interpretative dress? An experience must itself, one would legitimately suppose, be vague to a degree if the attempt to express it results in voices so discordant and changeful. And vague the earliest Christian experience of redemption most emphatically was not.

Moreover, another objection to the argument that because many are known to have experienced assurance of redemption through reliance upon Christ's death *taken alone,* therefore the

---

[11] Theories such as those of Duns Scotus, Grotius, and Limborch. These do not assert that Christ's death satisfied divine justice by offering an actual *equivalent* for the penalty which man's sin had incurred or, from another angle, by making payment of the *total* debt which man owed. The attempt to equate Christ's death with man's deserved punishment or with man's liability is held impossible. Christ's death becomes the offering of a sacrifice which God accepted *as if it were* the equivalent of sin's due retribution, or of a payment which God received *as if it were* the whole. On the first statement of the matter, the principle of necessary satisfaction to the demands of justice had been sufficiently affirmed on the Cross: on the second, a "token payment" had been made; and thereafter God was able to forgive.

earliest Church must have found assurance of redemption by
the same elusive reliance, rises up with arresting power. Even
if in face of the absence of any historical evidence in its favour,
the argument be still pressed, its supporters cannot go on to
assert that they have found the one and only indispensable
source whence the experience can spring. For if it were that,
how account for the unquestionable experience of redemption
possessed through the long stretch of time when that source
was untapped? We have seen that the early Church, when it
comes closely enough into view to permit our scrutiny, did *not*
sever Christ's death from all other constituent elements in His
ministry, past, present, and to come, nor proclaim "In that, and
in that alone, the secret of salvation lies!" Yet through all the
years and centuries the Church still rejoiced in the early experience, still knew the early peace, still possessed all the richest
treasures of the Christian life in as abundant profusion as the
earliest Christians had done. By the hypothesis, the experience
should not have been repeated—but there it is, written across
the history of those years and centuries in script as golden and
as glowing as ever! We seem faced by a reproduction of that
more ancient scene in which Egyptian enchantments performed
or seemed to perform the miracles which, it might be legitimately supposed, only Aaron's rod could work. How explain
it? To say nothing of the many who right down to and during
our own day have not accepted the programme put forward as
the only authoritative one, and who have made their contact
with Christ not only at the point indicated but at others as
well—confining ourselves to the Church of those times before
the programme had been formally drawn up or the exclusive
point invested with an unshared prerogative—is it to be asserted that the Christian experience of those times was not the
genuine thing? If it was genuine, by what magic, in the absence
of any duly-commissioned power, was the result produced? Did
some lying spirit pass off upon the disciples of those days a
counterfeit jewel for the authentic gem? In all consistency the
second alternative ought, it would appear, to be asserted by
those who employ the argument from experience in the way set

out. Yet to ostracize from the Christian fold men and women carrying so many marks of membership in it and wearing so patently the likeness of the Lord they profess to love and serve is, fortunately, repellent to many (would it were so to all!) even of those who press the argument strictly and far. Their hearts will not be ruled by their too austere logic; and the spiritual sensitiveness wrought in them by the Christian spirit refuses to lie quiescent under what consistency requires it to endure. Only, if adherence to supposed truth and the Christian spirit are thus openly at war, must there not be something wrong?

Of course the argument from experience is a most valuable one within its legitimate sphere,[12] but it is capable of plausible applications in spheres where its writ cannot run; and it may easily, unless careful watch be kept, take a leap over a difficult piece of logical ground and then as it were look back triumphantly from the other side, whereas, had it gone forward in more restrained fashion, it would have found its foothold insecure. It is a valid enough use of the argument if from the long-continued recurrence of some phenomenon at a given time or place or both, or under a given set of circumstances, we reason that the same phenomenon will continue to recur, even though no explanation of it be known. The frequent repetition of a possibility's fulfilment may reasonably turn the possibility into a probability for us, and turn probability into certainty, or at any rate into moral certainty, at last. In fact, it is upon such inferences that we rely for many of life's most familiar "certainties"—for example, for our certainty as to to-morrow's rising of the sun. It is an equally valid use of the argument from experience if, when two phenomena have repeatedly presented themselves upon our field as a first and second which never exchange places, we conclude (provided that the series has been sufficiently prolonged to obviate any suspicion of the *post hoc propter hoc* fallacy creeping in) that the first is the causal

---

[12] The argument from experience, in what I take to be its legitimate application along the line this book follows, will be referred to later on. See Chapter VII, § 4.

antecedent of the second.[13] If I have over and over again found
that the presence of fire causes heat, I am justified in concluding, when next I perceive fire and feel the sensation of heat, that
the sensation is caused by the fire. Again, once such a causal
relation has been established, it becomes a perfectly valid use
of the argument from experience if, on perceiving or feeling the
first or second phenomenon, we infer that the other, though at
the moment we do not perceive or feel it, is really present. If I
feel the sensation of heat, I rightly infer that one of the agents
duly certified by past experience as producers of heat—fire,
electricity, or some other on the accredited list—is doing its
part, even though at the moment I cannot locate it. Or conversely, if I perceive the presence of flame, I know that heat is
radiating from it, and, if I am unconscious of any sensation of
heat, merely conclude that I am outside the flame's circle of
radiation. The argument runs quite fairly from or to a force
which has repeatedly proved itself as productive of a particular
result. We may, moreover, stretch the matter so far as to say
that from what we perceive others to be doing or know others to
be feeling, the argument from experience will carry us safely to
an inference concerning the force or cause acting upon them;
for in such case *their* experience so to say telegraphs itself to *us*,
and thus in a manner becomes part of our own. All this is of
course the elementary alphabet of the thing, so elementary that
it may appear scarcely worth while to set it down. Nevertheless,
something even more self-evident must needs be added.

*An argument from experience, if it is to be valid, must start
from a platform demonstrably within experience, not from
somewhere outside of it.* To set this down may seem, not merely
superfluous, but almost farcical. And yet it is precisely under the
test thus suggested that the argument from experience breaks
down, as employed by those who reason that because multitudes
have found assurance of salvation following upon faith directed
towards Christ's death *taken alone,* therefore, by Christ's

[13] I am of course aware that according to the strict use of philosophical language one "phenomenon" cannot be spoken of as the "cause" of another. But for
our present purpose the expression may pass.

death, *taken alone*, salvation must have been brought to mankind. They claim that they are using the argument along the line indicated above as running from an effect to the force that causes it. They have themselves realized a consciousness of salvation consequent upon trust in something accomplished solely at the Cross: to their own testimony many others have said a loud "Amen," affirming that the same trust has for them produced the same result: is it not evident that at the Cross alone the redemptive act was wrought? But to reason thus is really to enact that logical or illogical "leap" which the argument from experience, unless closely scrutinized and kept in bounds, is apt to perform. All we have here is a *consciousness* of salvation produced by a *belief* that through Christ's death, taken in and by itself, and through its influence upon our relations with God, salvation is ours. In other words, we have at most a belief bringing about the feeling which it is naturally fitted to bring about—a sufficiently satisfactory example certainly, so far as it goes, of the relation between cause and effect. But the energizing force in the production of the feeling is the *belief,* and the belief alone; and the presence of the feeling can certify only the *presence and working* of the belief, not to its truth. Let us note carefully that all the formative facts or acts, so to call them, definitely asserted or implicitly suggested by the belief—for instance the framing of a divine "plan of salvation," accepted and fulfilled by Christ, to the effect that Christ's death was to be in itself the sole factor in salvation, or whatever else may be the facts and acts to which the belief professes to attach itself—belong to the order of *divine* experience, if the phrase may be employed, and are quite outside the range of our own. Nor can they by any strain of mind, or by any thinkable evolution of human mental and moral power or stature, ever be included within ours in such wise as to be subject to test. What we should require, therefore, in order to legitimize this "argument from experience," is to have stored up for us an actual *experience* or series of experiences wherein the effectiveness of a belief to generate its own appropriate feeling has repeatedly proved the truth of the belief, even when the belief has been directed upon matters wholly outside human ken. And such an experience we manifestly do not possess. For that matter, a belief in facts or acts or happenings surmised to lie somewhere behind us on the line of the purely secular historic process is not, in the absence of everything except the belief, authenticated because it can be depended upon to evoke a certain emotional reaction. I cannot argue that because a belief in some alleged by-gone event makes me glad or sorry, does so whenever I think of it, and acts in the same way on others when it is put before their minds, therefore the event actually took place. I may by the strenuous athletic exercises of a perfervid imagination persuade myself that a friend of mine came into a fortune so recently as a month ago; and I may, whenever I bethink myself of his supposed good fortune, feel myself transported with congratulatory delight; but my delight, and my knowledge of the belief that causes it, do not of themselves, let them visit me often as they may, provide proof that my belief is true. Were I to take them as guarantors, it would not be upon experience that I should be taking my stand at all. Of course subsequent information may reach me telling me that my friend has really received the pleasant windfall; and thereafter it *will* be upon experience (my experience of humanity's veracity and trustworthiness) that, in believing the fact, I base my belief. But otherwise, the quasi-logical "leap" involved in taking the conjunction of surmise and feeling for proof of reality is clearly absurd. Much more, then, failing within the range of merely human history, must such a "leap" fail when it attempts to find a foothold amid the eternal counsels of God. In fact the argument, professedly from experience, that on Christ's death *taken alone* salvation definitely depends according to the decrees of heaven shifts its starting-point for the second stage of its journey away from the platform of experience altogether, and becomes mere surmise. The *first* passage made by the argument —let it be conceded for our present purpose—may be legitimate enough. The presence of the *feeling,* let it be granted, indicates the presence of the *belief;* and if the *belief* be there, let it be granted also that the *feeling* is sure to ensue. But the *sec-*

ond passage, supposedly capable of bringing us to a conviction that the belief is true, lands us amid happenings and transactions of the eternities where neither our own experience nor that of others has ever been or can ever go; and the so-called "argument from experience," unless "subsequent information" (in this instance revelation) be called in to furnish a new platform from which it may take off on this its second flight (though, to be sure, by the use of this the argument in its original form would be destroyed), ceases before it has reached its goal to be an "argument from experience" at all. The contention for whose sake it has been constructed, if it is to be upheld, must build its defence along other lines than these.

We may return, then, with some confidence, as to a platform whence our thought may start on the next stage of its progress, to the statements previously made. Christ took His death as inevitable and His Resurrection as sure; and He took them both as essential for the discharge of the mission given into His hands; and, inasmuch as Resurrection is in and by itself a new beginning, He, taking them *together,* looked beyond them *both.* And, reverently following Christ in so reading the matter, we trace a further organic and vital connection *from* Christ as possessor of the new life-dynamic, *through* the Christ who died and rose again, *on* to the Christ who by His dying and rising remained no longer the Christ of a limited geographical area and of a transient ministry, but became the Christ of the whole world for the whole world's entire after-time. And, still reverently, we repeat the "must" which, though death could not force it upon Him, Christ imposed upon Himself, and say that, for the local Christ to become the universal Christ, Christ *must* die.

4

It is difficult, if not impossible (I think the statement may be ventured without presumption) to show the absolute necessity, for redemptive purposes, of Christ's death, its vital and organic relation with the redemptive scheme, except by drawing some such line of connection—from Christ the Life-Giver, through the Christ who died and rose again, on to the Christ universal—as we have sought to draw. We may *affirm* it, of course, without *showing* it, on the authority of Scripture, for one thing, and within that on the still more conclusive authority of Christ Himself. And indeed some theories of the Atonement hardly seem to pass beyond the mere affirmation. But that will not satisfy, and ought not to satisfy, a Christian disciple who is anxious to give a reason for the faith that is in him. If Christ's death was indispensable to the carrying out of His redemptive purpose, the task of showing some necessary connection between the two must be faced. We must be able, in giving an account of ourselves, to some extent to answer the question, "Why *must* Christ die?" To *some* extent only, granted. Mystery may gather, and gather even thickly, upon the problem long before we have reached anywhere near its ultimate borders. But here and there mystery's cloak must be drawn aside. Mystery must not be so impenetrable as to deserve the title of magic or to turn our use of Christ's death into the mere manipulation of a charm. That may have passed muster when joy so masterfully thrilled us in the hour of new-born enthusiasm whose tumultuous gusts whirled all questioning spirits away. But those spirits will return, stubbornly inquisitive, if and when normal calmer weather sets in and we set ourselves (as sooner or later most of us must) to re-build our faith, not on the shifting sands of feeling, but on the rock of a conviction tested and sure. Then we have to discover at least some suggestion, clear enough to free us from utter bewilderment, as to the *necessary* relation, the *vital* and *organic* connection, between the Cross and the redemption in which by common consent it plays so out-standing a part. Such a relation we have attempted to trace. Can it be done, on any of the generally current theories as to what the Cross signifies? Can they answer the inquiry, "Why *must* Christ die?"

The forensic theories of Atonement—speaking as they do of satisfaction to God's justice or of homage to God's outraged majesty, or of an appeasement of God's wrath, or of an endurance of sin's penalty in man's stead, performed at Calvary—come nearest to establishing such an organic relationship between the Cross and redemption, or at least to the appearance of doing so. If by Christ's death God was enabled to offer to man a salvation which without that sacrifice He would have been compelled (we speak after the manner of men) to withhold, it would seem that at any rate something like a causal connection is satisfactorily set up. Yet on closer analysis the connection appears to be *affirmed* rather than *shown*. For one thing, one has hardly had time to settle down upon the apparent plausibility of the contention before it begins to shift unsteadily beneath one's feet. The thought (it is no piece of hypercriticism) springs to one's mind that in such theories provision is indeed made for the removal of an obstacle, but scarcely for the establishment of a positive and effective cause. Salvation, on these theories, is a thing wrought out by God on condition that some other thing is previously done; but while the presence of an effective cause is in itself a condition, the fulfilment of a condition *quâ* condition is not necessarily in itself an effective cause. A whole multitude of conditions may require discharge before any cause can do its work, while their discharge may nevertheless do no more than clear the space and open the door for the fulfilment of the *final* condition—the entrance of the actual cause itself. In the case given here, what is suggested for cause simply makes salvation *possible,* but does not *give birth* to it in any real causal sense. There is in fact no *vital* and *organic* connection between the alleged cause and the alleged consequent result. Further, when we inquire into the precise usage and meaning of the words "salvation" and "redemption," the early appearance of plausibility, already impaired by the consideration just referred to, wears off still more. For, in effect, the theories under notice sever the redemptive process into two entirely distinct parts—the first consisting of the offer of pardon, consequent upon Christ's death, from God's side, and of the acceptance of it from the side of man; while the second consists of a spiritual development into the likeness of Christ Himself, or of "growth in grace"; and so entirely distinct are the two sections of the process that the second section calls for a quite fresh starting-point of its own in the operations of the divine grace. The sinner is first of all delivered from punishment by his trust in the Cross; and then the grace which has provided the deliverance takes the matter up from a fresh angle, comes in by another door, to cultivate the flowers and fruits of holiness in the soul. This statement has to be qualified by the admission that perfect reliance upon Christ's death for pardon is sometimes held to bring automatically in its train such an opening of the human heart to God's grace and to the influences of the Holy Spirit that the pardoned soul will start out upon the second stage of its progress without pause or break. Dr. Denney claims that the sense of debt to Christ under which the pardoned soul will lie "is so profound that the whole being of the Christian is changed by it: it is so strong as to extinguish and to create at once; under the impression of it, to use the apostle's words, the aim of Christ's bearing of our sins is fulfilled in us—we die to the sins and live the life of righteousness." [14] One can only say, Would that it were so! But while there are many chapters of human history and experience which appear to lend support to the statement, there are many also which emphatically contradict it: all down the ages from the time of the apostle James till now it has been glaringly proved how faith can be so dead as to have no following works; and it is scarcely possible to accept as valid a view which so often and so manifestly breaks down under practical test. Moreover, in another place Dr. Denney explicitly sets up a guard against a possible—at first sight perhaps the natural—interpretation of his words. A life of goodness lived under a sense of obligation might seem to imply nothing more than the development of purely natural good qualities, of a purely natural righteousness, under the stimulus and spur of overmastering emotion; but Dr. Denney puts it, "We may say that we have received the Atonement, and that the Atonement *regenerates;* or that we have been justified by faith, and that justification *regenerates.*" [15]

[14] *The Death of Christ*, p. 101.
[15] *Op. cit.*, p. 332.

It is obviously, then, a supernatural life that is born within the sinner under the consciousness of debt he feels; and as a supernatural life cannot be born out of a sense of debt (the very phrase is meaningless), it must spring from an entirely new outflowing of supernatural grace. For that matter, Dr. Denney, so far from questioning this, would doubtless have asserted it with emphasis. And that the new out-flow is opened to shed its blessings only upon the sinner conscious of his debt to the Cross does not alter the fact that it is freshly-opened and new. We are back accordingly at a redemption (if we take the term in its fullest sense) derived from two separate and distinct sources and experienced in two entirely separate and distinct ways. Usually, in fact, the matter is explicitly so stated in connection with forensic theories of Atonement, whether the energizing power at work in the second stage of redemption's process be the "irresistible grace" of extreme high Calvinism (of which view Dr. Denney's may perhaps be ranked as a later counterpart, expressed in terms more adapted to the modern mind) or the Holy Spirit acting with the co-operation of our own surrendered wills. For this last standpoint, the following quotation may be taken as representative. "Sanctification therefore can only mean that we take care to let the latter power (the Holy Spirit) rule us, instead of the former (the evil tendencies within.) What we are told is that we are to receive into us a new power—a real living force from heaven moving in the line of holy obedience; a divine, helpful, inspiring, indwelling Spirit Whose impulses must in the end prove mightier than the downward drag of our fallen hearts. . . . What we are called upon to do in the matter is to encourage and trust to the action of that mighty holy Power of God. We are neither to grieve Him nor quench Him. On the contrary we are to 'mind His things'—as our version has it: that is to say, to study how we may by all means invite and welcome and yield to the action of Christ's Holy Spirit within us." All this, be it remembered, is the programme for *sanctification,* a second programme which the Christian man must set himself to pursue *after* he has "won salvation." [16] Whatever

[16] Dr. Oswald Dykes, *The Gospel According to St. Paul,* p. 231.

way it may be put, on the forensic theories the redemptive process falls into two parts, each with an originating-point of its
own. To question the validity of this is by no means to refuse
recognition of any distinction between justification and sanctification: it is merely to say that they should not differ as do two
plants of different seed and grown from diverse soils, but only
as two shoots springing from a single stem. And once the severance is made, hope is gone of making that vital and organic
connection between Christ's death and salvation (in its fullest
sense) whereof we are in search. For the second stage of the
saving process the Cross becomes merely the *prius,* not the
effective *cause*—putting aside the suggestion previously made
that for the first section also much the same thing may be said.
Of the second, at any rate, the statement holds good. At the
utmost, a claim to have traced a causal relationship between
Christ's death and salvation can only be maintained if salvation be interpreted in the narrowest sense of deliverance from
penalty and wrath. Of the bearing of this failure upon Christian
experience something will be said in another chapter: [17] at present we are concerned only with its bearing upon thought. Under
the forensic theories we fail to reach that unity, as of things fitly
framed together, which the very constitution of our minds con-
strains us to seek between Christ's death and the full content of
the redemption He brings. The "vital and organic connection"
may on their basis indeed be *affirmed,* but cannot be *shown.*

But the "moral" theories which, in reaction from the cruder
forms of the forensic theory reduce the effect of Christ's death
to a persuasive appeal, also fail to suggest such a vital connection between the Cross and redemption as we require. Amid all
their variations, they follow some such line as this—that certain
revelations of God and His character had necessarily to be displayed before human vision, with a magnetism in them powerful
enough to win man back from his servitude under sin to yearning and aspiration after goodness, and that by embodying these
needed revelations in His life and teaching Christ threw Himself inevitably into death's grip. And as they all wear to so great

[17] See Chapter VII, § 6.

an extent similar characteristics, so do they all suffer a similar break-down. The assertions that Christ came principally to make the special revelations suggested by the various theories, or that if He did, they necessarily involved His death, are difficult, if not impossible, to sustain; and even if this point were waived, there is no such "dynamic" implied in the given revelations as would suffice for the redemption of the world. It will serve sufficiently if we glance at the failure in the first respect of two or three different theories in vogue: to their failure in the second respect—their non-provision of any real redemptive force—an allusion may be made (no more than an allusion is necessary after what has been said in a previous chapter) when this has been done.

It is sometimes put thus—that there was imperative need for a revelation of perfect holiness if man was to be raised from sin's miry slough, and that this revelation, given as it was in Christ, was bound at its impact against the world's evil to issue in Christ's own death. One notes at once that this assertion, in common with the "moral" theories generally, ignore the voluntary character of Christ's sacrifice on Calvary. One might fairly ask also how the assertion can consistently find a place in a "moral" theory of Atonement at all, since on that theory it is by that same revelation of perfect holiness—with the added revelation of what holiness, in proportion as it heightens its degree towards the summit of the scale, must lead to—that the world is to be saved. Will the abandoned and the devil-ridden be softer-hearted when they have learned that if, instead of slaying goodness, they yield to its reproof and its appeal, they simply transfer to themselves the doom they proposed to inflict? The supposition is on the face of it incredible. But apart from these considerations, the theory will not bear close scrutiny. For as a matter of fact, it was not sin in its more violent or even in its grosser forms that drove Christ to the Cross, but ecclesiastical hatred and pride. Christ had pierced the armour of self-complacency within which the religious authorities of His time and place were encased, and had torn off the robes of ecclesiastical arrogance under which they had concealed their shame and had so left them naked to the mocking eyes even of men who had looked up to them reverently and submissively before. Such people as these they were, not the adulterers and the harlots and the criminals deeply dyed in blood, who as opponents and accusers and judges acted the tragedy through. On the other hand, we see the violators of every law, moral and juridical, hearing Christ gladly; we see the ice of obduracy that lay thick upon the hearts of the rougher elements of society melting into swiftly-flowing streams of repentance at His word or His look; we see the evil spirits of almost every denomination of wickedness shrinking back in self-confessed defeat as His voice touched the ear or His hand the form or His influence the soul of those in whom those spirits lurked. Once again, it was most emphatically not sin in its most extreme forms, as usually reckoned, that drove Christ to His Cross. To affirm that the revelation of perfect holiness which Christ flashed upon the world must inevitably have led Him to His death is to make an affirmation which even human experience, viewed on the long and large scale, and still more the recorded facts of Christ's ministry, loudly contradict.

Along a different line, the statement is sometimes offered that there must needs be a convincing demonstration of God's hatred towards and triumph over sin, and that only by Christ's death and Resurrection could such a demonstration be given. The argument touches one at once with a sense of its unreality. It certainly raises more questions than it solves. For one thing, why should any new proof of God's power and determination to crush sin beneath His feet, were the proof never so arresting, be required at all? If there was one thing which above all others the elect nation already knew full well, it was that Yahweh loved righteousness and hated iniquity and that He would by no means clear the guilty. When one recalls the long-drawn catalogue of judgments fallen like devastating lightnings from heaven, of prophetic denunciations thundered against individual and national apostasies and fulfilled to the last jot and tittle, of famines and pestilences and calamities of all descriptions streaked with fire and blood, recorded on the Old Testament scroll, there seems but little that even Christ's death and Resurrection could do by way of adding to a witness so eloquently borne. Moreover, the suggested purpose lies aside from the usual line of God's working where the relations between Himself and the human race are concerned. Signs and wonders He did indeed perform over and over again, but not merely for their own sakes and for what might be termed purposes of something like scenic display. He never (if it may be said with reverence) came upon the stage to enact a part. The wonders and the signs were always related to a specific occasion—sprang out of it, came back upon it to mould and master it and conduct it to an issue designed. Christ Himself abjured the mere doing of marvels by way of "demonstration"; and "an evil generation" clamouring for them only moved Him to hold His supernatural powers under severer restraint. The mere acting out of a drama is not the divine way. Yet again, why the Incarnation for an end such as the one suggested? The death by violence, followed by a resurrection, of a perfectly holy man (a gift which God might have given to the world if He had so willed) would have possessed cogency equal to, probably greater than, the death and resurrection of incarnate God, as a proof of goodness triumphant over its foes. A greater miracle it certainly would have been, and in proportion to its heightened greatness, it would have driven the lesson more effectually home. And yet again, can it be controverted that God's determination to foil sin's power and bring its works to naught would have received even more immediate and imposing a proof if those who designed and carried out the tragedy of Calvary had been arrested at mid-career, paralysed just as their arms were raised to strike? Had the "twelve legions of angels" deployed upon the scene when the "great multitude with swords and staves" came in sight at Gethsemane to seize their prey and had they scattered the presumptuous forces in rout, or had Christ smitten to earth the High Priest before whom He was arraigned or the soldiers who bound and nailed Him, or had He astounded with swift compliance those who sneeringly bade Him come down from the cross—that surely would have been

a supreme manifestation of divine displeasure upon His opponents and a triumph fitted to make His enemies His footstool!
While on the other hand not even the Resurrection, once the
tragedy was accomplished, was sufficient for a vindication to
the sight or hearing of north, south, east, and west, of the
Christ who died. It would indeed almost appear as though any
such result had been designedly warded off. The risen Christ
showed Himself on a stage far less public than the stage on
which He died. There was no attempt to convince the crowd
which had heard His last cry and watched Him draw His last
breath. Only to the chosen few was the revelation vouchsafed.
Besides that, those who had slain him would not have been—
we are entitled to say were not—at a loss for some specious
argument to explain the whole thing away. They who had blas-
phemously declared that Christ cast out devils by Beelzebub
the prince of the devils could easily wave off even a resurrection, or a seeming resurrection if they preferred to call it so, by
similar sophistry; and Christ's voice echoes clear in this connection from that utterance of His in which He declared that
if men believed not Moses and the prophets, neither would
they believe even though one rose from the dead. We know,
too, that the ecclesiastical authorities, as if in anticipation of
the event which, we are told, was to convince them of God's favour to their victim, obtained permission from the secular powers to set a watch upon the tomb where He lay; having evidently
—with memories of Old Testament prophecies ringing in their
ears and snatches of Christ's words stirring uneasy ripples on
the surface of their satisfaction in the deed they had done—
hardened their hearts beforehand against what they feared
might befall. In fact, if Christ's death and Resurrection were
designed for a demonstration of God's hatred towards sin and
of His determination to put it to shame, one is driven to say
that it was a demonstration likely to fail—and which did actually fail—in respect of those who needed it most, and a demonstration fitted to succeed only in respect of those already
prepared and anxious to be convinced.

Yet another frequently-made assertion is that there lay in the

nature of things, if the world was to be redeemed, the necessity
for such a surpassing revelation of God's love as only Christ's
death could give. That Christ's death provided such a surpassing revelation is of course beyond question. But when we have
said that, have we shown the Cross to be a *necessary* factor in
redemption, or constructed any vital and organic relationship
between the Christ who died and the Christ who saves? It may
be said of this line of thought, as was said of the theory that
the Cross and Resurrection constituted together a supreme
revelation of God's hatred towards sin, that the *necessity* of
such a revelation is by no means proved. Men and women of
the older generations had learned that "like as a father pitieth
his children, so the Lord pitieth them that fear Him." They had
known full well how "in His love and in His pity He redeemed
them": they had been told by a whole chorus of clarion prophet-
voices that He was a God ready to pardon, gracious, merciful, and that with everlasting kindness would He have mercy
upon them. Nay, one unwilling prophet, anxious to launch the
thunderbolts of heaven, but entrusted with a mission of grace,
had rebelled because God purposed to be *too* tender-hearted
towards those whom the prophet himself wished to see destroyed. That God loved His people was no new lesson. And if
further testimony were needed, surely the life of Christ, quite
apart from His death, proclaimed the fact of divine love in such
wise as to scatter all questionings from the minds of anybody
open to testimony at all. Moreover, we must press insistently
the point that if we are to be content with the theory under consideration, what we require and what it must provide is a definite relation between a Christ who died as Revealer of divine
love and a Christ who is Redeemer of the world. Does the
theory provide it? *How* does Christ's revelation of love, made
by the endurance of suffering and death, redeem or help
towards redemption? The question cannot be put by. For unless it be answered, and the definite relation spoken of be established, Christ's death—especially when its voluntary character
is borne in mind—assumes something of the nature of a display.
Self-sacrifice, unless it be patently related to some verifiable

and tangible result which it furthers for some one's benefit,
loses all character, indeed all rationality, as a revelation of
love, and becomes merely histrionic. Dr. Denney's forcible illustration runs thus. "If I were sitting on the end of a pier, on
a summer day, enjoying the sunshine and the air, and some one
came along and jumped into the water and got drowned 'to
prove his love for me' I should find it quite unintelligible. I
might be much in need of love, but an act in no rational relation to any of my necessities could not prove it." [18] The Cross
cannot have come out of any necessity inherent in redemption
unless, besides revealing God's love, it accomplished something
which without it could not have been achieved. The question
must be stressed. *How* does the revelation of love, given in
Christ's suffering and death, redeem or help towards redemption? What absolute *necessity* does it satisfy? Why is it a *sine
quâ non?* Of course an answer has been given—usually to the
effect that so transcendent a demonstration of lovingkindness
cannot fail to draw the sinner by the cords of adoring gratitude
and waken in him such a tempest of enthusiastic responsive
affection for the Christ who died on his behalf as to engulf and
drown all the evil spirits within him in its tides. The assertion
is questionable from more than one aspect. A gesture of affection, made on a scale appropriate to a mere gesture—for example, an embrace, a kiss, a kindly look or word—may well win
thanks from its recipient. It is in fact an actual gift, and as such
fitted to evoke the emotion of thanks. But a gesture, meant as a
mere gesture and yet invested with the tragic colours of self-
sacrifice, made at tremendous cost and yet establishing no direct
contact with the person before whom it is displayed (and it is
not unfair to say that this is what Christ's death comes to on
the theory under notice) can scarcely rouse gratitude. Dr. Denney's man on the end of the pier could hardly feel that particular emotion towards the individual who got drowned ostensibly
to prove his love, whatever other emotions the spectacle might
stir. Surprise, pity, regret, a half-dozen of other emotions, such

[18] *The Death of Christ,* p. 177. There is another illustration in the Preface to
the seventh and subsequent editions of Dale's *Atonement.*

a gesture might waken, but scarcely gratitude. Nothing is bestowed: there is only a demonstration made, and that a quite disproportionate one if intended as a demonstration of love. So with the assertion that the revelation of love offered in Christ's death is enough, merely as such a revelation, to kindle gratitude sufficiently powerful for the up-lifting of human hearts out of evil into good. It may hold good in some instances, but it is quite inadequate as an account of Christ's redemptive work. And if it holds good in some cases, it is belied by more. One remembers Bushnell's remark that gratitude is one of the emotions which the soul case-hardened in evil cannot feel; and one reflects—reluctantly as one may set the door ajar for the reflection to enter—that whatever qualifications the remark may require, it is undoubtedly true in the main. Questionable indeed, then, the theory we have been considering turns out on closer examination to be. In company with other "moral theories," it fails to supply us with what we need.[19]

For beyond the dynamic of *persuasiveness* these theories have none; and of this, and of its insufficiency for meeting God's "problem" of redemption, we have already spoken. When we touch the question of forgiveness, they show us a God who forgives just as man forgives. They certainly paint into the picture

[19] It is worth noting that Bushnell, himself a powerful and fascinated advocate of a "moral theory" of Atonement, confesses that previous attempts to construct such a theory have led to no satisfactory result. He describes it as "one of the most remarkable facts in the history of Christian doctrine, that what the critical historians call the 'moral view' of the Atonement, in distinction from the expiatory, has been so persistently attempted, and so uniformly unsuccessful. . . . They have been partial, they have not included matter enough to make any complete Gospel, or to maintain any permanent hold, as a power, in men's convictions. They begin to wane as they begin to live, and shortly die for want of any complete apparatus of life. One proposes Christ as an example. Another imagines that His work is exhausted in correcting the superstition, or false opinion, that God will not forgive sin; and so allowing God's paternity to be accepted. Another shows Him to be the teacher of a divine morality that must needs restore the world. Another beholds, in His life and death, the manifested love of God. Others follow in varieties that contain some, or all, of the proposed methods of benefit, and fill out, as they conceive, the more complete account of His moral efficacy. The inherent weakness of all such versions of the Gospel is that they look to see it operate by mere benignities—something is either to be shown or done, that is good enough to win the world." (*The Vicarious Sacrifice*, edition 1880, pp. 336, 337.) Bushnell's explanation of previous failures is not the one which is offered in these pages. But his admission of them merits attention.

a God who makes a preliminary appeal to man, but that is all. They show us a God who seeks to persuade men—by fear, if we take the Cross as being a demonstration of God's hatred of sin and of His determination to beat it down; by a gentler magnetism than that of fear, if we take the Cross as being the supreme demonstration of eternal and changeless love; by some influence for which it would be hard to find a name, if we take the Cross as being a revelation of the fate which perfect holiness was by its very nature doomed to face. But they do no more. It really comes to this—that God, at the crisis of the world's spiritual destiny, met it simply by an appealing gesture more vivid, more dramatic, more tragic, than any He had made before. And we must face the implication of this. It implies that the Cross, whatever it may have meant and whatever it may have accomplished, formed no part of any *redemptive* scheme deserving the title; for redemption—one must recur to and emphasize the idea—involves the application of a new *force,* in the strictest sense of the word, to the existing condition of man. So Christianity ceases to be a religion of redemption, and becomes a religion of inspiration at most. And God in Christ was merely seeking to restore the life-movement of the world from the wrong lines along which it was straying to those His will would have it travel by nothing more than a clearer revelation and a louder call to come back.

By none of the theories we have been reviewing, then, is there any vital and organic relationship established between the death of Christ and the redemption of man. They offer no adequate answer to the insistent question "Why *must* Christ die?" It is not going too far to say that they seem to be fumbling, more or less at random and with haphazard keys, at a lock which remains invincible, and in which the tentative keys are found so pitifully small that they turn round and round without catching in the wards. The thing is too big (so a persistent instinct affirms) for facile interpretations like these. The whole reading is on too slight a scale. And an instinct so aggressive and so enduring cannot be lightly waved away. But may we not escape from the helplessness in which all these theories seem to leave us by saying once again that only through Christ's dying and rising could the life-dynamic in Christ become and be proved a universal and enduring power?

5

What must death have meant to Christ? One fears that one is treading too heavily upon sacred ground in even putting the question: yet, if one clothes oneself in garments of reverence as one approaches it, and if one asks and answers it in subdued tones, one may venture a little way. Only, of course, one must ask the question, too, with recognition of the fact that a full answer is beyond our reaching. None but God can know the secrets of the dark valley through whose passes, impenetrable by us, God trod in those last days and hours of God manifest in the flesh. One can but catch at some straying shafts of light that fall upon the inquiry's edge.

At least we can say that to Christ death must have been a very different thing from what it is to us. It is not putting it too strongly to affirm that in the usual sense of the word He could not die at all. We have already stressed the truth, implicit in His Deity, that He did not have His life rent from Him, but laid it down. For He had life in Himself as the Father had life in Himself: the very creative life of God dwelt in Him. And we can go on to say that for Christ there could be no terror as to the beyond, no trembling wonder as to what might be hidden behind death's dark doors, none of the many things which make death a riddle to our hopes and fears. Being already Lord of life, He was of necessity Lord of death as well. But we cannot go on to say, as superficial haste might mislead us into saying, that for Christ this freedom drew death's sting or muffled to a gentle murmur the reverberating sound of its chariot-wheels. For He dreaded it, we know. More than once His utterance becomes tinged with pathetic shrinking from the fast-nearing call: more than once—in spirit if not in words—He seems to brood with sadness on the fact that He, like the corn or wheat which is to bear its fruit, must first fall into the ground and appear to die; and although the transient recoil always ended in a "Father, Thy will be done," that note in quiet acceptance of what was to be was sounded only after His soul had been troubled and the wistful prayer "Father, save me from this hour" had been stayed just as it was about to start its trembling flight to heaven. At these moments of Christ's soul-trouble we shall presently take a reverent look again. What lay behind this shrinking from the cup which was to be set to Christ's lips? Not, of course, fear of the physical accompaniments of the death He was to die. Had that been the explanation, Christ would wear a less shining halo than that which encircles the brows of countless martyrs who have gone to their doom as to a bridal feast; and one spurns the suggestion as an absurdity—nay more, as an irreverence—deserving only to be stamped down. What, then, constituted death's supreme pang to Christ? Is not the answer this? *Being what He was, He could only die by the passing from Him of the creative life of God.*

It is necessary to fix this firmly in our minds; for this is one of the junctions, as it were, at which we may easily set the points mistakenly for our thinking and either doom it to wreck or at least turn it on to the wrong line and afterwards, in prolongation of the erroneously-chosen route, send it further and further astray. Much of the haziness surrounding the whole of our theme results from imagining an equivalence between death as we know it and death as it came to Christ. Death *itself,* death as it enters into our own human experience, or at any rate death with the added accompaniments involved in the Cross as death's instrument, is what we are apt to think of in connection with Calvary. That will not get us very far on the road to a comprehension of what Calvary means. Death *simpliciter* is a purely negative conception, a conception which erects a barrier across the mind's progress and from which no lead in a further advance can be obtained. If, then, it be death, *quâ* death, that we take as the experience which Christ went through, we have subsequently to find, *outside that death itself* (in some such ideas as that of satisfaction to justice, vicarious bearing of punishment, and the rest), something which we can throw back *into* or *beside* the conception of death in order to furnish it with a unique redemptive significance. For death, *quâ* death, even the death of a Christ, can have no redemptive meaning or power. You can only impose such meaning or power *upon* it by setting alongside of it another entirely different set of ideas fetched from elsewhere. You cannot discover such meaning or power *in* it by the closest reading of its implications or the most strenuous extraction of the inferences it supports or permits. We may of course continue to assert that Christ's death is an essential factor in redemption; but if, after making the assertion, we want to reach also to the significance of the assertion for our conception of Christ's redeeming work, we have to start that second stage of our thinking as it were from a fresh platform, since out of the assertion itself we can get no push to start us along our road. The utmost we can do on this method (the method which equates the conception of death for Christ with the conception of death for man) is, after declaring Christ's death to be an essential factor in His redemptive work, to cut ourselves loose again from the declaration for a moment, begin afresh, construct a series of conditions which His redemptive work must fulfil, and then seek to make a connection, backwards as it were, from the resulting construction to the declaration previously made. In point of fact, that is what many theories—though quite probably unknowingly—attempt to do. And they consequently leave the mind sub-consciously aware of a hiatus in the system it is required to accept. The theories, it is vaguely felt, are *brought up* to Christ's death, placed beside it—attached to it, so to say, but leaving some unfinishedness or even some gap at the point where the contact is supposed to be made. It is beyond the power of human thought to make in this way any "vital and organic" connection between the death of Christ and redemption. Death, *quâ* death, is too negative a conception to bear the strain. There is no passage from *mere* death to *redemption*. But we may fare better if we can fill the negative idea with some positive content—if we take death to have been for Christ not simply what it is for man, but that and something more; if we take it as having been that *plus* something which, because He was what He was, made death for Him an experience entirely unique. What was that something? Once again, may we not say—along the line of thinking these chapters seek to trace—that the answer is this? *Being what He was, He could only die by the passing from Him of the creative life of God.*

What *that* meant to Christ is a question which flings us into an ocean wherein thought, spite of its strongest strokes, can only sink and drown. We cannot by the intensest exercise of imaginative sympathy fully picture, nor in words at all express, what death so construed involved for Him to whom it came. But while we watch Him as here and there the anticipation, and at last the reality, of it seized upon His soul, and while we trace something of His spirit's deepening pain, we can, even through the blurred vision which is all that our straining sight achieves, discern the fitness of the phrases used. On Mount Hermon first we may see Him, after the realization had possessed Him that the Galilean ministry, so promising once, must be abandoned, and that only by carrying His holy challenge to Jerusalem and daring the supreme issue there could He discharge His Father's Will—we may see Him on Mount Hermon wrapped in prayerful preparation, quiet and with no element of agony in it, for the ultimate trial, and conversing with Moses and Elias [20] as to how for Him the glory which He had with the Father before the world began must for a desolate hour be eclipsed by death. But there the shadow was still only approaching the sun, and had not as yet touched its rim. It was rather for the encouragement of His disciples than for the strengthening of His own spirit that Christ had sought the mountain-top. As regards Himself, the transfiguration of His soul, so intense that it revealed itself through the incandescence of His very robes—the

[20] "Conversing with them," not "learning from them," as it is sometimes put. Compare Godet's remark, *"Comment certains théologiens se sont-ils imaginé que Moïse et Elie venaient instruire Jésus de ses prochaines souffrances, lui qui, six jours auparavant, en avait instruit les Douze?"* Godet goes on to suggest that, so far from instructing Jesus, Moses and Elias were instructed by Him—Elijah as to a greater glory than that of being taken up into heaven, namely, the glory of renouncing such an ascent; and Moses as to a higher fate than that of dying "from the kiss of the Eternal." (*Commentaire sur l'Évangile de Saint Luc,* I, 600.)

throbbing of the eternal creative life within Him and His consciousness of its regnant dominion over His personality—His
essential Deity in short—these things were then at perhaps the
highest point they touched during His earthly life.[21] The
shadow had not touched the sun's rim as yet. And though it was
of the decease which He should accomplish at Jerusalem that
Christ talked with His celestial visitants, the darkness which
was to swathe Him in Gethsemane held aloof. Later on, when
"certain Greeks," having heard of Him by the hearing of the
ear, and anxious to have knowledge of Him through personal
contact, sought Him out at Jerusalem, the shadow crept a little
closer. By the renown of His wondrous words and mighty
works, He had drawn these few. A triumph, surely! Ah, but
they were so few! It was a mightier and more widely-spreading
magnetism He was to exercise. He was to draw, not a few, but
all—only first the Cross! And as upon the momentarily-gilded
sky the prophetic finger traced the sign of Calvary, Christ's
soul was troubled. The dark hour that lay ahead as it were an-
ticipated itself, thrust itself forward so visibly as to take the
place of the hour that was and to become for Christ's consciousness *this* hour; and with the dark hour's anticipation there
swept over Christ something of the dark hour's pain. What
wonder, if in that dark hour the very creative life of God was
to pass from Him? Yet the trouble quickly vanished. "Now is
my soul troubled; and what shall I say? Father, save me from
this hour? But for this cause came I unto this hour. Father,
glorify Thy name." A little nearer indeed the shadow had
crept, but only to make a swift retreat again. Later still, in the
solemn hour spent in the Upper Room, as the moment struck
for the traitor to go out into the night and consummate his
crime, and all things told that the end was near, once more Jesus was "troubled in the spirit"; and though even now it was the
treachery of one who had been His professed disciple rather
than His own approaching fate that smote and stabbed His

---

[21] As J. P. Lange finely phrases it—"*Das himmlische Wesen Jesu brach aus
seinem irdischen hervor: es war als stände er jetzt schon auf den Höhen des
Jenseits, als gehörte er bereits der Geisterwelt an.*" (*Leben Jesu*, Book II, 905.)

heart, it meant that the shadow had crept nearer still. What wonder that His spirit was troubled, if the treachery which betrayed Him was to bring Him to a death in which the very creative life of God within Him must be given up? And this time the shadow did not go back. From the Upper Room Jesus passed to the garden not far away; and there the shadow all but eclipsed the sun. One's heart is shaken now, after nineteen hundred years and more, as one sees Him kneeling there in such nameless anguish that "His sweat became as it were great drops of blood falling upon the ground," and as one hears the echoed phrases come trembling down through the long corridor of the ages—"My soul is exceeding sorrowful, even unto death"—"O my Father, if it be possible, let this cup pass away from me: nevertheless not as I will, but as Thou wilt"—"O my Father, if this cannot pass away, except I drink it, Thy will be done." It must have been under the horror of a great darkness indeed that such words as these were wrung from Christ's soul. What wonder, if we have construed rightly the awful experience involved for Him in death—if death implied for Him the passing from Him of the very creative life of God? Yet it was only almost, not quite, that even in Gethsemane the sun was eclipsed. That utter eclipse came later. "My God, my God, why hast Thou forsaken me?" It was an agony now far beyond that of anticipation, sharply-fashioned to a thousand spear-points though anticipation had proved itself to be. It was the reality now of the experience which had been approaching with such inevitability in its threatening step for so long: the shadow conquered the sun's total disc and quenched its last quivering glow; and the lifted cup reached Christ's lips at last. For we must not take the words as some, afraid for very reverence to believe in their literal truth, have taken them—as meaning that Christ merely *imagined* Himself to have been forsaken. It was not that a dense passing cloud hid from Him a sun which nevertheless shone the while. The sun went out. This thing really happened. If it seem daring to say it, it surely requires greater daring still to think that Christ was deceived, a daring indeed for which presumption would be a more fitting name. The

Father, of Whom Christ had said that He was always with Him, veiling His face—the very God forsaken of God—the consciousness of Sonship ebbing away in swift tide from the soul of Him who had so confidently, and surely so truly, declared "I and my Father are one"—these things, and much more than these, were behind that cry. These things, and much more than these, were what death meant to Christ. Do we not construe them aright when we translate them thus—that to Christ death meant the passing from Him of the very creative life of God? What else, what less, can they have meant?

So, for the redemption of the world, He laid down His life, and (we may dare to say it, while knowing that all human speech on such a theme cannot help swerving from final truth both to the right hand and to the left) let His very Godhead go. *Laid down* His life, for to the last the power of keeping it was at His command. So for the redemption of the world He laid down His life in order that, for the redemption of the world, He might take it again, and might out of that renewed creative life within Himself give eternal life to men.

6

Along this line we find in our conception of Christ's redeeming work a valid place for the substitutionary idea, and indeed invest that idea with new significance.

It lies on the surface that according to the reading of Christ's saving work which has been suggested—as we see in it the very transference of Christ's life to man—Christ is our substitute as *agent* in redemption. The appropriateness of this phrase might well have been stressed in the previous chapter; for if Christ be in very truth the Life-Giver, the Creator of a new personality in man out of His own, He is *ipsissimis verbis* declared to be, as agent in redemption, man's substitute indeed. Perhaps, however, it is in the present connection that the point may more fittingly be made, since we are specially viewing the Cross and the Resurrection as the means whereby Christ became, as *agent* in redemption, man's substitute *for all time*. He is substitute in deeper senses still, as we shall presently see; but it is from this aspect of the matter that the start must be made in our effort to construe the substitutionary idea, else we may easily be led astray. The confusions and complications which have clustered round the idea of substitution arise very largely from this—that at any rate since the Reformation era the idea has been taken to imply the substitution of Christ for man primarily as regards penalty; [22] as though a culprit, duly found guilty, should be suffered to step down from the dock when sentence is impending and another should voluntarily accept the court's decree of doom. Behind this lurks of course the misconception (as I at least must deem it, holding it passing wonderful that any one for whom seeing Christ means seeing the Father should for so much as a fleeting moment entertain it) that Christ's first purpose in saving man is *to shield him from God*. With this misconception moving to and fro across the dark background of the mind (it is only there, I think, that it can have its home, for forced into the open daylight it could not survive the indignant protest of the instructed Christian intelligence, not to say of the enlightened Christian conscience), and from its half-hidden recess whispering its directions as to the lines on which thought about the matter must travel, it is small wonder if the substitutionary idea should translate itself into terms of penalty and doom. The second error follows naturally enough from the first: it is indeed no more nor less than the fruit which the seed might be expected to bear. But if, with that fundamental mis-

---

[22] It is perhaps worth while to point out that the idea of an actual transfer of sin's punishment from man to Christ must not be fathered upon Anselm, as it frequently is. Anselm's doctrine is that God's honour, rather than His justice, was satisfied by Christ's death. Man could not make amends for the dishonour he had done to God, because everything man could perform was already no more than God's due; and so man must remain in God's debt to the end. There could never be a surplus wherewith the debt might be discharged. But the God-man, by His endurance of sufferings which He need not undergo, satisfied the demands of God's honour; and God, as a reward for Christ's voluntary suffering, consented to forgive man. Of course in the last analysis a penal element is discernible in the theory, though in a qualified form, for Christ suffers in order that, following upon His suffering, the Judge who would else have condemned may forgive. Certainly Christ's death is interpreted in a forensic fashion as releasing man from divine wrath. But, as stated in the text, it was not till Reformation times that the conception of an actual transference of penalty was definitely formulated.

conception cast out, we take Christ's salvation of man to be, not the *shielding of him from God* but the *making of him one with God* in the sense of making him partaker of God's very life, then the consequent error of construing substitution in terms of penalty, having lost its support, drops of its own weight; and it is as substitute in the capacity of *agent* in redemption that Christ at once stands forth. Yet the reading of Christ's redeeming work which we have been following requires us, when we have said that Christ is substitute as *agent*, to say further that He is agent as *substitute*, with the emphasis falling heavily upon that final word. For He is not agent in the limited sense of holding a commission on man's behalf and bringing back to man the fruits of its triumphant discharge. That, of course, does not carry us to the substitutionary idea (though, very curiously, some who claim to hold the substitutionary idea in all its strictness really get no further than that), and certainly does not match the conception of Christ's redeeming work which we have traced out. Taking Christ as the One who, having the creative life of God within Himself, bestows the divine life upon man, creates or re-creates it in man, we take Him as One who *within* man actually and literally substitutes Himself *for* man: He is "agent" in redemption in the sense of transferring His own personality to the place of man's when man makes room for Him so to do; and thus the entire redemptive process is wrought out by Christ *in* man and yet *instead of* man, nothing being left for man to perform save the one act of will whereby He yields himself up to Christ and bids Christ live in him. On the surface of the conception of Christ as the source and spring of a real "life-dynamic" there lies the substitutionary idea.

But the idea clamours for fuller recognition than this; for persistent through the ages has been the feeling that Christ's work on man's behalf involved more than the doing of something for man, even in the sense of substituted agent just set out—that it somehow implicated Christ's whole Personality in the task, and brought Him into a veritable sympathetic experience (reading the word "sympathetic" in its strictest and fullest connotation) of what the unredeemed sinner must himself go through. There is justification enough. For one thing, it is beyond controversy that many New Testament utterances at any rate adumbrate (to employ no stronger word) the deeper aspects of the substitutionary idea—and this quite apart from discussions concerning the precise meaning of ὑπέρ and περὶ and ἀντὶ, the final closing of which would leave the matter just where it is now. When we find Peter declaring that Christ Himself bore our sins in His own body on the tree—when from Paul come the tremendous affirmations that Christ was made a curse for man and that for man He was made sin—we know that the minds of these apostles were ranging in realms where Greek prepositions matter very little and where literalism's minute dissection of paragraphs and clauses can be of little avail. As we listen to them, and so to say let our minds go with theirs, we realize that behind their phrases lies the conviction of a veritable "sympathetic experience" (to use the phrase again) on Christ's part of the unredeemed sinner's fate, an experience endured by Christ in order that by man it might never be endured. The very phrase "He gave Himself for us"—repeated as it is with many variations in the New Testament, page after page—hints, and not obscurely, at a relationship between Christ and man which goes far beyond something on man's behalf even in the fullest "agency" sense, though that is necessarily involved, and which views Christ as identifying Himself with the fate which for man's sinfulness hung threateningly over man's head. And to the voice of the New Testament the voice of nearly all profound thinking on the topic adds its everrecurring refrain. It is true, as we have seen, that early Christian thinkers did not find in Christ's death *taken alone* the focal point whence radiated all the beams of redemptive light; but whenever they spoke of it, they spoke of it as an event in which Christ's experience as Saviour travelled an orbit in some fashion and in some degree coincident with that appointed for the sinner's experience of doom. Somehow, Christ's road, in that stage of it which stretched from Gethsemane to Calvary, led Him into the dark region where unredeemed souls wander lost.

And ever since the same thing has held good. Even those who have sprung back in most startled recoil from certain interpretations of the term "substitution," on the ground that they violated the dictates of the moral sense, have not been able to free themselves from the haunting impression that the term itself cannot be summarily thrust out of doors when thought upon the great theme is furnishing its house. Through the centuries the idea of substitution—with some mysterious significance in it which substitutionary agency does not exhaust—has won response from the sensitiveness of the Christian Church, and any systems which have wholly banished it from their purview have seemed to leave an "unexplained residuum" in Christ's redeeming work and in the experience it involved for Him, while at the same time rejecting a suggestion which, if only its depths could be probed, might have helped to illuminate what was left shrouded in the dark. It is from Christ as "substitute-agent" that we must begin our interpretation of the substitutionary idea.

The deeper significance of substitution has been suggested, at least hinted, in what has already been said. Christ, in that awful moment when He sent His cry of forsakenness palpitating to heaven, felt God's creative life go from Him. God forsook Christ, not in Christ's imagination, but in actual fact. One may not pitch the statement in any lower key. Turn the statement round, and we must dare to say, if we can bring ourselves to say anything at all, that He lost God. *But that is sin's dread penalty for man.* It was the experience of dread penalty, then (the experience *associated* with it, one might more accurately say, since for Him in His sinlessness the experience was no penalty, but an indispensable antecedent condition of His Saviourhood) that Christ went through. He endured the experience of it in order that man might be freed from its present threat and its ultimate clutch. Whatever the loss of the divinest element within him—sin's direct judgment—would mean to man, Christ knew, though on Him no judgment could fall. To add anything to that statement seems almost like sacrilege. Indeed, even in regard to man one would scarcely dare, nor would it be possible, to fill up the outline and to say what the loss of the divinest element in him—the loss of the divine within him and by consequence the loss of the divine without him, the loss of God Himself—involves. Amid the materialisms of our life, and under the blunted sensitiveness which they induce, the idea forfeits something, perhaps much, from the piercingness of its thrust. Yet, if so much may be said, there are hours when the material veil which hides the eternal realities wears thin, when the soul realizes itself to be gazing upon or even in some measure carried into timelessness, when it feels upon itself a faint prophetic touch of the hands that wait to grip it there; and then conscience may rise to some partial guess at what it means for God to be lost, for God to go. Then we may dimly understand that it means to have the very self rent asunder by the departure of the diviner element within and the consequent paralysis of all effort after communion with the divine without, at last so passionately desired; that it means to be in a very real sense face to face with God and yet separated from Him by impassable gulfs; that it means to be blind while the helpless eye-balls strain in futility to see the vision known to be near, deaf while the orchestras and choirs of the heavenly hosts are making their anthems pass ringing by ears fain and yet unable to hear; that it means to be adrift on eternity's wide seas alone.[23] And if we say that when Christ in the last agony made His call "My God, my God, why hast Thou forsaken me?", God's creative life passed from Him, we say that His experience was *this*. It

[23] I do not, in this purely incidental allusion to the topic, express or hint at any opinion as to whether such a loss of the soul is for ever irreparable or not. I do not know that I have one. But I confess that Whittier's sombre words (in *The Answer*) haunt me sometimes—

> "A tenderer light than moon or sun,
>   Than song of earth a sweeter hymn,
> May shine and sound for ever on,
>   And thou be deaf and dim.
>
> "For ever round the Mercy-seat
>   The guiding lights of Love shall burn;
> But what if, habit-bound, thy feet
>   Shall lack the will to turn?"

The bare possibility of such a thing surely lifts everything contended for in this book far above the plane of mere theoretical interest, and makes any theological question involved in its pages one of vital import indeed.

was substitution indeed. True, as has been said, there can have been in the experience for Christ nothing of what sin must infuse into it for any man whom it befalls, no sense of a retributive ingredient in it, no touch of remorse for opportunities missed or for divine invitations rejected or for grace refused. Of course not. One shrinks from mention of such things, even though they are mentioned only to be denied. But, unless we insist on an almost mathematical calculation of the constituents in a substitutionary experience and will not be content with anything else than a perfect series of identities, that does not make the substitution any the less real. And for that matter, on any theory, even on the most strictly forensic one, the same reservation must be made. But the *experience* was in the final and essential make of it one with the experience which at its journey's end awaits the Christless and Godless soul whence the divinest and best has passed away. Our own earthly days bring or show us instances enough of an experience which is penal in one case and not in another, yet equally searching and dread in both. An innocent sufferer may endure precisely the same sum-total of pain as a wrong-doer who is receiving the due reward of his deeds; and the *experience* is in each instance the same. Nay, if it be true that in the innocent sufferer's case the very fact of his innocence adds to the intensity of his suffering, much more must this hold good of Christ. He who did no sin, and in whose mouth there was found no guile—He to lose God! But that is what Christ endured. Him who had from all eternity been in the bosom of the Father, Him God forsook. That is the stark reality of the thing. Once again, it was substitution indeed. So, for man's deliverance from the impending doom, Christ submitted Himself to its sword. So, to re-open for man the door to heaven which sin was threatening to close, Christ let it close against Himself, and descended into hell.

It was previously remarked that in the reading of Christ's redeeming work suggested in these pages the substitutionary idea not only finds place, but receives added emphasis. The claim may surely be held justified in view of what has now been said. In fact, it can hardly be denied that in other conceptions of Christ's redemption—except indeed in those framed on the most strictly forensic lines—the substitutionary idea, in spite of all efforts to preserve it, is at the least beclouded, often so far whittled down as to be almost lost. For let us clear our minds as to what substitution really involves. Substitution, in human experience, can only be alleged of cases in which one man actually performs an act which another is due to perform, or suffers what another is appointed to suffer, or surrenders something in order that another may gain or keep it; in cases, in short, in which the words *"instead of,"* stretched to their fullest extent of meaning, may be legitimately employed for description of the substitute's act. The man who benefits must veritably drop out of the transaction; and the substitute must veritably go through the experience or endure the loss from which the beneficiary is freed. This much, at least, the term "substitution," if employed with any exactitude, must be taken to imply.

On the line of thinking we have followed throughout, this condition is fulfilled in regard to Christ's death; and in the full-blown forensic and juridical theories of Atonement it is (with some qualification) fulfilled in another way. If thought's constructive effort lays down its starting-point on the idea that Christ's saving work is to *shield us from God,* and if it goes on to declare that Christ accomplishes this by enduring the divine wrath which would else have fallen upon man and, in order to appease that wrath, by suffering the actual penalty which must somewhere find its victim, then it may fairly be claimed that the substitutionary principle is worked into the substance of the scheme. And for those variants of the forensic theory which circle round the terms "satisfaction" or "debt," the same acknowledgment may be made. In support of these theories, certainly, Bronson Alcott's practice of taking himself the punishment which refractory pupils had incurred may be instanced, as it frequently is instanced, for illustration of Christ's work on behalf of men.[24] To be sure, even in these theories the illustration does not fit with the meticulous accuracy one is entitled to

[24] Sanborn and Harris, *Memoir of Bronson Alcott,* I, 194, 195. Alcott seems to have sometimes gone so far as to let punishment fall on innocent scholars.

demand; for while in Alcott's case you have a precise equivalent between what the master experiences and what the pupil
escapes, it is not clear how Christ's *physical* death on the Cross
can be the equivalent of the death—much more than physical,
surely—which sin brings for penalty in its train; so that thought
still as it were leaves its equation unresolved, one of its terms
remaining in algebraic rather than integral form. That, however, may pass with no more than bare mention of it as a flaw.
But there are many theories which, while sheering off from
such crude statements as those just quoted, and while admitting
that the conception of Atonement must be construed in a richer
and more ethical sense than that of throwing up a shield between man and God, are nevertheless quite rightly unwilling
to empty themselves of the substitutionary idea, and which seek
to open a door for its re-entry after it has seemingly taken its
departure in company with the repudiated extreme forensic
formulas. The precise form in which the idea of substitution
is to be brought back is usually left undetermined. The theories
in question propound various analogies, drawn from human experience, whence some suggestion as to a possible fuller, though
indefinitely future, formulation may be obtained. Moreover,
the analogies advanced are supposed to support the contention
that the penalties of sin may be to some extent vicariously borne
—not indeed in the strictly forensic sense, but in some milder
sense not yet ascertained. Not only the substitutionary idea
itself, but the substitutionary idea with some flavour of the
"penal" element in it, though not a flavour that will offend the
conscience, is to be saved. But the suggested analogies do not
really carry us any distance toward the substitutionary idea:
any contact with it they appear to establish turns out to be only
verbal in the end; or if from any suggested analogy the substitutionary idea does emerge, it is found impossible to apply
it to Christ's death for man. We are referred, for instance (the
illustration is fairly typical of those commonly adduced), to
the wife who in her efforts to reclaim a besotted or immoral
husband endures "vicarious" misery through long heart-break-
ing years, refusing to accept the deliverance which the law

would afford her if she asked, and who at last succeeds in bringing him to a better mind; and we are asked to see in such an
incident proof that the penalties of sin may fall in part, not
upon the transgressor, but upon an innocent head. But surely
the incident supplies no such proof. That the *consequences* of
sin may light upon the innocent, it undoubtedly does demonstrate. But that is not the same thing. What we have is the
self-sacrificing wife paying for the opportunity of reforming
her husband a price she need not have paid. We have voluntary
suffering *with* the sinner—nothing more. Consequences, if you
will; but not penalties. The wife's affectionate and forbearing
ministry will not suffice to release the sinning husband from the
natural penalties—the loss of health, the blunting of brain, the
paralysis of faculty, the coarsening of soul—which follow upon
his continual debaucheries, though it may mitigate them, of
course. We may indeed assert that the husband *deserves* to
suffer what he has brought upon his wife in addition to what
he has brought upon himself. But that, again, does not mean
that there has been substitution. There is here no experience of
the wife to which the phrase *"instead of"* might be properly
applied. To speak of such an incident as offering even a hint of
"substitution" is surely a playing with words. Another illustration frequently employed is that of the man who refuses to take
the last remaining place in the life-boat when on a sinking vessel
the *sauve qui peut* resounds, and who unselfishly meets death
in order that some one else may be saved. The analogy appears
so plausible. One man dies that another may live—a statement
which seems to lie exactly edge to edge over the statement that
Christ died in our stead. Substitution emphatically asserted in
both cases, surely! Well, certainly, in a sense. But how apply
the analogy? Is it really a help to any understanding of the
thing? Actually, the very simplicity of the analogy has been a
snare: the fact that the word "die" occurs in both its parallels
has produced a false impression of a correspondence which
does not actually exist. Let us see. The word is heard *four* times
when the analogy is drawn out. The man who flings away his
chance of life *dies* in order that the man to whom he gives place

shall not *die;* and Christ *dies* in order that we shall not *die*. It is simplicity itself. But lay the second parallel of the analogy alongside the first, and difficulties start up. In the two parts of the first parallel the word "die" certainly bears identical meanings. It is in both parts quite literally employed. But, passing to the second parallel, or contemplated parallel—even if we can equate the meaning of "dies" in the statement that Christ "dies" with its meaning in the statement that the self-denying man on the wreck "dies" (and even that much is open to the objection previously noted in regard to the forensic theory), we cannot by any skill complete the process and equate the meaning of "in order that we shall not die" with the meaning of "in order that the man to whom he gives place shall not die." For obviously, Christ did not die in the natural sense in order that in the natural sense we shall not die. The common doom falls still upon those for whom Christ's life was given. The perfect parallelism refuses to appear. The second line of it, as we attempt to lay it down, sheers off in an intractable curve. We can equate the meanings of "die" in the first and second usages of the term: we may perhaps, though doubtfully, equate its meaning in the third usage with its meaning in these two; but we cannot possibly equate the meaning of the term in its fourth usage with the rest. The simple analogy, it would seem, has broken down at the first touch of cross-examination. The illustration, therefore, does not satisfy the conception of a substitution consisting in the performance of some act which another was due to perform or in the suffering of what another was due to suffer. Nor can we say that it satisfies the conception of a substitution on Christ's part consisting in the surrender of something in order that man may gain or keep it. According to the proffered analogy, the man who *surrenders his life* does so in order that the beneficiary from his act may *keep his life;* and if we attempt to bring the substitution of the illustration into line with the redemptive substitution of Christ for man, we end —since redemption must have man's redemption into holiness for its final purpose—in the grotesque conclusion that Christ surrendered His goodness in order that man might preserve or recover his own. Under this further test of what substitution must mean, the analogy, plausible as it appears, breaks down as utterly as it did under the first. We are entitled to assert that, except on the strictly forensic theory, the substitutionary idea of Atonement (still putting aside the interpretation of it set out in this book) is not preserved in any sense that the mind can grasp. It crumbles under any attempt to arrest and grip it. It floats before us like shimmering vapour instead of beaming like a fixed and shining star. Thought not pressed into solidity and definiteness, and expression content to hide rather than to reveal, may have disguised the fact. But the fact is so. When one makes an effort to seize the idea, one feels as if one were trying to catch melting flakes of snow. But we are equally entitled to assert that on the line of thinking we have laid down the substitutionary idea comes into its own; *and on that line of thinking, moreover, the analogy which we have just seen so lamentably failing, justifiably re-asserts the competence and fitness it was previously proved to lack.* For—let the solemn and awe-inspiring words be set down once more—Christ lost God in order that by man God might not be lost. He surrendered the essence of His self-hood in order that man's divine self-hood might be preserved or regained.

7

After the Cross, the Resurrection. Of this comparatively little need be said; for the special significance of the Resurrection from our point of view has been implied in what has been suggested as the special significance of the Cross. By way of preventing the thread of our thought from hanging slack, a few phrases previously employed may be set down once more. The Cross and the Resurrection of Christ (or perhaps it is better to add another factor to the statement, and say the *life,* the Cross, and the Resurrection of Christ) must be taken *together* in order to the full appreciation of any one of them; for each is not so much an isolated event as an element in one event inclusive of them all. At the Cross, when, forsaken of God (for He meant what He said), the cry of His broken-heartedness went up, Christ surrendered the creative life wherewith His Father had endowed Him: in the Resurrection He received it again. So by the Cross and the Resurrection the local Christ became the universal Christ, the Christ of a swiftly-transacted earthly ministry became the Christ of a ministry for the world's entire after-time; and this ministry is the communication of the very life of God from Christ Himself to man. And so through Cross and Resurrection there came into play the universal life-dynamic whereby God corrects the world's erring life-movement and draws it back towards Himself. And again, on this reading we make and keep a vital and organic connection from Christ's life, to and through His death and His rising, to His redemptive work.

It is worth noting, as we pass, that the Resurrection of Christ, set in this context, gives a guarantee of immortality for us far more strong than any which the mere fact of the Resurrection, taken *per se,* can give. It is as thus evidential for our own victory over death that Christ's Resurrection is commonly taken and dwelt upon, after it has been noted as a vindication of Christ's power over those who slew Him. But it becomes much more forcibly evidential along that line when it is looked upon as the resumption by Christ of the very creative life of God, surrendered at the Cross. Indeed it is doubtful whether, without that context, the guarantee is complete. For the loftier our estimate of what Christ was, so much greater does the improbability grow of any outstanding *fact* or *experience,* regarded *merely* as a fact or an experience, coming to an exact repetition for ourselves. How should our life's footsteps, when Christ treads the high hills of transcendent experience which lay open to Him, keep in step with His? What would be a matter of course for Christ, He being what He was, may well be altogether outside the reach of our utmost hope, we being what we are. He rose from the dead—yes, but He was very God of very God; and that might well appear to make too daring the inference that we too shall conquer death because He put it beneath His feet. But if the creative life of God which had been offered to man in Christ through His earthly life, in His Resurrection, once the Cross was past, baptized Him again and in Him and through Him set its fountain flowing full and free for man once more, then immortality is guaranteed indeed. Receiving that life from Him, then because He lives, we shall live also —we may sing the triumphant psalm without a quaver in any single note. Not only so, but the Resurrection of Christ, set into this context and read with this significance, guarantees an immortality worth having. For not any and every kind of immortality is worth having. Mere continuance of life, if that were all of which we were assured, might be a gift of uncertain value. But in this context, immortality means and includes all that God's creative life can make of us and all that God's creative life can pour into the vessel of the human soul. Christ's Resurrection, read as we have read it, guarantees immortality, and guarantees an immortality which must be not merely endless, but in the fullest sense of the term "eternal," life.

In the Resurrection the divinely creative Christ is given back to all the world and to every age. "My God, my God, why hast Thou forsaken me?" That was the transitory eclipse of Christ's Sonship. But the eclipse passed. He was once again declared to be the Son of God with power, according to the spirit of holiness, by the resurrection from the dead. Resurrection came because God's creative life, baptizing Him anew, made resurrection come. For it must be remembered (the point is not without significance) that the record and the reference always keep in view *God* raising Christ from the dead, not Christ raising *Himself;* it is always the exceeding greatness of God's power, not primarily of Christ's own, that the Resurrection is declared to display. And being thus raised from the dead, the risen Christ dieth no more.

Chapter VI

CHRISTUS CREATOR: CHRISTUS REDEMPTOR

We have found, or are finding, a "cosmical" significance in the redemptive ministry of Christ. It restores the life-movement whereto God had in the beginning of things committed the world, the life-movement whereon sin had set its grinding brake so forcefully as to bring it to a halt at last, the life-movement which suffered actual reversal in the end and in which under Christ's life-giving dynamic the counter-reversal came into play. A "cosmical" redemptive work, in truth. But is it possible that the term "cosmical" ministry may be used of Christ's in an even larger and wider sense? Did Christ's redemption mark the birth of an entirely new activity—new not merely as to the direction whence it impinged on the world which was to be redeemed, but as to the source from which it sprang? Was it the assumption by Christ of an office He had exercised before, or the resumption, as it were under a fresh commission and ordination, of an office which He had held from creation's earliest day? If we could take at least a few steps towards finding, in the ages antecedent to the time when the incarnate Christ was born in Bethlehem of Judaea, the *same* Christ who, born there and slain on Calvary and risen the third day, is ever-present now—if we could come within measurable distance of realizing that the Christ we know is the same Christ, not only *to-day* and for ever, but through the longest backward reach of the word *yesterday*—it would not be a wholly useless thing. For surely the jewels in Christ's crown must be multiplied manifold, and glisten with glory intensified a thousand times, if we can discern Him as so to say embedded and regnant in the "eternal order," not only in regard to the immeasurable stretch of it that lies ahead, but in regard to the equally immeasurable

136

stretch of it that lies behind. So a new wreath of empire would be added to those that meet upon His brow; and it would be with a fresh accent in our words of homage, perhaps with a fresh and richer glow in our hearts, that we should approach Him as for His renewed coronation and hail Him Lord of all. Did He first take the "eternal order" into His keeping to set it right when it had gone astray, or had it been His charge even from that far-off time when God created the heavens and the earth? [1]

Admittedly, much of what is said on such a theme must be tentative—speculative, if that word be preferred. It carries us into realms where almost every movement must be one of exploration, with hardly any milestones or guide-posts to indicate the way. And it is not suggested that the possession of any views on the topic is necessary to the ordinary man in order to his realization in experience of Christ as Redeemer, or even for that matter to the preacher for the forcible presentation of his appeal. Yet if it be asked, Why then vex ourselves about a mystery whose attempted probing promises a reward so small? the answer (at any rate so far as the preacher is concerned) is clear. For the exploration of the topic may at the very least prove of assistance to the preacher in his effort to "think things together," and may thus indirectly reinforce the strength of his appeal after all; and in yet another way, as we shall see, it may serve to quicken the heat of his zeal for the souls of men, inasmuch as it may waken in him a keener realization of the world's great need for what Christ has to bestow. And if it can do *that,* it is assuredly no useless thing.

I

We have to begin at a point somewhat remote from our main theme; so that some measure of patience may be asked for if the immediate relevance of what first falls to be said is not clear. For the question under consideration allies itself closely with

[1] It will be seen that we return here to the subject mentioned in the footnote on p. 27 as being temporarily postponed.

the fundamental question which philosophy has through the centuries been striving to solve; and though philosophy and its problems are not our chief concern, it is necessary to turn a glance in their direction in order to obtain the adequate and proper background for our view.

The true relation between "the one and the many" has formed thought's basic problem almost since thought in any philosophic sense began—at any rate almost since the conception of an original source of all temporal and visible things, and the effort to find it and ascertain its name, took their places upon the field. Of course the effort to discover what the "original source" actually was came first. True, there were in the East religions or philosophies which, deeming the riddle of one original source insoluble and abandoning it in despair, settled down for refuge into "dualism," as when Zoroastrianism portioned out the creation of the world between Hormuzd, the creator of all that is good, and Ahriman, the creator of all that is evil—though even Zoroastrianism held that behind both these deities there lay the abstraction "Zarvana Akarana," which was Eternity itself, altogether "absorbed in his own excellence." But in the line of thinking down which western philosophy traces its ancestry, the "original source" was diligently sought—to be found, for instance, by Thales in water or by Anaximenes in air. Then, however, close upon the heels of this primary problem came another, soon to run parallel with the primary one, and soon indeed to blend itself so intimately with the primary one that the two became wholly fused. For the very statement of the first problem, with the two terms employed in its formulation, straightway raised the second; and the second speedily showed itself to be even more intractable and searching than the first. What the human mind by its very constitution deemed itself bound to seek after was not merely an original something which was as it were a manufactory whence the "all things" were sent out, but a "whole" which put forth the phenomenal universe from itself and yet *at the same time* retained that phenomenal universe within its embrace. Of course the very idea of the "source of all things"—of the *one* thing which lay behind the phenomenal world with its manifold constituents and diversities—necessarily implied that the original source of all things had in the far back of time, or before time began, held the "all things" within itself; and thus the idea involved at any rate the *original* unity of the entire "whole." But when closely scanned it involved more than this. Thought demanded, not only an *original* unity whence all temporal and visible things emerged, but a unity unbroken by their emergence. Notwithstanding the multiplicity of appearances which might present themselves on the field of the world and in the processes of history, they must still be held in, and while apparently sepparated from, nevertheless still form part of, the one indivisible (quantitatively indivisible) "All." Thought could not be content with picturing a source out of which all phenomenal things had sprung, to be sent spinning round and round in their separateness through the void: to have been so content would have been for thought to endow things phenomenal with an independent existence of their own, and so to prove itself guilty of violating its own primary demands. All that had ever been, all that actually was, all that might ever yet be, had to be gathered into a unity out of which all emerged, within which nevertheless all remained, and by which all was at last reclaimed; and all the elements constituting the "many" must be discerned as but a succession of waves rising and falling along the tides of an infinite sea. It was unity that thought craved—not only a unity which had been, but a unity which persisted in spite of all that appeared to impair or destroy it. So the problem of "becoming" reared its head. How could the "one" become the "many" in such wise that only the "one" should still remain? Diversity forced itself against thought's craving for unity as a fact not to be gainsaid; and somehow a reconciliation of the contradiction and the contrast had to be found. Long before the Christian era thought had been engaged in this Jacob's wrestle for Being's ultimate secret. Perhaps Pythagoras and his disciples (Pythagoras himself originated the title "philosopher") may be regarded as the earliest thinkers to tread this road. Above all, Socrates the master and Plato the disciple, with a marvel of insight never excelled and seldom approached in any subsequent age, had wrested their priceless jewels from philosophy's reluctant mine, and had bequeathed them, framed in golden settings of the spoken or written word, as abiding treasures for the possession of all the centuries to come. However, the old philosophical solutions of the problem are not our concern. It is only the background for the study of our own special theme that we are seeking to construct; and these things are mentioned only in order to show that Christianity, when it came, found this supreme riddle of philosophy pressing itself insistently on the minds of men.

Christianity, it is often and quite truly remarked, is not primarily a philosophy, but a religion of reconciliation. Yet it may imply a philosophy and, since it is itself an interpretation of one part of the eternal order, must fit in with a true interpretation of the totality of the eternal order when that true interpretation is found. It is not putting it too strongly to say that it must *become* a philosophy when its implications are drawn out.[2] It asserted at the very least, continuing the assertion from that made by the older Judaic faith, a humanity definitely created by God—an assertion, by the way, at which strict philosophy (intent upon preserving a "whole" wherein "the many," while emerging from it, was still embraced) would be inclined to look askance. It asserted next a humanity alienated from the God who created it. And it asserted above everything else a reconciling Christ. In philosophical language, it asserted a severance of the "one" from "the many" (a moral severance certainly, but all the more emphatically a severance for that), and a bringing

[2] "Every religion implies a particular view of God's relation to the world, and has therefore a philosophy behind it. And in process of time this philosophy needs to be expressed, for men think as well as act, and their action depends upon their thought, as well as their thought upon their action: and thoughtful men, in proportion as they are in earnest with their religion, must ask themselves what general theory of the world it involves, what attitude towards contemporary thought it obliges them to take. And this was doubly necessary in the case of Christianity; from the fact that it arose in a philosophic age, and had to be preached in philosophic centres. Educated society in the first centuries of the Christian era teemed with philosophy of various kinds, which with the more serious minds took the place of religion as a guide of life. And it was necessary, if Christianity was to appeal to the educated world, that it should define its relation to this philosophy."—Illingworth, *Reason and Revelation,* pp. 112, 113.

of the severed parts together again. So it touched the age-long problem at once; and it could not be long before the contact became clear. If Christianity were to be adjusted to the claims of philosophical thought, how was its emphatic assertion of creation, alienation, and reconciliation, to be brought into harmony with that unity which philosophy so ardently craved? There seemed only one road to take. Somehow, creation, while remaining the deliberate act of God's personal Will, must be so construed as to indicate the creation of a humanity which, though set up to live its own proper and partially independent life, was nevertheless in some way held, or was meant to be held, within the life of God Himself. And somehow, alienation, in spite of the extremity to which according to the Christian message it had gone, must be so construed as to leave some point of contact between God and man unbroken—or to show how, if the last contact snapped, the re-establishment of it immediately began. And somehow, reconciliation, however it might appear to mark the entrance of an entirely new operative factor in the developing scheme of things, must in its turn be construed as really marking the return of the former operative factor—redemptively re-constructive now in a sense not applicable to it before—to take up its work again. It is not suggested, of course, that for the earliest preachers of the Gospel or for the apostolic writers the problem was thus definitely formulated or its lines thus precisely laid down. They were consumed by an evangelistic passion which could yield scarce an inch of space and scarce a moment of time to such interests as these. Only, perhaps, by a passing side-glance could they indicate that such interests had so much as swum into their furthest ken. But this was the problem which, only dimly recognized though it might be (it was at least that before Christianity had run through a few decades), had sooner or later to be faced. God had created man, yet had not wholly separated man from Himself by virtue of the creative act, and must still be in some sense within the humanity He had made; and however far during history's course man's forfeiture of the divineness in him had proceeded, the moment of its total loss must be also the

moment at which the divineness which had been in man re-
sumed, or offered to resume, its occupancy and its hold. Christ
had become incarnate, had lived and died and risen to live again,
in order to be the agent in instilling divineness into humanity
once more; and the divineness He imparted must be the same divineness which humanity through its sin had cast away—which
meant that the Christ who offered Himself for man's redemption must be a Christ who had lived in man before. It was along
a line something like this, in fact, that the long pondering of
Christian thinkers upon the problem led them to the doctrine of
the Trinity at last; but we have not here to trace the steps
whereby that goal was reached. It is, let it be repeated, only
the background for the study of this chapter's main theme that
we are attempting to construct; and all this is said only to give
some hint of the specific form—necessitated by the primary
ideas and assertions of Christianity—in which the problem of
"the one and the many" clutched from the outset at the skirts
of Christian thought.

Hints of its dimly-discerned presence, in fact, lay their touch
upon us from more than one New Testament page. The prologue of the Fourth Gospel, with its reference to the "Word"
or "Logos" which had been in the beginning with God, which
was God, which became flesh and dwelt among us—together
with its declaration that this same "Word" was the world's
Creator without whom nothing was made that was made—
leaps to one's recollection at once. Or in Paul's magnificent
phrases written to the Colossian Church, telling how the Son
of God's love, in whom we have our redemption, is Himself the
first-born of all creation—the One in whom all things were
created in the heavens and upon the earth, things visible and
invisible—the One through whom and unto whom all things
have been made—the One who is before all things and in whom
all things consist—in these phrases, piled up as if striving to
scale the pinnacles of thought whose summits touch the very
feet of God, and so resounding that "they go through one like
the clang of steel," we catch an echo of the great problem

again. And equally unmistakably, if less loudly, the echo sounds
in another phrase of Paul's, flung as if half-casually upon his
page, to the effect that "for us there is one Lord, Jesus Christ,
through whom are all things, and we through Him." The great
cosmic problem, in all the vast imperial sweep of it, looms up
not far away when the apostle bids the Ephesian Christians
rise to the conception of a Christ in whom God had chosen
them before the foundation of the world and in whom all
things, the things in the heavens and the things upon the earth,
should be summed up when the fulness of the times had come.
Or when we listen to the writer to the Hebrews asserting that
in these latter days God, who had previously spoken through
the prophets, had by Christ spoken in a Son, and moreover
through a Son whom He had appointed heir to all things and
through whom also He made the worlds, committing their
upholding to that Son's word of power [3]—then we are lifted
up into the same high latitudes once more, and seem to overhear
the ultimate eternal secrets whispering to one another in their
hiding-places close by. It is easy to see that subsequent Christian
thought, in endeavouring to fill up the outlines which these New
Testament utterances sketch and in drawing out more fully the
implications which these utterances suggest, must find itself
moving into the region where in philosophy's court the problem
of "the one and the many" was already being tried.

2

It will be well, before looking at these subsequent developments of Christian thinking, to obtain a precise idea, so far as
that is possible, of what is meant by the New Testament utterances at which we have glanced. We may select from them
Paul's great message to the Colossians as the typical New
Testament expression upon the theme, since the others do but
repeat that message with non-essential variations of colour and

[3] For these passages see Colossians i. 14–20; 1 Corinthians viii. 6; Ephesians i.
4–10; Hebrews i. 1–3. I have not cited Ephesians iii. 9 as the best authorities
omit "by Jesus Christ" in that verse. The Revised Version excludes them.

tone.[4] Let it be said once again, however, that there is no suggestion of any deliberate "philosophizing" on Paul's part. He was primarily a preacher of Christ as the Redeemer of men. He may not have envisaged—we may probably affirm that he did not consciously envisage—the "cosmical" conception of Christ which his message implied as being a reply to philosophy's central problem: any relation between that message and that problem is incidental—accidental in fact would perhaps so far as Paul himself is concerned be a more fitting word. The relation is striking none the less, as we shall see; and, as we shall also see, it did not escape the notice of those who worked round Paul's words later on and dug beneath the surface to find the roots from which they sprang. But what did Paul's "cosmical Christ" actually imply?

His movement of thought towards the conception was forced upon him by the necessity for combating certain "gnostic"

---

[4] The passage should be carefully studied with the help of Alford's *Greek Testament* or the *International Critical Commentary* or some other equally authoritative work. The precise significance of its cardinal expressions must be fully appreciated. The chief points are these.

Verse 15. εἰκὼν. This word, translated "image," means much more than "likeness." The εἰκὼν represents an original archetype of which it is an actual manifestation. A second thing, merely made *like* to a first, would not be the εἰκὼν of the first. Perhaps the reflection of the sun in water may be taken as a fair, though imperfect, illustration.

πρωτότοκος πάσης κτίσεως is very imperfectly rendered "the first-born of every creature," as in the Authorized Version, or "the first-born of all creation," as in the Revised. These renderings seem to make Christ simply the first of created beings, and the phrase was in fact so understood by the Arians. The actual meaning is "born first before all creation." The phrase connotes both priority and sovereignty in respect of creation. πάσης κτίσεως is a genitive of comparison—"earlier born *than* all creation" might pass as a true, though partial, rendering of the whole phrase. A full discussion of the matter will be found in the commentaries mentioned above.

Verse 16. ἐν αὐτῷ. Not strictly *"by Him."* Rather *"in Him."* He was the conditioning cause of all creation, containing within Himself all that is found in creation. The idea of "by Him" is given a little later, in the δι' αὐτοῦ of the same verse. δι' αὐτοῦ really means *"through Him."* Christ was the mediating cause through which God did His creative work.

ἐκτίσθη. "Were created." The aorist tense points to a definite creative act in time.

ἔκτισται. "Have been created and now exist." He maintains still the creation which He framed.

Verse 17. συνέστηκε. "All things consist"—"are held together" or "are kept coherent and harmonious." An assertion of Christ as the *immanent,* as well as the creative and upholding, Power in respect of the entire creation.

heresies which, as Epaphras had informed him, were infecting the Colossian Church. Gnosticism in its full development was of later date than that of the Colossian Epistle; but the speculations, theosophic and other, out of which it grew were rife in the Lycus valley where Colossae stood, long before Paul wrote, indeed before the Christian era dawned.[5] In the guise it wore when it made its assault on the Colossians it evidently asserted this much at least of the more mature gnostic theories—that matter was evil; that since this was so, God could not Himself be the Creator of the world; that from the Absolute Eternal Being, whatever or whoever He might be, there ranged downwards a long and many-tiered hierarchy of "aeons" or "angels and principalities and powers" from the last of which (or from more than one of which) the world emanated; that the Incarnation of God in Christ had no reality, since of course the inherent evil of matter made the Deity's assumption of flesh an impossible idea; and that redemption was not the work of Christ alone, but must be accomplished by aid which only the intermediate "aeons" or "angels" could give. Obviously such teaching as this swept Paul's entire gospel away, depriving it of its very essentials at both ends. To Paul it rang like a challenge to mortal combat on behalf both of the faith in which he had been born and of that fuller faith into which he had been brought by his experience on the Damascus road, which had opened its secrets to him during his lonely meditations in the Arabian desert, and under the inspiration of which he had ever since lived. And under the stimulus of the challenge he leaped to a reading of Christianity profounder in some respects than that which even he had entertained before, though he had caught half-glimpses between the pages of the book wherein it was inscribed,[6] and found—found with startling suddenness, would not be too strong an expression—the "Christus Creator" "Christus Redemptor" conception, a conception which counterattacked the new heresy both in front and rear, stretching the

---

[5] On this see Lightfoot, *Epistle to the Colossians,* pp. 73–113.
[6] As for instance in Romans viii. 19–22, where the idea of a "cosmical" redemption is adumbrated.

immeasurable curve of its rainbow-arch above his head. Belief
in Christ's pre-existence had of course been part of his faith's
equipment from the first; but under the new illumination pre-
existence became a richer idea. It was no longer merely a necessary corollary from other elements of the Christian faith,
though it might possess that justification still: it had itself become a capital article of faith from which further elements
might be deduced. Paul looked upon it now no longer as a
branch-stream issuing from its parent river, but rather as a
mighty tributary almost over-brimming its banks as it rushed
on to feed the main river's flow. Naturally, it was from the
conception of "Christus Redemptor" as his starting-point that
he still worked, for it was this conception that had been his
major theme, the "master-light of all his seeing," since his
ministry began; so that it was in a sense *backwards* to the conception of "Christus Creator," though the conception itself
must in any systematic use of it be initial, that his journey was
made. But the goal once reached or leapt to, he took his stand
there, one foot firmly planted on the new ground, the other
keeping its place equally firmly upon the old, and the entire
space between dominated by the implications which the old and
the new conceptions, thus linked up, were seen to involve.

Paul's counter-thesis against the false teaching prevalent
at Colossae worked itself out on some such line as this. First
and foremost, as might be expected, he re-asserts that salvation comes, not through the intervention of any "aeons" or
"angels," but through the Christ who had for so long been the
central sun in the apostle's sky. No other subsidiary luminary
need offer its rays to supplement, far less to render secondary,
that supernal glory. "In whom we have our redemption." It is
Christ Himself, and Christ alone, who re-instils into man the
divine life which man had lost. Against the new doctrine, so far
as concerned the devastating lie with which its system closed,
nothing could or needed to be done except to re-affirm the
mighty and magnificent truth. But what of that other lie with
which its system began? Was the outward and visible world an
evil thing, born from a series of ever-degenerating and progres-

sively attenuating gods or "principalities and powers"? That idea came defiantly into collision at once with the monotheism which was engrained in Paul's nature, as in that of every Jew, like the vein in the granite rock, and which proclaimed that in the beginning God created the heaven and the earth. To Paul, this was a commonplace so unassailable that he does not in this Colossian passage think it worth while to repeat it in set terms, though it is of course implicit in all he says. But if he does not do that, he does more. The wing of inspiration carries him far beyond the elementary assertion that God made the world. Like the pre-existence of Christ, that primary article of faith is transfigured into a far more incandescent splendour as he comes back to it from his reiteration of Christ's Saviourship of the world. God *in Christ* had been the Redeemer—or, to put it the other way round, Christ *as God* had redeemed. Now, as if carried back in a chariot of fire, blazing its revealing trail across the cosmic horizon from history's end to history's beginning, the Christ who redeemed the world is found in the God by whom the world was made. As God *in Christ* had redeemed, so God *in Christ* had created; or, to set it in the reverse order again, Christ *as God* had redeemed, and Christ *as God* had created too.[7] "In Him were all things created, in the heavens and upon the earth, things visible and invisible"—ay, and all those other quasi-deities, the "thrones or dominions or principalities or powers," if such there were, of which the new teachers made so much. The Christ who was the Last was also the Christ who had been the First. And the gap between? Paul had caught the answer to that inevitable question already. It had been given in that same revealing flash which had shown him how in and through Christ all things had been made; and Paul springs to the seizing and the proclamation of the answer as if eager to press out to the last drop the fulness of the new

[7] In one of those earlier "half-glimpses" of the cosmic Christ to which reference has been made Paul had caught sight of the "Christus Creator" idea, and had spoken of Christ as the "one Lord, Jesus Christ, through whom are all things." (1 Corinthians viii. 6, R.V.) But at that time the conception was evidently hanging somewhat loosely at the outskirts of his doctrine, and had not been worked into the wide sweep of context wherein he framed it when he wrote the Colossian Epistle.

revelation's content. If it was God in Christ, or Christ "the image of the invisible God," that made the world; and if it was God in Christ, or Christ "the image of the invisible God," that redeemed the world; then it was in and through God in Christ, or in and through Christ "the image of the invisible God," that during all the intermediate stages the world's very life had been grounded and sustained. Not only is He "before all things," but "in Him all things consist." To Paul "immanence" was as true as to any thinker it has ever been. Christus Redemptor had been Christus Creator; and Christus Creator, destined from the foundation of the world to be Christus Redemptor at last, had been the all-sustaining Christ throughout. So the great synthesis stands out complete and clear, as Paul's backward progress of thought, starting from Christus Redemptor, had framed it. The eternal Christ created. The same eternal Christ sustained. The same eternal Christ redeemed. And finally, as if with one waft of the wing, Paul retraces the long flight across the cosmic spaces from his new standing-ground at their commencement to his old standing-ground at their close, and in magnificent summary declares how it "was the good pleasure of the Father that in Him should all the fulness dwell; and through Him to reconcile all things unto Himself." Call it inspiration—call it quickened spiritual insight—call it what we will: under the new revelation Paul beheld Christ's ineffable glory, as a glory radiating from "the image of the invisible God," flaming out upon him from suns and stars, from mountain and sea, from field and flower, and knew it for the same glory which shone, even though with brightness more subdued or veiled, from Calvary's Cross; and the one eternal Christ was all in all from Alpha to Omega, from the Beginning to the End.

But one point in the apostle's synthesis needs, in view of subsequent developments, to be particularly stressed. Christ had been Creator in the beginning, Sustainer and Indweller throughout, Redeemer at the end. *But the last term of that series implied by its very presence in the scheme that in the immanence of Christ there had been a break, or at any rate a change in approach of the life-giving impulse out of which it*

came. Christus Redemptor had been Christus Creator; but the
fact that Christus Creator had had to become Christus Redemptor meant that the Christ who created had had to re-
create, and consequently meant also that somehow and
somewhere the original creative and sustaining power had been
resisted and had broken down. In Paul's thought-series, as it
threaded itself on this wide arc which his mind was traversing,
this fact could never cease for an instant to thrust itself into a
foremost place. Indeed, the first and last terms of the series, as
they acted and reacted upon one another, forced him to interpret the middle term not only as permitting, but as actually
demanding, an interruption or violation of Christ's original
relation to the world. Christ had redeemed. That assertion
could point to nothing else than a definite and purposed act in
time. The same Christ had created. Creation had also been a
definite and purposed act in time, not a mere effluence out of
some unconscious or impersonal source.[8] And since upon the
first act in time there had followed the second, the first must
have failed to fulfil its aim. If Christus Redemptor had been
Christus Creator—and equally so if Christus Creator had been
Christus Redemptor—the historic process had suffered arrest
on its predestined road; and between the creation as Christ
shaped it and the creation as Christ redeemed it Paul saw a
creation which had failed.

Nevertheless—and this also must be stressed—Paul had
risen to a true unified conception of all things; not indeed to a
conception wherein unity is held to be necessarily synonymous
with mere singleness, but to a conception wherein unity is
equally entitled to its name—a conception which, while allowing to all the factors of the world-process, as the mind reads
them off, their own individuality, throws round them something out of which they all came, which in their emergence dis-
tinguishes itself from them and them from itself, which after
their emergence pervades them, and which at the end takes
them back into itself again. (For that matter, it may be noted
in passing that the distinction between unity conceived as mere

[8] See the reference to ἐκτίσθη in note on p. 144.

singleness and unity conceived as just described is one which philosophic thinking has too often failed to make, as if forgetting that *unity* in the sense of separateness transcended is a thing which a *unit* in the arithmetical sense cannot provide). He had girdled all things with Christ. To the Christ from whom all things proceeded all things went back; and the Christ who had started them on their course was the Christ who had been within them while they fared forth upon it, who was in them still because in His redemptive work He had regiven Himself to them and had once again become the life-Creator within them, and who would at last bring them home. The entire process shaped itself into a perfect round: travel in thought which way you might, forward to the goal or backward to the starting-point, it was Christ—Christus Redemptor or Christus Creator united in a Christ who was the same yesterday, to-day, and for ever, that you reached. Christ was all and in all. And we may affirm that Paul, in these resplendent phrases of his, evangelical and in no wise intentionally philosophical as they were, provided an outline which, had it been filled up with due regard to all its parts and proportions, might have led to a theology both philosophical and evangelical at one and the same time. But the opportunity was missed, and missed more than once.

3

For in the development of the Greek theology—to take that first—the middle term of Paul's "thought-series" came to be too exclusively stressed. The look backward to the first term was only occasionally and casually taken; and of the look forward to the last term the same thing is true in but a slightly less degree. It was probably due to the influence of Greek philosophy that the failure befell. Greek philosophy, with its craving for unity in the sense of "singleness," had accustomed thinking men to the conception of a world which emanated from rather than was created by the Eternal Reality lying at the back of all things, and which even in its very emergence remained in the

last analysis rather another aspect of that Reality than something in any measure distinguishable therefrom. The world was
as it were but a pulse-beat, made visible, in the infinite Source
of all. Of course Christian thought could not run on such a line
as this. To accept it would have involved the absolute exclusion
of Paul's ἐκτίσθη from the Christian vocabulary. Greek theology
could not affiliate itself with Greek philosophy in this respect.
It is true that Plato had called the world the "only-begotten"
from the original source of all things, had also used of it the
expression "the Son," and had spoken of it besides as "the
created image of the everlasting gods." [9] It is true also that
Neo-Platonism, so widely spread and influential in the earlier
centuries of the Christian era, had disseminated far and wide
the idea of an "out-flowing" of all things from the ultimate Being by a sort of internal dynamic. In one Neo-Platonist at least
—Numenius [10] of Apamea, a disciple of Plato who calls his
master "a Moses breathing the Greek spirit"—Plato's title for
the world as "the only-begotten Son" re-appears, used in more
or less Plato's sense. But the entire trend of both Platonism
and Neo-Platonism makes it impossible, in spite of the occasional recurrence of the word "created," to suppose that anything like creation in the Christian sense was intended. Reference to the most elementary philosophical text-book will put
this beyond range of doubt. It was out of the question, there-

[9] *Timæus* 31 B, 50 D, 37 C. In 31 B the word is μονογενής, the same word
afterwards used in the New Testament. In 50 D the word is not υἱός but ἔκγονος,
which however has precisely the same meaning. In 37 C the expression is τῶν
ἀϊδίων θεῶν γεγονὸς ἄγαλμα. Of course the coincidence of Plato's expressions with
those used in the New Testament and later in connection with the Christian
Trinity is merely verbal.

[10] Numenius was born in the reign of Antoninus Pius (138–161). His phrase
in regard to the likeness between Moses and Plato is τί γάρ ἐστι Πλάτων ἢ Μωσῆς
Ἀττικίζων. It should be said, however, that the genuineness of the quotation
is questioned by some scholars, notably by Reinach (*Textes d'auteurs grecs et
romains relatifs au Judaisme*, p. 175, note). It is of interest to observe that a
similar comparison was made centuries later by Maimonides (1135–1204) between Moses and Aristotle. The fragments of Numenius' writings which have
been preserved are scattered about the pages of the *Evangelica Praeparatio* of
Eusebius. They are from the work περὶ τἀγαθοῦ, comprising six books in Platonic
dialogue form. The fragments have been collected and translated in *Numenius
of Apamea*, by K. S. Guthrie. Numenius is alluded to by Clement of Alexandria
(*Stromata*, I. xxii).

fore, that at this point Greek philosophy and Christian thought should link up. Christian equivalents for philosophy's language would be sought after in vain in this field. The idea of a world "emanating" from God in a sense which excluded God's creative activity could have no place within the borders of the Christian faith. But the idea of a divine life all-pervading and immanent—there contact could be established between Christianity and philosophic thought! That idea was already included, as we have seen, within the framework of Paul's doctrine; and the Greek theology fastened upon it with eager intent. The obvious translation, from the Christian standpoint, of philosophy's terminology was "Christ immanent in man": to speak in those terms was to set a sort of philosophic seal upon that second member of Paul's thought-series to which the apostle had given the rendering "in Him all things consist"; and to strike this note became Greek theology's dominant and preoccupying concern. And naturally, with absorbed insistence upon this second member of Paul's synthesis came a growing lack of insistence upon the first and third. In the almost blinding light wherein the middle member was viewed the others became wrapped in shade. "Christus Creator," and (more important still) "Christus Redemptor" in the full New Testament sense, dropped into the background of thought—with the further consequence that as these two terms of Paul's series faded into comparative obscurity, and as the consciousness of their mutual action and reaction therefore became feeble, Greek theology failed increasingly to recognize, as we saw that under the consciousness of their mutual action and reaction Paul had recognized, how at some point in history a break in Christ's immanence within man must have taken place.

The process was gradual, it is true. One can discern lying back in the years of Greek theology's early growth utterances which sound more nearly like full echoes of Paul's. In the anonymous second-century *Epistle to Diognetus,* for instance (*circa* 150), we find the "Christus Creator" conception starting into clearest expression when the author calls Christ "the very Creator and Fashioner of all things, by whom He (God) made

the heavens, by whom He enclosed the sea within its proper
bounds, whose ordinances all the stars faithfully observe," and
piles phrase upon phrase to similar effect.[11] And the "Christus
Redemptor" theme rings out with equal decisiveness in the
same document. "He Himself (God) took on Him the burden
of our iniquities. He gave His own Son as a ransom for us—the
Holy One for transgressors, the Blameless One for the wicked,
the Righteous One for the unrighteous, the Incorruptible One
for the corruptible, the Immortal One for them that are mortal." [12] But these voices by degrees died away. A century later
the tendency to lay almost exclusive stress upon the middle term
of Paul's thought-series had reached its height in 'Clement of
Alexandria (d. *circa* 217) and in Origen (185–254), Clement's
pupil and his successor in the Alexandrian catechetical school.
For these great theologians, the whole essence of Christianity
was to be found in the conception of the divine life—the Logos
who was the eternal Christ—immanent, and changelessly immanent, in the human race.[13] Christ was necessarily and permanently in man, and therefore no need for Him to re-bestow
Himself upon man could ever arise. The whole story of Redemption was the story of God's education of man, through the
agency of the indwelling Christ, up to a realization of the fact
that Christ was within him; and for the individual, salvation
was a matter, not of becoming a son of God, but of recognizing
that he was one already. The historic Christ did not come to
re-fashion a broken relationship between man and the divine
life, but to re-affirm a relationship of whose existence man had

---

[11] *Epistle to Diognetus*, § 7. *Ante-Nicene Christian Library* (ed. by Roberts
and Donaldson), I, 309, 310. I am tempted to show the whole resplendent passage in its Greek dress. The writer says that God sent αὐτὸν τὸν τεχνίτην καὶ
δημιουργὸν τῶν ὅλων, ᾧ τοὺς οὐρανοὺς ἔκτισεν, ᾧ τὴν θάλασσαν ἰδίοις ὅροις ἐνέκλεισεν,
οὗ τὰ μυστήρια πιστῶς πάντα φυλάσσει τὰ στοιχεῖα, παρ' οὗ τὰ πέτρα τῶν τῆς ἡμέρας
δρόμων (ἥλιας) εἴληφε φυλάσσειν, ᾧ πειθαρχεῖ σελήνη νυκτὶ φαίνειν κελεύοντι, ᾧ
πειθαρχεῖ τὰ ἄστρα τῷ τῆς σελήνης ἀκολουθοῦντα δρόμῳ, ᾧ πάντα διατέτακται καὶ
διώρισται καὶ ὑποτέτακται, οὐρανοὶ καὶ τὰ ἐν οὐρανοῖς, γῆ καὶ τὰ ἐν τῇ γῇ, θάλασσα
καὶ τὰ ἐν τῇ θαλάσσῃ, πῦρ, ἀήρ, ἄβυσσος, τὰ ἐν ὕψεσι, τὰ ἐν βάθεσι, τὰ ἐν τῷ μεταξύ.
τοῦτον πρὸς αὐτοὺς ἀπέστειλεν. (Lightfoot's *Apostolic Fathers, Texts*, p. 495.)

[12] *Epistle to Diognetus*, § 9. *Ante-Nicene Christian Library* (Roberts and Donaldson), I, 312.

[13] One of the best short accounts of Clement and Origen may be found in
Allen's *Continuity of Christian Thought*, in the chapter on "The Greek Theology."

through sin fallen unaware—a doctrine which, by the way, sounds modern enough. That in Christ "all things consist" became a truth which, with its necessary implications and its kindred truths, practically elbowed most other truths from their place, or at any rate left them with but bare standing-room on the far edges of the Christian scheme. Glimpses may occasionally be caught of them stirring fitfully on their dimly-lit footholds, as when Origen speaks of Christ's death. But he speaks of it hardly more than casually or as in asides: he alludes to it as having been a ransom paid to the devil; [14] and it lies outside the real process of redemption as Origen conceives that process, in no vital connection with Christianity's central idea. Christ is in man, and man needs to recognize the fact—that is the sum and substance of the whole matter. Even with fourth-century Athanasius, though the "Christus Creator" conception does every now and then appear, as when he speaks of Christ as the One by whom all things have been made, or declares of God that He created His works through the Son,[15] it is the conception of the immanent Christ on which he lays most emphatic stress. (Of course the supreme work of Athanasius was wrought out along quite other lines, and was concerned with the true idea of Christ's Person and essential nature; but that is not at present within our range.) On the immanent Christ, indeed, his phrases are as splendid as those already quoted from the *Epistle to Diognetus*.[16] It is true that Athanasius does not hold this *orig-*

[14] It was not Origen, however, who initiated this theory. Irenæus, whether or no he started it, certainly held it.

[15] *Contra Arianos*, § 4. See Robertson's translation in the *Select Library of Nicene and Post-Nicene Fathers* (ed. Wace and Schaff), IV, 313, 316. Similar phrases may be found in many other places in the same treatise.

[16] The reader may care to see an extract from Athanasius in this vein. "The Holy Word of the Father, then, almighty and all-perfect, uniting with the universe and having everywhere unfolded His own powers, and having illumined all, both things seen and things invisible, holds them together and binds them to Himself, having left nothing void of His own power, but on the contrary quickening and sustaining all things everywhere, each severally and all collectively; while He mingles in one the principles of all sensible existence, heat namely and cold and wet and dry, and causes them not to conflict, but to make up one concordant harmony. . . . Obeying Him, even God the Word, things on earth have life and things in the heaven their order. By reason of Him all the sea, and the great ocean, move within their proper bounds, while, as we said above, the dry

inal immanence of Christ in the world and in man, changeless
though it be, sufficient to make man in the full sense a son of
God; nor does he, like Origen, take mere recognition of that
immanence as being all that is required of man in the experience
of redemption. The point—a very important one—will be mentioned again in the next section. Nevertheless the "Christus
Redemptor" factor of Paul's synthesis—at any rate as Paul
conceived it—becomes, even in Athanasius, of comparatively
minor account. So, with the "Christus Creator" factor feebly
held or in some cases almost dropped (it receives passing mention in the Nicene creed) and with the "Christus Redemptor"
factor reduced to what the Greek theology made it, the apostle's
great thought-series was ruthlessly shorn at both ends; and the
opportunity of a theology both philosophic and evangelical
was flung away.

The Latin theology of the West, successor to the Greek theology of the East, came by a different road to the same final
loss. It is true that even in the West the Greek theology
retained some influence for a time. In Justin Martyr, for instance (died *circa* 166), who is usually looked upon as the
thinker from whom the Latin theology traces its descent, one
comes upon utterances which might well have issued from
the lips of Clement of Alexandria or of Origen. The conceptions which moulded the Greek theology still retained some
hold upon his mind—not a surprising fact when one remembers that he was familiar with Greek philosophy, and that just
before his conversion to Christianity he had found a transitory

---

land grows grasses and is clothed with all manner of diverse plants. . . . There
is nothing that is and takes place but has been made and stands by Him. . . . For
just as though some musician, having tuned a lyre, and by his art adjusted the
high notes to the low and the intermediate notes to the rest, were to produce
a single tune as the result, so also the Wisdom of God, handling the Universe as
a lyre, and adjusting things in the air to things on the earth, and things in the
heaven to things in the air, and combining parts into wholes and moving them
all by His beck and will, produces well and fittingly, as the result, the unity of the
Universe and of its order, Himself remaining unmoved with the Father while
He moves all things by His own organizing action, as seems good for each to His
own Father." *Contra Gentes,* § 42. (Robertson's translation in *Select Library of
Nicene and Post-Nicene Fathers,* ed. Wace and Schaff, IV. 26, 27.)

satisfaction in a very definite Platonism. He even goes so far, when maintaining that God had given witness of Himself in that reason which dwells in humanity, to speak of Socrates and Plato as Christian men; and moreover, his identification of the incarnate Christ with that indwelling reason as its supreme revelation is indisputably clear. But his chief emphasis is not on such points as these. In the main, it is of Christ as the giver of a new law that he speaks; and acceptance of Christianity, with Justin, means acceptance of truth rather than submission to and participation in a divine life wherewith Christ inspires and suffuses the souls of men. Two diverse and more or less discordant currents of thought crossed one another in him, the second so far overwhelming the first as to give volume and direction to the main stream. As a comparison of the given dates will show, Justin wrote not many years after the author of the *Epistle to Diognetus*. It is a fair statement, that while the Greek theology can be traced back to the Diognetian Epistle, it is in Justin that the genesis of the Latin theology—more legal, less philosophical, than the Greek—is to be found.

It is no matter for surprise that theology in the West took the course it did. For just as in the East philosophy pressed hard upon theology's development and to a large extent laid down its lines, so in the West the Roman systems of State organization and of jurisprudence exercised a pressure no less formative and compelling. So far as the structure and function of the Church were concerned, the highly-organized Roman State—the entire system of government, so methodically articulated and ordered from the highest levels to the lowest, by which the Empire was ruled—provided a model, or at any rate a very definite outline, for a similar organization of the Church. On the theological side, the marvellously full and widestretching fabric of Roman law, with its civil and penal enactments and all its machinery for the settlement of issues between creditors and debtors, between property-owners and heirs or claimants, between criminals and society, and the like, could not but determine very largely the forms in which as time went on the Christian formularies gradually came to be shaped, moulding the Latin theology till it settled down to the form which in Augustine it at last assumed. Perhaps, before we turn to Augustine, we may note Tertullian's name (*circa* 155–222) as that of a thinker who thrust Western theology swiftly forward upon its way. In Tertullian we find the constant recurrence of legal terms such as "satisfaction," "debt," and the like, employed in connection with the relations between God and man: he sees nothing strange in calling the Church's faith her "property"; looks upon heretics as criminals who seek to filch it from her, and prophesies for them an adverse verdict with its consequent sentence at a great final assize; the doctrine of original sin receives in his writings its first moulding towards the shape into which Augustine afterwards fashioned it: for Him, God is emphatically and exclusively the Ruler and Judge whose one function is to guard His prerogatives and to vindicate His laws. But it is Augustine (354–430) who is quite rightly looked upon as the greater artificer of the theology of the West. He as it were throws all the points just mentioned into a cauldron of fiery thought which kindles them into a far more glowing heat. And to those mentioned he adds many more. Augustine saw God throned far away from the world of men and at enmity with it; for the sin of Adam had by its catastrophic consequences involved the entire human race in its doom. All its members were like prisoners tried and condemned already, only waiting for the appointed day on which justice would execute its decrees. A certain number, indeed, might have their sentences remitted in virtue of the work which Christ's death had in some way (not very clearly defined, for Christ really occupied a subordinate place in Augustine's redemptive scheme) accomplished; but this was only because the Supreme Judge had selected them out of the rest to be examples of a mercy which He extended or withheld as if at the bidding of caprice. The word "grace" is indeed frequently upon Augustine's lips; but the grace which God bestows upon its recipients is conferred simply because God so ordains, and comes, not from any essential gracious character in God, but by the fiat of God's arbitrary will.[17] The whole thing is systematically legal through and through. Through the unwinding of the entire scheme one can see the wheels of the legal machinery turning regularly and remorselessly round; can hear the proclamation of heaven's edicts of arrest against man, the clank of the culprit's chains as stern warders hale him to the bar, the reading of the indictment, the sentence passed. God the judge, man the prisoner in the dock, Christ One whose intervention is in certain cases permitted to prevail with the result that the favoured criminals go free while the rest pass out to their doom—so Augustine saw the drama staged. And the Church of the West—which means the only Church that played an appreciable part along the principal lines of the world's history—was held captive by the Augustinian theology for centuries beyond Augustine's own age. Through the Dark Ages, through the entire mediaeval period, through the times of the schoolmen and onwards, the standard theology of the Church retained its legalistic form. It is true that on this doctrine or on that speculations sprang up—as for instance in Anselm's doctrine of the Atonement and in the counter-doctrine of Abelard; true that in some doctrines certain modifications were made, as when election was taken to signify election to salvation only, not election to doom. But such speculations and discussions were carried on within the legal framework which always surrounded theology as a whole. The theological building stood all the while, so to say, on the same foundations and was bounded by the same walls, whatever movement there might be from room to room. It is true, also, that at intervals the voice of mysticism was heard—of a mysticism, however, which ignored the legal theology rather

[17] Augustine's doctrine of grace had several aspects. There were "prevenient grace," and "operative grace," and "co-operative grace," each with its own special mission and effect; but they were all bestowed upon man, if bestowed at all, in the way indicated in the text. It is worth while adding that for Augustine grace came near to being almost materially conceived, something conveyed to Christians through the sacraments. Along these lines Augustine prepared the way for the future full sacramentarianism of the Roman Church. Is it possible that beneath this there was some haunting sense (and if the case is so, we may well exclaim *O corruptio optimi pessima!*) of the truth that for a real Christian experience there must be a real self-communication of the divine life to man?

than opposed it and claimed that not by the acceptance of a legalistic faith, but by a "contemplation" of the Divine Essence which was to lead to a selfless union at last, was the way of salvation for human souls to be found. In the mediaeval mystic school Ruysbroeck, Eckhart, and Tauler will leap to every one's memory as bearing representative names.[18] But when all these allowances are made it still holds good that the Augustinian theology remained in possession of the field for centuries after Augustine's day. Even the Reformation brought no change in this respect. Indeed, while in both of its principal forms—Lutheran and Calvinistic—the Reformation made strenuous protest against a Church which had substituted itself for Christ, its interpretation of the *rationale* of redemption was if anything yet more legalistic than that of pre-Reformation times; for it established as orthodox the doctrine of an actual bearing by Christ of man's destined punishment for sin, so making the substitutionary idea definitely penal—an interpretation of it which, though it may have been hinted at before, had not previously won its standing-place on a list of the authoritative articles of the Christian faith. This was of course "law," rendered still more sternly frowning-faced than ever in its insistence on the uttermost farthing of its demands and in its readiness to accept that uttermost farthing by whomsoever paid. Long after Augustine, through ante-Reformation and post-Reformation times, Augustine's legalistic theology kept possession of the field.[19]

[18] The mystics necessarily held a doctrine of the divine immanence in the human race, of a divine indwelling in virtue of which and by development of which a perfect union with the Divine Essence became possible along the "contemplation" way. "The soul finds God in its own depths" is a typical utterance of Ruysbroeck's. Without this, their system could hardly have found a platform from which to start. But with this school it was not on Christ as the mediator of a divine immanence that any special stress was laid: in fact, Christ was to its members rather the exemplar than the mediator of God's immanence in man, the perfect instance of what man experienced only in part. This is quite a different thing from Paul's conception of God immanent in man through His Son. It should be understood, however, that in what has been said here it is the mediaeval mystics who are particularly in view. Later on it was to become manifest (for instance in William Law) that "mysticism" and "evangelicalism" are not necessarily incompatible.

[19] There were certainly occasional whispers indicative of hunger for something which legalism could not offer. Osiander (1498–1552), for example, while fully

How far off this entire world of thought lay from that through which the Greek theology ranged is at once apparent; and how much further still the whole system had travelled from the great thought-series of Paul is equally clear. Christus Creator, Christus Redemptor, and the immanent Christ from the beginning to the end of the vast process whose orbit links the two—of these three elements only the Christus Redemptor element survived, and this in a form removed by celestial diameters from that into which Paul had shaped it. The Christus Creator conception did indeed receive occasional mention from the schoolmen, though a mention only feeble, and a mention which left it out of all relation with the redemptive scheme. But except for this slight qualification, it is true to say that only the Christus Redemptor factor in Paul's synthesis survived, and this in altered form. Altered its form necessarily was. For the conception of God with which the Latin theology began involved an almost purely external view of what redemption meant. God sat now "on the glittering summit far withdrawn," watching the world beneath Him as it went spinning on its round, touching it when He would and keeping His hand aloof when He would, speaking to it when He would and letting the silence brood unbroken when He would, reckoning up His stern count of the growing total of man's transgressions against the day when the divine wrath should fulminate through the skies, and having little else to do with the world He had made. The Latin theology's God was in fact a God very much like the deist's God of later days. And it was man's judicial status in His sight that was the supremely important thing. That break in man's relations with Him which the Christus Redemptor idea, even in its altered form, necessarily implied was not for the Latin theology what it had been for Paul. It was not by the loss from man's nature of a creative Christ that the break had been made: it had been made by man's positive infraction of commands which declared "thou shalt not" and by

endorsing Luther's doctrine of justification by faith, held that faith not only secured deliverance from penalty, but also brought in some sort of magical way an infusion of Christ's nature and righteousness. But such voices were declared heretical, and soon died down.

man's negative infraction of commands which declared "thou shalt." It was as a culprit in the legal sense criminal, not as a nature in the spiritual sense fallen from a pure and lofty estate, that man was arraigned. In spite of the Latin theology's insistence on original sin, it is not too much to say that it was rather with sins than with sinfulness with which God was concerned, and that theology had consequently to deal with the penalties of the first rather than with the correction of the second. Necessarily, therefore, this externalism with which man's relation to God was viewed led to a corresponding externalism in theology's view of Christ's redemptive work. Salvation became something wrought outside man, *for* man rather than *in* him. Legal status was the matter to be weighed; and consequently the Christ who, in Paul's synthesis, had by restoring *Himself* to man also restored man to Himself, was not the Christ whom the Latin theology proclaimed. And of course with the disappearance of the Christus Creator conception in any sense connected with Christ's redemptive work, with the disappearance of God immanent through Christ in the world and in man, and with the attenuation also of the Christus Redemptor conception to that of a correction of man's status by Christ, the apostle's great sweep of thought had been contracted to a single point. There was nowhere any suggestion of a cosmic process to which Christ, from Creation to Redemption, belonged; in which He was the First and the Last; which hung in utter dependence on His hand. The need of such a suggestion was not felt. Theology lost all connection with a universal scheme of things. It worked itself out from its premises to its conclusions in loneliness, and was content so to do. Under these conditions a theology both philosophical and evangelical could not be born. Once again the opportunity of constructing such a theology had been lost; and there was no hope that under these conditions a renewed offer of it would be held out.

It was in the early nineteenth century that the opportunity offered itself again, only to be lost once more. There had been religious movements and theological debates during the interval, of course; but none of them had in any degree looked

towards the remote region whither Paul's thought-series had
been relegated or shown any disposition to call it back. In England there had been the deistic controversy; Chillingworth's
assertion that human reason had rights which were unjustly
denied when the standard creed was forced upon men by ecclesiastical authority or at the point of the sword; and the declaration by the Cambridge Platonists [20] that the mind of man was
participant in the mind of God Himself and that the divine
mind was in-dwelling in the human, and their endeavour to
translate the accepted doctrines into language whereby the fact
of that union should be brought out. In Germany there had been
the rationalist movement of Reimarus [21] and others; the be-
ginnings of a critical movement towards the Bible in Semler
and Eichhorn; and a more distinctly spiritual revolt against
the hardness of the Latin theology in the pietistic school among
whose leaders Spener bears an outstanding name. And both in
England and abroad Socinianism had reared its head. But none
of these movements so much as opened a window whence a
new rising of the Pauline sun might have been discerned.[22] It
was not till after the appearance of the idealistic philosophy in
Germany that even so much as this took place; and this brings
us, as has been said, to the nineteenth century's early decades.

The German philosophy of idealism, initiated by Kant [23]

[20] Perhaps I may be permitted to refer any readers desiring a compressed account of these thinkers and of others—such as Dorner, Erskine, and Maurice—
mentioned later in this section, to the relevant chapters in a previous book of
mine, Liberal Orthodoxy.

[21] Reimarus was the author of the Wolfenbüttel Fragments which Lessing published in 1774 and subsequent years. Lessing did not himself defend the rationalistic conclusions of Reimarus, though maintaining that the truth of Christianity
could not rest upon the letter of Scripture alone.

[22] The Cambridge Platonists are the only group in respect of which exception
to this statement might with some plausibility be taken. They are frequently
spoken of as having marked a return to the Greek theology. I have in the book
previously mentioned (Liberal Orthodoxy, p. 47) given my reason for thinking
this view untenable. A return towards Greek theology, or the beginning of such
a return, they admittedly did mark. But that is not the same thing.

[23] I put the matter in this way, because it appears to set Kant correctly in the
philosophic succession. But Kant is sometimes counted among those against
whom the idealistic system reacted instead of as having himself been the first
exemplar of the reaction. This is due to the excessive emphasis laid by some upon
that negative element of his system mentioned in the text a few lines further
on. Some who professed to be his followers interpreted him as denying the exist-

(1724–1804) and developed by a succession of thinkers with
Fichte (1762–1814), Schelling [24] (1775–1854), and Hegel

ence of the super-sensible world because he maintained that reason could not
find or grasp it; and these developed that side of his philosophy in forgetfulness of the other. And this one-sidedness of interpretation in the philosophical
sphere had its effect in the theological also, producing thinkers such as Tieftrunk
and Wegscheider, who in varying degrees held that the supernatural factor in
Christianity must be eliminated since pure reason failed to justify it. But this
was really to ignore Kant's more positive side. Kant's system is not really a
rationalistic, but an idealistic one; and he belongs therefore to the idealist line.
It is worth remark that Pfleiderer, with special reference to Edward Caird,
Hutchison Stirling, and Thomas Hill Green, asserts this relation between Kant
and the idealists to have been more fully recognized in England and Scotland
than in Germany itself. (*Development of Theology since Kant in Germany and
Great Britain*, p. 343.)

[24] Schelling is sometimes interpreted as having been more or less in accord
with Christian doctrine, especially in regard to the article of the Trinity. Thus
Matheson, while admitting that "in the case of Schelling there was *at first* a
strong leaning towards the view of an impersonal God who became a Trinity in
the world" (*Aids to the Study of German Theology*, p. 98), goes on to affirm that
Schelling in his later stages passed from this position to one far more orthodox.
I do not think that this can be made good. Schelling went through three marked
phases, but in none of them did he come anywhere near the accepted Christian
faith. At the beginning, in fact, he treated it with what can only be called scorn.
Matheson's phrase "a stong leaning" seems very inadequate as to Schelling's
early period, in view of Schelling's definite assertion that the finite world is *itself*
the Son. "*Der Ewige aus dem Wesen des Vaters aller Dinge geborene Sohn Gottes
das Endliche selbst ist, wie es in der ewigen Anschauung Gottes ist.*" (*Sämmtliche
Werke*, Abth. I, Band I, p. 294.) And from this position Schelling never travelled
far. In his second stage of thought he spoke of the Son as the Wisdom which,
from being a mere "potency" within God, came into actual being before the
Creation for the purpose of being afterwards manifested to a humanity yet to be
and of taking over the world's lordship from the Father; and this construction of
the matter is further complicated by hypotheses as to how out of the "dark
background" of the Absolute God Himself came to exist. Moreover, for Schelling
God even so is not yet really complete; for "the era of the Spirit is still to come."
"A completed God is no God" is a phrase repeatedly on Schelling's lips. The
difference between the earlier and the later renderings amounts to no more than
this—that in the earlier the impersonal God has got further towards becoming a
Trinity than He has in the later. And in Schelling's latest work, not published
till after his death, he holds this position still. In this work he is explicit enough
in declaring that before the creation the Father ruled, that during the entire
period of creation the Son rules, and that after the period of creation (still of
course in the future) the Spirit will rule. "*Es ist erlaubt zu sagen: Die Zeit vor
der Schöpfung sei in besonderem Sinn die Zeit des Vaters, da das Sein noch aus-
schliesslich in seiner Hand ist, die gegenwartige Zeit sei in vorzüglichem Sinn die
Zeit des Sohn, von dem eben darum gesagt ist; er muss herrschen, bis er alles
ihm Widerstrebende zum Schemel seiner Füsse, d.h. zu seinem Grund, seiner Basis,
seinem Hypokeimenon, gemacht hat. Die dritte Zeit, die während der ganzen
Schöpfung die zukünftige ist, in die alles gelangen soll, sei die Zeit des Geistes. Es
ist also auch erlaubt, die drei Personen als die successiven Herrscher dreien verschiedener Zeiten zu denken.*" (*Sämmtliche Werke*, Abth. II, Band I, p. 71.) All
this is far from the Christian Trinity. It is true that in his latest writings Schelling

(1770–1831) in their foremost ranks—was a reaction against the *Aufklärung,* prevailing at the time. Kant had affirmed in his *Critique of Pure Reason* that knowledge was reached neither by the mind's passive reception of experience, as the empirical philosophers declared that it was, nor by the mind's self-searching within the realm of its own innate ideas, which the strictly rationalistic school asserted to be the true programme, but by the united action of both receptivity and activity; and he had affirmed, further, that knowledge of "things in themselves," of any super-sensible world, was consequently put out of "Pure Reason's" reach. But he had nevertheless gone on to affirm with equal emphasis, in the *Critique of Practical Reason,* the existence of a super-sensible world which only the "Practical Reason," contrasted thus with the "Pure Reason" and its powerlessness, could and must somehow discover; and his successors in the idealist line took this super-sensible world as their starting-point—took it for granted, one might almost say—and proceeded to demonstrate how the entire system of things was evolved therefrom. They returned in fact to the old philosophical problem of "the one and the many"; and it is as a resurrection of the Greek philosophy, or at any rate of the Greek philosophic method, a re-positing of the Greek philosophic

---

abandoned the lofty scorn which he had earlier poured upon the Christian faith, and by a very strained exegesis sought to square his ideas with certain Bible texts. And it may be true that, as Twesten puts it, Schelling provided a bridge over which some passed from scepticism to an ultimate acceptance of Christianity. *"Sie ist für Viele der Uebergang zu einer Christlich gläubigen Ueberzeugung geworden."* (*Vorlesungen über die Dogmatik der Evangelisch-Lutherischen Kirche,* p. 180.) But this cannot justify a putting of Schelling upon the list of definitely Christian thinkers. Schelling's works have not, so far as I know, been translated into English. Dr. Richard Garnett says (*Life of Emerson,* p. 101) that a translation of Schelling's introductory lecture to his final course appeared in the *Dial,* the short-lived organ of the New England Transcendentalists. But though I have searched all the numbers issued through the four years of the *Dial's* existence, I have not been able to trace it. The only reference to the philosopher that I have found is a statement, given merely as a news-item, that his final course of lectures had begun at Berlin. (*Dial,* III, 136, issue for July 1842.) O. B. Frothingham does not, in his pages on the *Dial* in *Transcendentalism in New England* (pp. 132 ff.), make any reference to such a translation, though he tells earlier (p. 116) how Schelling was introduced to the United States through the writings of Coleridge. Nor is there any mention of it in the exhaustive list of contributors to the *Dial* given by George W. Cooke in the *Journal of Speculative Philosophy* for July 1885.

enigma, that their system-making must be viewed. There were differences, certainly—for instance, the term "emanation" cannot with propriety be employed in any description of the German-born philosophic schemes. But spite of differences, Greek philosophy and the new idealism were alike in this capital point: both looked at the universe "as but a pulse-beat, made visible, in the infinite Source of all." The old question between "the one and the many" (or the seeming many) was again to the fore. Of the idealist systems, Hegel's has attained to the loudest fame.[25] It is impossible here to give anything like an adequate summary of a system so vast and complicated. For anything beyond what the following few sentences can suggest, information must be sought in books specially concerned with the history of philosophical thought.[26] Here only a hint or two can be given. For Hegel all is Thought. The entire universe is the unfolding of the Absolute Reason, which is the one reality. Also, as the Infinite Mind comes to at least partial (in religion to complete) self-consciousness in the mind of man, so the mind of man, in an apprehension of its own dialectical processes, comes into touch with the Absolute; or rather, such an apprehension *is* only the Absolute coming into touch with, returning upon, itself. Now all progress of thought is on this wise. The mind puts forth, discovers, a truth; and for a time this newly-born truth holds the field as it were by its own right. Presently, however, the opposite of this truth is in its turn discovered or put forth; so that there is a clash of contending "rights." Finally, the opposition is lost in a higher truth reconciling the two erstwhile foes and combining them into a unity. This, because it is the "dialectic" of the finite mind, and because the finite mind mirrors the Infinite, is the "dialectic" of the Infinite Mind as well; and it is along this line that the eternal and original Idea thinks itself toward perfect self-consciousness. Moreover,

[25] I have ventured in the following explanatory sentences to quote from my own *Liberal Orthodoxy* instead of seeking for fresh expressions, as the old ones were at hand to serve my turn. In one or two other places in this section I have taken the same liberty.

[26] *The Secret of Hegel*, by J. Hutchison Stirling, is the profoundest study in English. If a briefer exposition be desired, there is the volume by Edward Caird in Blackwood's *Philosophical Classics*.

while the finite mind mirrors the Infinite, it is itself in all its
"dialectic" an actual part of that "dialectic" which is the Infinite Mind's own; from which it follows that every concept
emerging in the process of human thinking is an item in the
process of the eternal Thought as well. The universe in all its
historic processes is simply the Absolute Reason thinking itself
out. It should be said that Hegel conceived himself to be, not
an assailant but a defender, of Christianity; and it is not surprising that certain theologians should have been eager to enrol
this desirable-seeming ally and to grasp his outstretched hand.
True, the greatest theologian of the time, Schleiermacher
(1768–1834), whose work was to prove the most powerful of
all and to produce the most permanent results, was building
his system from a non-philosophical base. Starting from the
feeling of "dependence upon God" as the basal fact, Schleiermacher followed the path of speculation only so far as was
possible while that basal fact was kept in mind and allowed to
hold speculation under its control.[27] But many yielded in greater
or less degree to the Hegelian spell. Was it possible, these
asked themselves, to find for Christ in the Hegelian context a
place which should at the same time satisfy the demands of
both philosophy and the Christian faith? The situation was in
general outline a reproduction of that which we saw in the
earliest Christian centuries—philosophy concentrating upon
the fundamental problem of problems, and theology seeking to
adjust its step so that it might march at philosophy's side. And
this is to say that once again the opportunity of recovering
Paul's great thought-synthesis presented itself, and that a theology both evangelical and philosophical was once again clamouring to be born. But the opportunity passed unseized as it
had passed unseized before.

It might have been expected that under the circumstances a

[27] Scheiermacher was, however, largely influenced at some points by his early
study of Spinoza. (See on this Pfleiderer's *Developmnt of Theology in Germany
and Great Britain since Kant*, pp. 110–115.) His enthusiastic apostrophe to the
philosopher "Join me in reverently offering a tribute to the manes of the holy
and despised Spinoza" is often quoted. (*Rede*, II, pp. 47, 48, ed. 1831.) But
Dr. Selbie justly remarks that "the Spinoza whom Schleiermacher knew and
reverenced was in some respects a creation of his own." (*Schleiermacher*, p. 241.)

return to at least the early Greek theology would have been achieved, even though Paul's vast horizon remained hidden from sight. But as a matter of fact it was only in Britain that even this half-way house was attained. In Europe it was the Hegelian doctrine of "thesis, antithesis, and synthesis" that proved supremely magnetic for theology's eyes; and it was under its spell that their theological scheme was framed by the thinkers with whom we are dealing. From the list of their names perhaps those of Dorner (1809–1884) and Rothe (1799–1867) in Germany, and Martensen (1808–1884) in Denmark, may be selected as outstanding, Dorner's being the most widely known. It was from a conception of the Trinity framed on a somewhat Hegelian basis that Dorner,[28] and for that matter others as well, set out on their quest. With Dorner and the rest it is not, however, the coming of an Absolute to self-realization that is in question but the coming of a *Revelation* to its fulness; though it must be remembered that for theologians of this school "revelation is a *creative* act of God upon the human heart," [29] an actual self-impartation of God to man. God is at the same time a self-maintained or self-sufficient Personality and a Personality which must impart itself to others —wherein we have the basis for the doctrine of the Trinity with its Father and its Son and its Love uniting both. In the

[28] Dorner is usually classed as an "eclectic," into whose system elements from various systems are gathered. The description may be accurate, but is not very informative inasmuch as it does not indicate from what systems the gathering has been made. He is thus classed by Pfleiderer (in *Development of Theology in Germany and Great Britain since Kant.*) On the other hand Frank (in *Geschichte und Kritik der neueren Theologie*) puts him among those who sought to carry theology back towards the faith of the Church, while Adams Brown (in *The Essence of Christianity*) makes him a Hegelian. In point of fact, he must be reckoned as a disciple of Schleiermacher who tried to bring back philosophy into the partnership from which his master had expelled it. Rothe is classed among the "speculative theologians," as a disciple of Hegel with leanings toward Schleiermacher, by Pfleiderer, and as a disciple of Schleiermacher with leanings toward Hegel, by Frank. A case can be made for all these methods of placing the men; but on the whole it seems to me that it is behind Schleiermacher they fall in.

[29] This is Pfleiderer's apt phrase. (*Development of Theology in Germany and Great Britain since Kant,* pp. 160, 161.) I have again used, in regard to Dorner, some explanatory sentences from my book *Liberal Orthodoxy.* See also Pfleiderer in the book just named (pp. 156–164) ; and for an excellent condensed summary, Principal Sydney Cave's *The Doctrine of the Person of Christ,* pp. 182–186.

nature of God Himself, therefore, "thesis, antithesis, and synthesis" are duly given. But God as self-imparting necessarily reveals Himself as He is—that is, both as self-maintaining *and* as self-imparting; and Revelation is the action of this double process upon the world. And revelation's completion—the final "synthesis" revealing at the same time what God is in Himself and what He is to man—could only occur through a real incarnation of God in Christ; for the gradual self-impartation of God to man must end, Dorner holds, if mankind *as a whole* is to experience and benefit by it, with an *individual* in whom God and man are one. Incarnation had been a gradual process through the ages: the historic Christ was its culmination and its crown. It will be seen that the accents, so far as the treatment of Christ's place in the cosmic order is concerned, had been quite shifted from the places on which they had stood in the early Greek theology. To find a place for Christ in the Hegelian context meant to follow out a self-revelation on God's part which reached its apex in the historic Christ rather than to establish Christ as having Himself energized in the historic process throughout. He stood at the summit of Revelation's ascent, but was hardly Himself the essential factor within that ascent throughout, as the Greek theology had taken Him to be. In one degree or another, in various forms, all the thinkers of the "eclectic" school pursued this line. And this shifting of the accents meant a great deal. The dominant interest being now Revelation pure and simple, it was Christ as Revealer that took precedence in theological thought over Christ as Saviour. Soteriology could no longer occupy the foremost place. True, the "Christus Redemptor" idea was by no means utterly lost. By the very fact of His being the perfect incarnation of the Divine, Christ was held to become in some way the Redeemer of humanity. Besides this Dorner, for example, clung more or less fast to the Church's general doctrine of atonement by vicarious satisfaction, though this was so to say tacked on somewhat artificially to the main line of theological speculation rather than shown as a necessary constituent in it or corollary from it. In sum, the general run of thinking on such lines as these was not likely to strike, and as a matter of fact did not strike, a path back to the early Greek theology's conception of a Christ who had from the beginning dwelt in man to save him if only man knew himself as he really was. And the possibility of a return to the whole content of Paul's synthesis was still more remote. The "Christus Creator" conception hung far back in the distance. An occasional glance or word was flung back in the direction where it hid, but no more. The "immanent Christ" conception had been exchanged, as we have seen, for that of a God perfectly revealing Himself at last *in* the historic Christ— though of course any criticism of this conception as inadequate implies no denial of the truth which it most certainly contains. The Greek theology, still more emphatically Paul's thought-series with its far-flung sweep, were both very far away. Whether, had the movement persisted with anything like its first energy and finally found itself, some real return to either or both of these positions might have been accomplished, it is impossible to tell. However that may be, it lost its noon-tide brilliance soon. For Hegelianism, at first accounted theology's friend, was before very long found to be an acid dissolvent of the Christianity which Hegel had so confidently set out to secure: the theology it had so largely inspired became as a nat-ural consequence suspect; and the "eclectic" school, though it kept and still keeps its adherents, yielded chief place on the theological side to a different order of thinkers, Ritschl and the Ritschlians, who, erecting their theological edifice on a totally changed foundation and to a totally re-drawn architectural plan, carried their reaction so far as to declare for a complete divorce between theological and philosophical thought. And a similar attitude, with modifications and qualifications at this point or that, has subsequently been maintained by the "Posi-tive Theology" of the early twentieth century and by Barth and his school. Thus in Germany the issue was worked out.

In Britain the course of things ran to a different close. The romantic movement, so powerful in the fields of poetry and lit-erature, had sent its vivifying winds across the theological terri-tories as well. One thinks at once of Coleridge (1772–1834), poet, philosopher, theologian, and great in all three departments; perhaps the foremost of his age in a line of thinkers whose vision was wide and acute enough to attempt the marrying of religious with philosophical ideas. Something of German influence came upon him, for he had spent fourteen months in Germany and had heard some of the lecturers in the new movement there; but whatever debt he might owe to them, he was of far too original a mind to be their slave, and he struck out and followed a line of his own. In some respects he may rank as a disciple of the Cambridge Platonists: indeed, he explicitly avows himself indebted to John Smith and Henry More. But if he set out from their starting-line, he outdistanced them before long. The Cambridge men, we saw, insisted on the indwelling of the divine *mind* in man; and they may be credited, we saw, with initiating a return *towards* (*towards,* not *to*) the Greek theology. But Coleridge took a further step. With him the idea was that of a moral and spiritual, rather than of a merely intellectual, correspondence between God and man. God in His wholeness, and therefore in His holiness, not simply God's mind in man's mind—that was the note. A further step in the direction of the old Greek theology, which had been predominantly moral in its emphasis, this undoubtedly was. In the theological sphere, Coleridge, though he was not in any real sense a systematizer and one can scarcely speak of any system of his, rested upon the idea that Christian doctrines could not fail to be found valid when they were viewed alongside the conception of a real correspondence between man's spiritual nature and the nature of God, because, thus matched, they were discovered to speak of a redemptive scheme whereby that correspondence may be deepened and enlarged; and it was along that line that he found new meanings in the doctrines of sin, salvation, the Deity of Christ, and the rest.[30] Another thinker looking in the same direction was Erskine of Linlathen (1788–1870), a Scotch contemporary of Coleridge's, who began with

---

[30] It is in the *Aids to Reflection* (1825) that Coleridge's treatment of these themes is chiefly to be found.

ideas similar to Coleridge's own, and then in his later books [31]
passed on to assert the conception, soon to be widely spread,
of "Christ as the Head of the Race" in the sense that in Christ
and through Him, not otherwise, all humanity had as a literal
fact had its life since human history began; from which it followed that in Christ's sinless life and in His sacrificial death
Christ had carried all the members of the human family with
Him *if they would have it so,* and that a consciousness of the
pardon and reconciliation they possessed was all that men really
required. It was the first outstanding declaration since the
Greek theology had faded, in anything like the key afterwards
to become so familiar, of the immanence of the Christ-life in
man. The same note was struck by McLeod Campbell (1800–
1872), a Scotch minister and a friend of Erskine, in a book
still famous and still deserving to be read,[32] with its doctrine
that reconciliation means not so much the reconciliation of man
with God as man's realization and consciousness of the reconciliation which Christ as the Race's Head had already accomplished. In Britain it is however the name of Maurice
(1805–1872) which stands out most prominently in this connection. Before Campbell's book appeared Maurice had found
in the conception of Christ as the Head of the Race the central
conception of Christian truth, and had made it the touchstone
for all the rest. Christ was in every man and consequently every
man was in Christ: there was no necessity for man to become a
child of God, because he acquired that status by the very fact of
human birth; and sin lay in refusing to recognize this fact,
while *per contra* salvation lay in awaking to its glory and its
truth.[33] So strenuously indeed did Maurice press this idea that
he did not hesitate to characterize any questioning or negation
of it as "the devil's lie." [34] Of the value of the "Christ as Head

---

[31] *The Unconditional Freeness of the Gospel* (1828) and *The Brazen Serpent*
(1831).
[32] *The Nature of the Atonement* (1856).
[33] See *The Kingdom of God, Theological Essays,* and *The Doctrine of Sacrifice.*
[34] In a letter to his mother. (*Life of F. D. Maurice,* by his son F. Maurice,
I, 154–157.)

of the Race" conception something will be said a little later
on.[35] At this point it is spoken of only to show that by Erskine
in his later books, by McLeod Campbell and Maurice, it is
clearly upon the platform of the early Greek theology that we
are summoned to stand. But Paul's synthesis was still far away.

So, down the centuries, the chances came and went. At no
point did the three constituents of Paul's thought-series hang
together in a triple constellation on the horizon of theological
thought. The "Christus Creator" conception was well-nigh lost
and forgotten in the void. The "Christus immanent" conception
was dropped from the Latin theology, and, though stressed
in the Greek theology and in the later thinking of Maurice
and his school, was stressed in lonely detachment, and consequently took on little or nothing of the significance which Paul
had given it. The "Christus Redemptor" conception shared a
similar fate, forfeiting what had been on Paul's view its chief
characteristic; offering for the Latin theology merely the means
of securing an acquittal verdict in the law-courts of heaven, and
for the other schools of thought a revelation of what man was
rather than a dynamic under whose working man was to become what he ought to be. And Paul's "break" in the immanence
of Christ? The Latin theology substituted for this—for never
having possessed the conception, it could scarcely lose it—the
conception of a law broken by man, while thinkers of the other
school denied that any such "break" had ever occurred. The
chances came and went. It is a chilling summary. Verily Paul's
synthesis remained at the end of the days far, very far away.

4

Can we beckon it back out of its distance till its rainbow arch
stretches above our heads once more? The attempt is worth
making. Humbly and tentatively indeed it must be made, as
must be any attempt which seeks to establish contact with truths
whereof only dim glimpses through the haze covering the far
eternities can be won. But it is worth making none the less.

[35] See the next section of this chapter.

The Christian doctrine of the Trinity is here assumed. Nor are the readers of this book, already holders of the Christian faith as the majority of them will probably be, likely to cavil at this. A few words may however be said by way of allaying the haunting fear, which now and again returns upon most of those who take the Trinitarian formula upon their lips, that it may in the end lie open to the charge, should adversaries choose to make it, of being little more than a plausible guess. The occasional return of the haunting spectre is nothing whereof to be ashamed, for in the very act of sending thought into a region outside of space and time we are necessarily shutting ourselves away from attaining knowledge in the strict sense of the word; and it is small wonder if a sense of our incompetence should now and then make us doubtful and afraid, perhaps even a little inclined to deny any particular value to what thought brings back to us from its distant quest. But if we cannot finally lay the spectre, we can at least arm ourselves beforehand with certain considerations sufficient to keep it at arm's length.

To put the matter at its lowest, even were it true that the doctrine of the Trinity is no more than a guess at the unknown, it might at least be said that it is in this respect on no lower level of probability than any others. (The reference is of course to scholarly formulations of it, not to the popular tritheistic misconceptions of it resulting from interpreting the term "Person" in its ordinary sense). For indeed philosophy, in all those stretches of it which prepare some prescription for extracting "the many" out of "the one," does little more than guess. All philosophies save the purely materialistic varieties admit the necessity of acknowledging some sort of distinction in the "ultimate Reality," whatever their ultimate Reality may be; for an Absolute constituted in mere "singleness" can yield nothing in the way of a possible world, however long and arduously it may be twisted and turned about within the mind. Philosophical Unitarianism, with all its insistence on the unity of God as against the Trinitarian scheme, has to make a similar confession. Martineau, for example, affirms of the Reality behind all things that "Mind, to think out its problems—unless those problems are a dream—cannot be monistic—a mere subjective infinitude—its tides and eddies all within"; and then proceeds to declare with certainty that Space, and with slightly less certainty that Matter, are co-eternal with God Himself.[36] Some sort of "objectivity" to God, it is thus allowed, there must from all eternity have been. To those who do not feel the force of this, if such there be, may be passed on the counsel of Bishop Horsley to Priestley, "If you imagine that the absolute unity of the Divine substance is more easy to be explained than the Trinity, let me entreat you to read the 'Parmenides.' " [37] Well then, granting that we must affirm distinctions in the Eternal Reality and Source of all things—or must at any rate affirm something that is not mere "singleness"—is the Christian Trinity of Father, Son, and Spirit any more of a guess, or a less plausible guess, than Schelling's "dark Basis" (designated $A°$)

[36] Essay on "Nature and God" (*Essays, Reviews, and Addresses,* III, pp. 175–177). Martineau goes on to explain that of course he does not mean to contend for the eternal existence of "the particular material objects we see around us." This doctrine of Martineau's as to the eternal existence of Space and Matter has been a source of some perplexity to the historian of his philosophical opinions, Professor Upton. (*Life and Letters of James Martineau,* by Drummond and Upton, II, pp. 361, 362). Rather strangely for a thinker usually so superlatively clear, Martineau appears to have spoken with varying voices on this theme. In another place, while still asserting the eternal co-existence of God and Space, he seems to sheer off from asserting the eternal existence of Matter as well—this under the influence of Boscovich's theory. (*A Study of Religion,* 2nd edition, I, 381–383.) In yet another, after saying that a "Self" implies an "Other-than-Self," he holds that this "Other-than-Self" in regard to God is "the aggregate of rational and moral beings, represented in our world by Man." (*Ibid.,* II, p. 181.) This last statement appears to ignore the serious objection that this "aggregate of rational and moral beings," if uncreated, leaves us with two equally co-eternal beings, one of them outside God; if created, leaves us with a time when God was not Himself complete—an idea which Martineau would most certainly not have entertained. Finally, in his last work of importance, which may presumably be taken to embody his final conclusions on the matter, Martineau returns to his earlier view that both Space and Matter must be conceived as co-eternal with God. He asserts as emphatically as ever that "an 'absolute subject' is no less a contradiction in thought than a single-termed equation or an uncaused effect. . . . The moment we conceive of mind at all, or any operation of mind, we must concurrently conceive of something other than it as engaging its activity." Upon Space, accordingly, Martineau falls back as supplying in part the needed co-eternal thing. But it supplies it only in part. For "Space is not in itself an object, but only the opportunity for objects: so that there is, perhaps, still need of another *datum;* viz., matter occupying finite place." (*The Seat of Authority in Religion,* pp. 32, 33.) One observes, however, that even in this last pronouncement a "perhaps" occurs.

[37] *Tracts in Controversy with Dr. Priestley,* p. 287.

and its "potencies," successively termed A (pure subject), +
A (predicate and object), and finally ± A (subject-object), by
passing through which mysterious items philosophy finds itself
at last on the road to God? Or even than Hegel's "thesis, antithesis, and synthesis"? It would be difficult to point out where
the Christian scheme is at any disadvantage, if plausibility in
guessing is to be the test.

But further, the doctrine of the Trinity is much more than a
guess. The Church's thinking along the line which led to the
doctrine for its final goal started from an acceptance of certain
facts as historic and from an experience which those facts made
possible. The truth or untruth of the accepted facts is not here
in question: the point to be made is that it was from such accepted facts and from an experience consequent upon their acceptance that the doctrine of the Trinity at last emerged. It was
with the conception of the absolute Deity of Christ that the
Church's thinking upon the mighty theme began. The Church
found Christ to be in very deed "very God of very God," "God
manifest in the flesh," nothing other and assuredly nothing less;
and that "finding" of Him was held to be justified in the results
which, thus conceived, He wrought upon the Church's members. He must be, so the verdict ran (again, the truth or error
of the verdict is not here being discussed), not merely a revelation of God, but the Bringer and Embodiment of *"God's Presence and His very Self, and essence all-divine."* But then, since
God is One and must ever remain One, this same Christ, God's
"essence all-divine," must necessarily have been homed within
the God-head's Being while God's unbegun eternity had been
running its course; for any other theory would have involved
the grotesque assumption that God had at a point in historic
time created another God. Yet—again since God is One and
must ever remain One—this eternal "homing" of Christ within
the eternal Godhead must not be so conceived as to imply two
Gods: the relationship between the two must be a duality in
unity, each constituent of it, while necessary to and needing the
other, holding nevertheless the "fulness of the Godhead"
within itself. So did Christian thought reach the lofty concep-

tion of the Father and the Son and of the oneness of the two. But then there came a further step. For long before the coming of Him whom Christian thinking now recognized as "God manifest in the flesh," pre-Christian thinking had been familiar with the idea of the Spirit which was the influx into the world of God Himself; which had in the beginning brooded upon the face of the waters; which had informed the prophetic mind; which had made itself felt for warning in the human conscience, for promise in human aspiration after holiness, for judgment in human remorse for sin; which had been the lamp kindled by God within sight of earth to illumine at least the outskirts of the darkness wherein He dwelt, the voice to bring to earth at least the whispers of that more awful voice which no man could hear full-toned and live. To Christian thinking, no less than to the thinking of prophet and seer, the Spirit was as it were God coming forth from Himself. And since it was in Christ that God had made His last and supreme advent, and since Christ was God, it was but going a step beyond the stage already reached for Christian thinking to affirm that in some sense, most real however mysterious, Father, Son, and Spirit must be one. The whole ascent of thought was by steps of inference, not by way of unwarranted and hazardous surmise. It is true that Christian thought, starting out with no intention of philosophizing, but simply with the intention of accounting for an experience which Christians deemed themselves to have passed through, thus found itself upon a high peak whence some faint insight into philosophy's ancient problem of "the one and the many" could be obtained; but that fact did but provide for the inferential process whereby the summit had been attained an additional guarantee; and for that matter, one may boldly say, conferred upon Christianity a title to be heard as a competent witness in philosophy's court. At any rate, the ladder of inference had been climbed steadily step by step. The doctrine of the Trinity is no guess. Legitimately or otherwise so far as the soundness of its primary ground is concerned, Christianity reached the doctrine as the goal of a thought-process which had never lost touch with the experience whence it made its start. It is hardly possible to say similar things regarding philosophy's dealing with its ultimate question. Probably no one would contend that Schelling's algebraic-looking series, even when it reaches its climax in A°, represents anything like an ascent from human experience: indeed, if it may be said without disrespect, the entire speculation impresses one as being much like the Oriental conjuring trick of climbing a rope flung upwards without having any fastening to solid earth. Hegel's "thesis, antithesis, and synthesis" certainly appears at first sight to be in somewhat better case, for it does profess to argue from the known "dialectic" of the finite mind to a parallel "dialectic" in the Infinite. Yet Hegel's system takes, even here at its start, a far longer stride than any taken by Christian thinking on its way to the Trinitarian faith. Let it be accepted, at any rate allowed to pass unquestioned, that the "dialectic" of the finite mind is correctly described and that the description holds good for all processes of finite thought. But then the inference is not merely that Infinite thought must follow and be bound by the same *laws* of thinking as finite, but that its *method* also must be the same: what it comes to is that Infinite thought must pursue the same programme of trial and error as that which the mind of man pursues. An inference fairly long and large, one would suppose —so large and so long that, as it nears its end, it does not seem to hang very steadily against the breath of possible doubt concerning its title to be considered an inference at all. And the next inferential step, or what claims to be so, is larger and longer still. For we are called upon to believe that this "dialectic" of the Infinite Mind, itself inferred from the "dialectic" of the finite mind, constitutes *all that there is in Being, Infinite and finite alike*. Surely a long stride—so long that it merits the name of "leap" rather than stride! In fact, Christian thought has been far too apologetic upon this theme (as indeed upon many others), and has too lightly surrendered its claims to be the challenger rather than the challenged in the lists. And in view of all this, we may with quiet minds ignore philosophy's reproach—may ignore also, whenever and howsoever often it returns, the spectre of doubt as to whether our faith be not after all a "guess"—and settle down upon the declaration that we believe in Father, Son, and Spirit, One in Three and Three in One. In the Son, eternally begotten of the Father, God sets His creative power and life as it were outside Himself, yet holds it within Himself still. In the Spirit, eternally proceeding from the Father and the Son, God sets His self-communicativeness free (yet, again, holding it still within Himself) to flow forth upon the world.[38]

It was to the "Christus Creator" conception, we saw, that Paul travelled *backwards* from the "Christus Redemptor" conception with which he began: it is from the "Christus Creator" conception therefore that we make our start when we travel *forward* over Paul's thought-series to its close. The Christ who was the Eternal Son made the world. Does it matter whether this is grasped or not? Does it even matter or not this is true? The full reply to the inquiry will be reached presently. For the moment we may be content with saying that to the Christian whom Christ has redeemed the "Christus Redemptor" conception at least takes on an added magnetism and beauty when he realizes that the world which Christ redeemed is the world He made. Perhaps indeed it is not too much to say that it takes on, not merely added magnetism and beauty, but added significance as well, and that one cannot enter into the full greatness of the "Christus Redemptor" idea unless the "Christus Creator" idea has first been seized. The two truths, when set over against each other and as it were looking into one another's eyes, both receive and impart an added colour from the rays of light which in that mutual glance they exchange. "In the beginning God created the heaven and the earth." The first words of Genesis still remain, of course, the foundation truth from which as its base the entire edifice of Christian thought mounts skyward to its topmost stone. But

[38] The line followed in this book does not call for any special treatment of the doctrine of the Spirit. But it must not be inferred that I hold it of less than primary importance for theology. The "Binitarian" conception of God is equally with the conception of God as "singleness," unable to satisfy the demands of Christian or philosophic thought.

unless, under the impulse which God's self-revelation in Christ should impart, we pass beyond that affirmation and put it that *God in Christ* made the world and all that is therein, we can scarcely escape altogether from the sub-consciousness of a sort of "division of offices" (how often one has to regret the inadequacy, reaching to the point of grotesqueness, of all human words on these high themes!) between the God who created and the God who redeems. Certainly it is impossible to enter into such a full sense of rest, of redemption to the uttermost, in Christ as would result from a realization that the world has been His from the beginning, if we have anything like a feeling that He has been "called in" to save a world from which He was apart before. Questions apparently minor and insignificant turn out sometimes to have large consequences according to the side on which they are ultimately resolved; and it may be that the idea of a kind of "division of offices," to use the phrase again, between God the Father and God the Son—the idea which has done so much to turn theology's course along mistaken lines—may be due in part to forgetfulness of the truth that "Christus Redemptor" is "Christus Creator" too. At any rate it is from the platform of the last-named truth that we start, affirming with Paul that "by Him were all things made." Ruskin—a man who, poet as he was to the inmost fibre of him, was not likely to squander poetic expressions upon ideas he deemed valueless—avowed his faith that "the right hand of Christ first strewed the snow on the Lebanon and smoothed the slopes of Calvary." We may well take our stand beside him, giving with soberest conviction our assent and echo to his words. And we shall only be uttering the literal truth as Paul held it, not merely giving voice to an exaggerated ecstasy of adoration, when we sing with Faber

> Jesus is God! The solid earth
>   The ocean broad and bright,
> The countless stars like golden dust
>   That strew the skies by night,
> The wheeling storm, the dreadful fire,
>   The pleasant wholesome air,

> The summer's sun, the winter's frost,
>   His own creations were—

or when we call upon our souls to transport themselves on imagination's pinions back to the far-off creation morning, and bid them

> Hark! the voice eternal
>   Robed in majesty,
> Calling into being
>   Earth and sea and sky—

or when we declare our assurance that

> At His voice creation
>   Sprang at once to sight,
> All the angel faces,
>   All the hosts of light;
> Thrones and dominations,
>   Stars upon their way,
> All the heavenly orders
>   In their great array.

"By Him were all things made." It was He whom the morning stars acclaimed when at the dawn of the world they sang together for joy.

We pass to the "Christus immanent" element of Paul's synthesis. Not only is Christ "before all things," but "in Him all things consist"; and, as has previously been said, immanence was to Paul as real as to any thinker of ancient or modern times it has ever been. Does it matter for this second factor of the series, as it mattered for the first, whether it be grasped or not? Does it even matter whether or no it be true? To these, as to similar questions in regard to the first factor, the full reply will presently be reached; and the large value of the "Christus immanent" conception, as a stone doing its part in sustaining a building fitly framed together, will perhaps be perceived. The immediate answer may be that at least the idea of the Christ who created the world being also the Christ who sustains it by the ceaseless influx of His power, the conception of the world as being veritably only the externalized manifestation of Christ's ever-energizing will, in a most real sense the visible if partial embodiment of His invisible glory, makes the world more beautiful for the Christian worshipper, and sanctifies the pleasure which he finds in contemplating the magnificent panoramas which it sets in movement before his eyes, with their vivid colourings, their calm or tossing seas, their flowers and rolling plains and mountain-spires. The conception banishes all possibility of looking upon the world as common or unclean. "In Him all things consist." The entire range of things from tiniest grassblade to man's physical frame so fearfully and wonderfully made—nay, more than that, the entire range of things from what seems the dead stone by the wayside to the thinking and willing and emotional faculties of the human race —is kept in being only because Christ continues to clothe in these visible and tangible robes the ceaseless out-goings of His might. In and through them He not only speaks, but is. The Christian thinker will not be afraid of the phrase. It is of Christ that the Christian will think when he sings with Tennyson

> The sun, the moon, the stars, the seas, the hills and the plains—
> Are not these, O Soul, the Vision of Him who reigns?

And though in his half-blindness he must change down to the minor key and go on

> And the ear of man cannot hear, and the eye of man cannot see

—he will go further still and close the song as Tennyson closed it—

> But if we could see and hear, this Vision—were it not He?

Even the Christian whose gaze is but half-cleared will realize that "Something lives in every hue Christless eyes have never seen"; and alike in the lengthening bars of light which streak the eastern horizon at dawn, in the wide expanse of stainless brilliance which roofs the earth when noon-tide is at the full, and in the shimmering waves of splendour which in ebb and flow wash round the edges of the sun as it drops down to the west, he will behold "Christ whose glory fills the skies." "In Him all things consist."

But here there looms upon us that "break" in the immanence of Christ of which Paul was always and everywhere so acutely conscious. That he was thus persistently conscious of it is beyond dispute. It hangs cloud-like in his sunniest spaces of thought. This same apostle, who declared that in Christ "all things consist," declared with no less emphasis, and indeed with more frequent iteration, that the world and man, unless linked by freshly-forged bonds of faith to the Christ who had lived and died and risen again, were separated from Him by measureless gulfs. "Without Christ"—"without Christ"—the words or their equivalents ring out again and again, cutting the air like the sad strokes of a passing-bell. Paul beholds a world so utterly dissociated from Christ that He has in it neither part nor lot, a world whence Christ has turned away. For that matter, the same thing may be said of other New Testament writers, though as it is Paul's thought-series we are following here, it is specially to Paul that the present reference is confined. It may not square with facile theologies and diluted soteriologies to look the fact in the face; but on eyes wide-opened it strikes with a compelling vividness which makes refusal to acknowledge its presence an impossible thing. Nor is it enough to take Paul as meaning simply that the human race had been gradually losing its immanent Christ by reason of the steady and insufficiently resisted encroachments of sin, and that the last stage and the final crisis were at hand. That idea or something like it —as representing for Paul something that had taken place in by-gone history's course—may be there; but it is not the whole story. Had that been all, Paul could scarcely have affirmed the severance between those who are one with Christ and those who are not to be so absolute: it would have been a matter of degrees and of a sliding scale. He could hardly have employed of those not linked with Christ so uncompromising, so sombre a phrase as "dead in trespasses and sins." He could not have set Christ over against the world as definitely parted from it or thought of the natural man as one who in Christ had no standing-ground at all. He could hardly have said of those who link themselves with Christ that for them "old things have passed away, all things have become new." But it is so he speaks of both. It is a consummated catastrophe that wrings his soul. He has in mind something definite that has taken place at a definite point of time. There and then, whenever and wherever it may have been, the "break" in Christ's immanence befell. The new immanence of Christ in man is for Paul never merely the strengthening of a still existent immanence which has grown weak or the arresting of a deterioration whereby a still operative immanence is endangered: it is the reversal of a condition wrought out to its issue, the restoration of an immanence which has passed away. True, that *primary* immanence whereof Paul speaks when he affirms that in Christ "all things consist" cannot have come to an end, else the world had sunk into annihilation at the moment when it ceased. And yet a "break" in Christ's immanence there has been. Christ immanent still— Christ immanent no longer—can the paradox be resolved?

I do not know that Paul has anywhere given an explicit answer to the question as to where and when in his view the "break" in Christ's immanence took place. But as we turn his pages we come here and there upon expressions which, as we ponder them and their implications, fit them together, and frame them in their necessary background, may perhaps enable us to catch some glimpse of his thought. Even to himself it may not have stood out in clear-edged outline; but we may with all humility, and with ready admission that we may be wrong, seek to give fuller substance to the suggestions which look forth from behind his words. For instance, when we find him saying of Christ that "the death which He died, He died unto sin once," [39] we are immediately struck by the unusual ring of the words he employs. That Christ died *unto* sin—the statement seems with deliberate intention to slant off in a different direction from the far more frequent statement that Christ died *for*

---

[39] The references for this passage and those subsequently quoted in this paragraph are as follows: (Revised Version) Romans vi. 10; 2 Corinthians v. 14, 15; Romans vi. 11; Romans viii. 10; Colossians iii. 3; Romans vi. 3 ff.; Philippians iii. 10; Galatians ii. 20.

our sins. Why *"unto"* instead of *"for"*? Why *"sin"* instead of *"sins"*? Without falling into the error of attaching too much weight to single words or to changes in them, yet when two terms of a common phrase are altered as if with particular desire to avoid those ordinarily used, we may reasonably conclude that a change of idea as well as of terminology must be implied. Moreover, the new words are touched and tinged with something of mystery. *"Unto* sin" does not so readily as *"for* sin" yield its meaning to the mind's questioning; and *"sin"* instead of *"our sins"* seems to carry thought away from the individual transgressions of men to some totality of evil, as it were, which individual transgressions manifest only in part. We are back in fact upon the conception of a cosmic force with which, as we saw in a previous chapter, Christ was at grips. And the impression of being in contact with another range of ideas is deepened when we find Paul making a whole series of statements to the effect that those who experience the new immanence of Christ have actually died *with* Him. "We thus judge, that if one died for all, then all died; and He died for all, that they which live should no longer live unto themselves, but unto Him who for their sakes died and rose again." He bids his readers, "Reckon ye also yourselves to be dead unto sin, but alive unto God in Christ Jesus"; and he reminds them, "If Christ is in you, the body is dead because of sin, but the spirit is life because of righteousness." To the Colossians he writes, "For ye died, and your life is hid with Christ in God." To the Romans he gives a string of injunctions based on the fact that they have been "baptized into Christ's death," have "died with Christ," are "united with Christ by the likeness of His death," "buried with Him through baptism unto death." Of himself he speaks as aspiring to "become conformed unto Christ's death," and, more startlingly still, makes the tremendous assertion, "I am crucified with Christ." These utterances are not very easy to interpret; and perhaps even a moderately satisfactory interpretation is impossible unless, besides being thus interrogated, the phrases are set against some such background as that which Paul's "thought-series" provides. With that behind them they may perhaps grow more luminous, and be to some extent at least lit up by the light from the "thought-series," taken as a whole, in which they are framed. At the present point, however, it is not their actual interpretation with which we are dealing. They are quoted here because they may assist us to determine for ourselves where the "break" in Christ's immanence came in. For they hint, it is evident, at some revolutionary change in Christ's cosmic connection with the world. They look quite beyond His relation with any individual human soul. They speak—such a phrase as Christ "dying unto sin" forces the realization upon us—of some experience which Christ passed through as it were over and above the experience which human eyes perceived Him to pass through when they saw Him die. They seem to hint at a death behind that death, so making the very shadow of Calvary vaster in its sweep and denser in its gloom. And though those whom He redeems are in some sense to share in even that experience—for they too are to die *unto* sin and to die *with* Christ —it must be at something still more profound than the first experience of union with Christ involved in redemption that Paul is pointing. Yet, though that death lies in a manner behind Calvary's death as men beheld it, it was nevertheless a part of it, experienced in the same bitter hours, consummated at the moment when the cry "It is finished!" broke from Christ's lips. What if, over and above the answer given in a previous chapter to the question "What did death mean for Christ?", a deeper answer yet is at hand? What if, over and above that primary immanence of Christ by reason of which it is in Him that "all things consist," there were another immanence of Christ in humanity from which at Calvary Christ withdrew? What if for Christ death held this in addition to all its other meanings—*that Christ's cosmic relationship with humanity changed, by the withdrawal (in some sense) from humanity of His former immanence in it, at the Cross?*

Let us recall some phrases used on an earlier page to describe the line along which, according to God's original design for man, man's spiritual development was to proceed. There was, we saw, to be something more than evolution, something more than a development of personality *within itself*. There was to be *a movement of personality out of itself into God;* and it was by the progressive adjustment and submission of man's will, carrying the entire personality with it, that this self-identification with God was to be consummated at last. But this identification of the human personality with God could only come to pass if God Himself were present within man's personality to magnetize it and to draw it upward—and present within man's personality, not merely as permeating it with His creative and sustaining power (of course He was present thus), but as offering Himself for a further relationship yet to be set up. One may put it as a seeming paradox (it is only in seeming that it deserves the name) that God must be present within human personality and yet in that very presence separate from it, in order that a movement of human personality into union with God might become a possible thing. Personality could not pass out of itself into God by dint of any native push or impulse, even though that push or impulse existed and operated by reason of God's own energizing and sustaining power. However far along the path of development *within* itself it might by such a push or impulse be driven, it could not reach *beyond* itself or, having taken flight from its first standing-ground, alight and settle down upon another centre from which its life should thenceforward be derived. There must be a pull from outside itself as well as a push from within. With Paul's "thought-series" to guide us, can we now fill a little more completely the outline thus suggested? May we say that the Eternal Son, immanent in every man as Creator and Sustainer of all man's constitutive elements and faculties right up to those exercises of will whereby man was to decide his fate, was immanent in every man in another sense (we may call it, if we will, an incarnation of the Eternal Son in the race, as distinct from that incarnation of the Eternal Son in a historical Personality which was later on to come) as the appeal of the divine life to man to lift himself to a loftier plane and at last *consciously* as well as *unconsciously* to derive his life from that higher source? Up to those last choices that man had to make, up to and in the very power

by which they were made, Christ had been "Christus Creator"
and "Christus immanent" too; for in the beginning, as in New
Testament times, it held true that "without Him was not anything made that was made." May we say that He was present
also, and operative also as it were by another immanence from
a different direction, seeking to influence man in such wise that
man's choices might be rightly made, and that Christ might in
another and higher sense become "Christus Creator" and
"Christus immanent" through the free decision of the human
will? May we say that in every pulsing consciousness of the
presence of something higher competing with something lower
for his adherence, man was feeling the presence and drawing
of the Eternal Son of God? May we say that there was this
immanence over and above that primary immanence in virtue
of which it is in the Eternal Son that "all things consist"? And
if so, was this the immanence which was withdrawn when Christ
—the historic Christ—died?

It is to be conceded that, if this reading of the matter be correct, the recognition on man's part of the Christ-appeal within
him could only—even if the line of human development had
been drawn as God meant it to be—have been gradual; would
have begun with a dim dawn wherein the outline of the appealing Christ was but faintly and waveringly discerned; and would
have grown from that dim dawn to a perfect day in whose fulness man and Christ stood face to face. But the suggestion has
no real doubtfulness thrown upon it by this. We make no difficulty in admitting an unrecognized influence of the Holy Spirit
within man at any stage of human history from its origins until
now: in fact, it is one of the accepted truths of the Christian
faith that God has never left Himself without the Spirit's witness in any soul, be it that of Greek, barbarian, Scythian, bond
or free. Why make any difficulty, then, in admitting a similar
unrecognized influence and appeal from an indwelling Christ?
It is but providing another appeal which the indwelling Spirit
was appealing to man to answer, and but giving to that other
appeal its author's name. Besides, since it is on the wings of
God's self-communicativeness—which is the Holy Spirit in all

its multifarious activities—that every divine influence necessarily descends from heaven to earth, it is the Holy Spirit itself
that must have borne the indwelling Christ down upon and into
man; and if we vision a Christ in man and yet unrecognized *by*
man, to whom man was being pointed by the Spirit, itself unrecognized as such, we make our picture complete without intro-
ducing into it any element discordant or distorted or in any wise
strange. It is but to set back into earth's earlier ages a Spirit
who does not speak of Himself but who takes of the things of
Christ and shows them unto man. There is no inherent improbability in the suggestion of a Christ dwelling in man and calling
to man while man did but hear the calling without seeing the
Caller's face or shape, even without knowing how to speak His
name. Hesitation in conceding that the case stood thus there
need not be. Nor need we be disquieted because we cannot imag-
inatively trace for ourselves the process whereby that early unconscious response to the indwelling Christ was meant, in God's
purpose, to grow into a response conscious and full-orbed. How
could it be otherwise? It is surely natural enough that we, having come to the place where we stand by paths which, after
branching off from the main and rightful one long ago, have
branched and branched again till the last stretch has brought
us to a goal celestial diameters away from the one which a
straight advance would have attained—it is surely natural
enough that we should be unable to lay down on imagination's
map the line of that straight advance. How would sinless man
have come at last to recognize as the voice of the Eternal Son
that voice which from the beginning called him higher? We
cannot tell. We cannot expect to tell. We cannot even in thought
or fancy get back to the starting-point and construct an ideal
history for a human race kept pure. Behind us the doors are
shut. Would sinless man have reached at length to a knowledge
of the Eternal Son without such a revelation of Him as in actual fact the historic Christ has given? Was the Incarnation
necessitated by human sin, or would it have taken place if sin
had never been? We ask the question sometimes; and in support of both "Ay" and "Nay" plausible arguments may be ad-

duced. But certainty there cannot be. We cannot tell. But there is nothing in all this to prevent us from holding—if only the suggestion fits in with the entire range of Christian thought— that from the outset it was in the Eternal Son that God came down to meet and grip His evolving creatures; that even in the older dispensations it was only through the Eternal Son that man could rise to God; that long before the message was framed on His human lips the Eternal Son was saying, in a whispered language whereto man did not as yet hold the key, "No man cometh unto the Father but by Me."

It is to be conceded, also, that on the suggested theory man was not, in virtue of his primary constitution and spiritual equipment, in the full sense a son of God. There need be no reluctance or hesitancy in assenting to the statement. Indeed, it deserves to be made, not at all as a concession yielded after compulsion, but as indispensable in the interests of truth—this notwithstanding Maurice's severe censure of it previously quoted. In fact, this matter needs closer thinking than it frequently wins from those who lightly attach the label "son of God" to man as he was originally formed. It is not so simple as it appears. Men sons of God from the first? "Yes" and "No." "Yes"—in the sense of being born out of God's creative power. "No"—in the sense of a complete moral and spiritual affiliation with God, springing from the voluntary decision of man's own will. That had yet to come. Yet only by that would a full sonship be set up. Christ immanent in man from the beginning of time? Again "Yes" and "No." "Yes"—in the sense that "in Him all things consist." And "Yes" also (if the line we have indicated be correct) in the sense that the Eternal Son dwelt unrecognized and yet appealing within humanity in order that humanity might recognize the unrecognized Son in the end, hearken to and obey His appeal, and deliberately link itself with Him. But "No"—in the sense of an immanence all-possessive and all-pervasive of humanity, directive of it throughout, as it were filling it from base to top. That had yet to come. Yet only thus would a real immanence, worthy to be so called without qualifying word or phrase, be set up. These "Yes" and "No" distinctions count for much here, and must not be swept aside. Man was not as if by inevitable necessity or inalienable birthright a son of God, unless that title be so watered down as to lose half its strength. The potentiality and promise of a perfect sonship he assuredly had; and the power to realize potentiality and promise was offered to him in the beginning by the indwelling of the Eternal Son, as it was afterwards offered to him once more in the advent of the Son Incarnate; but he had, both in the older time and in the later, to *become* a son of God. He had to acquire his perfect filial status, not merely to recognize it as already possessed. For that matter, this cautionary note is struck by at least one commanding voice out of the midst of that early Greek theology which loudly proclaimed perfect sonship as man's native endowment and the full immanence of Christ as having accompanied man's birth. We may console ourselves for Maurice's reproach, if it irk us, by taking shelter under one of the Greek theology's greatest names. It was noted before that Athanasius did not hold the *original* immanence of Christ as sufficient to confer full sonship upon man. One quite definite statement, representative of many others in which a similar idea is expressed or implied, may be set down here. Athanasius says of the Old Testament transgressors that *"since they were not sons by nature,* they were capable of becoming degenerate and disobedient"[40]—the very structure of the sentence, be it noted, putting out of court the interpretation that the sinners alluded to *lost an existing sonship* through their sin. The affirmation is explicit that they sinned, or were capable of sinning, precisely because they were *not* sons. And indeed, if we think the thing through with care, it becomes increasingly difficult to see how, if man had been in the full sense a son of God from the

---

[40] *Contra Arianos,* I, 37. R. H. Hutton quotes another explicit statement from Athanasius to the same effect. In this, in addition to affirming that "we are not by nature sons of God," Athanasius goes on to present the same idea from the other side, and says "also God is not by nature our Father." Hutton does not give the reference. (*Theological Essays,* 3rd edition, p. 264.) It is perhaps worth noting that even Clement of Alexandria glances for a moment in this direction when he says "They shall learn from us that he (man) was not perfect in respect of his creation, but in a fit condition to receive virtue." (*Stromata,* VI, 12.)

outset, with the immanent Christ all-pervasive and all-possessive within, sin could ever have entered into human experience
at all; for under the given conditions every element and faculty
of man's nature would have been submitted to and would have
manifested the inspiration of the immanent and all-pervasive
Christ; and the entrance of evil could therefore only become
possible on the grotesque hypothesis of Christ's own will using
man's surrendered will as an instrument for flinging Christ's
control aside. Of a potential perfect sonship we may indeed
still continue to speak; but higher than that our assertion cannot be safely pitched.[41] Wiser, surely, it must be to keep to the
lower note—a note which for all its restraint is spur enough to
the soul's aspiration—and say that from humanity's birth
Christ the Eternal Son has offered to all men, and has given to
those who have received Him, power to become sons of God.

Accepting, then, the suggestion of the Eternal Son immanent in man from the beginning, with an immanence over and
above the immanence implied in the affirmation that "in Him
all things consist"—the suggestion of the Eternal Son immanent in man in order to woo man into perfect sonship—can we
go on to the further part of the suggestion, and hold it, if not
established, at least possible, that this immanence ceased when
Christ expired on the Cross? Was it thus and there that Paul's
"break" took place?

Obviously, the appeal of the Eternal Son, made as He dwelt
in man at the beginning (acceptance of the suggestion being
assumed) failed, and dropped to completer failure, as the years
and centuries passed on; and the entire world-order, slipping
from the grasp which should have guided and ruled it, went
astray. And the Incarnation of Christ at least implied, what-

---

[41] How (to instance another difficulty) could the terms "redemption" and
"salvation" be employed in connection with Christ's work if man were already
in the full sense a son of God? What could redemption or salvation mean if full
sonship were already possessed? Not a few ideas which hold their heads high
when they present themselves on a mental field otherwise vacant, are forced to a
humbler mien merely by being set into juxtaposition with certain fundamental
Christian conceptions. Introduced into that new company, they seem to shrink
and wither, as if suddenly finding themselves in an atmosphere they cannot
breathe.

ever other implications it may have held, that the moral and spiritual development of humanity must thenceforward proceed on other lines. The people whom God had planted "a noble vine, wholly a right seed," had finally become "the degenerate plant of a strange vine" unto Him. So the old husbandry could avail no more. God Himself proclaimed that its power was spent. It is but putting the same thing in other words to say that the Eternal Son, through whose immanence God had from the first sought to win men into sonship, Himself recognized that His appeal to men had been in vain. With reverence one may put it that Christ the Eternal Son, coming to inaugurate His new appeal to humanity, must have recognized that the new appeal had to be made because of the failure of the appeal made before.[42] If, with a quite natural and proper sensitiveness, one shrinks for a moment from ascribing a consciousness of failure to Christ, one may feel oneself at least absolved from any blame for so doing when one recalls Christ's lament over the city which was to reject Him, and hears the echoes of that "O Jerusalem, Jerusalem . . . how often would I have gathered thee . . . and ye would not!" in which Christ's own pathetic confession of failure found voice. That utterance looks both forward and back. It had a forward look in anticipation of the death which Christ was to accomplish at the city over which He wept. It meant recognition of and sorrow for the failure of that last earthly appeal He was about to make. Most true. But that "how often" means a look turned the other way, the backward way. It means, surely, recognition of and sorrow for the failure of earlier appeals. And who can say how far back that retrospective "how often" went? May not that backward look have pierced right into the long-drawn rejection of the Eternal Son in the centuries gone by? At any rate, failure Christ certainly could feel and confess. And if He had been immanent in man down the past ages to win him, and man had refused to be

---

[42] I have sometimes wondered whether this may be the ultimate truth behind McLeod Campbell's idea that Christ made a perfect confession of sin on behalf of man.

won—if He was to offer a new immanence to man after the Cross had been endured and the Resurrection had conquered the Cross—it is no extravagant suggestion that at the Cross He withdrew that earlier immanence from the humanity to which He had given it in vain. So for my part I read it. And I think it may fairly be claimed that by taking this view of Paul's "break" we bring round ourselves an atmosphere akin to that which Paul breathed whenever he thought or spoke of it—the atmosphere of a recollected catastrophe in which the whole world was flung in shock and storm from its hitherto established spiritual course, almost from its hitherto established spiritual base. The immanence of Christ withdrawn from humanity at the Cross! One seems to see the whole creation catching its breath, watching in fear and wonder as the moment of that catastrophic happening comes and goes. It means that Christ the Eternal Son has by that withdrawal brought the old order to an end; has added an entire era to the list of things done with for ever; has consummated an event cosmic in the fullest and widest possible sense; has altered the structure of the world and even the very constitution of man. Taking this view, we can enter into that deep emotion, that feeling as of high tragedy, with which Paul was filled whenever that "break" recurred to his mind. And from that haunting phrase about "Christ dying unto sin"—surely from that the cloud of mystery lifts at least a little way! From the humanity in which He had been immanent, but which in spite of His appealing immanence had become "sin," the Eternal Son withdrew; and though He withdrew only to offer Himself to humanity again, the withdrawal was made none the less. He died *unto* sin—died away from it, as refusing to have further part or lot in the spiritual order which sin had spoilt beyond repair. If even in the new spiritual order which He was going to set up sin should still intrusively rear its head and take up arms in dispute of His sovereignty, the battle should be fought on different ground under a different challenge and by a different plan of campaign of His choosing. Paul's hints grow clearer. The immanence of Christ withdrawn from humanity at the Cross! Does not at least a ray of light fall from the suggestion upon that stretch in Paul's "thought-series" which Paul left lying in the half-dark?

Over the final stretch of the apostle's sweep of thought there need be but little lingering, for over that no dimness of outline hangs. "Christus Redemptor" stands out as the ultimate whereto all else has led, its meaning defined in utmost clearness, the richness of its content displayed for all to see. And "Christus Redemptor" always bore for Paul, as its last and loftiest significance, the restored immanence of Christ in man. That in thus construing the phrase Paul was reproducing Christ's own conception of His redemptive ministry I have in previous chapters attempted to show. Cross and Resurrection indeed emphasized as indispensable—as to that there is no possibility of dispute; but Christ had died and Christ had risen that Christ might live again; and He lived again in order that He might give His own life to man. Words and phrases crowd upon one's memory. Paul's own conversion experience had been the revealing of God's Son in him; and to so commanding and overmastering a height had that revelation grown that it was no longer Paul himself that lived, but Christ that lived in him. The Corinthians are a new creation, Paul tells them, because they are *in* Christ. The Colossians are reminded that their life is hid *with Christ in God*. For the Galatians and Ephesians he prays that Christ may be *formed in them* and that Christ may *dwell in their hearts*. But indeed nearly all Paul's writings are luminously studded with phrases such as these: they run like interwoven threads through the stuff of almost every argument, break in with swift recurrence at every opportunity as though they had been waiting for entrance at the door. The restored immanence of Christ in man—man *in* Christ or Christ *in* man— that was what in his final apprehension of it "Christus Redemptor" meant for Paul. Perhaps, were Paul inditing an epistle to Christian readers of our own time, he would prefer a more exclusive use of the phrase "man in Christ" over the other phrase "Christ in man," as emphasizing more strongly the fact that

Christ is *not* in man till man has by the deliberate exercise of his will thrown himself into Christ. For if our tracing of Paul's "thought-series" is valid, that other phrase "Christ in man" stands for something which did indeed hold good in the world's earlier ages, but which ceased to hold good at the Cross; and Paul, writing now, might well desire to guard himself against a misconstruction he would have reckoned most grave. The apostle's message was this—that Christ was once again to be in man *when man had set himself in Christ.* To be sure, the two phrases come to the same thing in the end; and so long as misconstruction be avoided, it matters not which be used. Whichever interpretative expression be preferred, "Christus Redemptor" stands for the restored immanence of Christ in man. One may venture to speak of a first and second incarnation. Christ had been incarnate in the race. *That* incarnation had reached its term. But He had become incarnate, next, in the historic Christ in order, after Cross and Resurrection, to become incarnate in the race once more. "Christus Redemptor," it can hardly be too often repeated or too strongly stressed, stands, not for the recognition of an existing and inalienable immanence, but for the restoration of an immanence which has been lost—the restored immanence of the Eternal Son in man. But for this it *does* stand and for nothing less; and it stands for this, not in poetic metaphor, but in the most literal interpretation that words can bear.

It is only by careful remembrance of this that we can protect ourselves against being misled when we use or hear others use such terms as "Christ the representative man" or "Christ the Federal Head of the Race." Allusion has been previously made to these expressions, so ever-recurring in the language of more than one present-day theological school. They have an indisputable attractiveness. But they imply only half-truths. And the danger of a half-truth—which at the best implies a half-truth reserved and at the worst may easily pass into a half-lie—needs no emphasis. If we are going to make these expressions work in harmony with the suggestions of Paul's "thought-series," and particularly in harmony with Paul's interpretation of its final item "Christus Redemptor," we must set up close against them a warning notice that, so far as they have any truth at all, they indicate not what *is* but what *is to be*. The warning notice is specially required because the first suggestion of the expressions is precisely the opposite of this.

For instance, to speak of Christ as "the representative man" causes us—since we naturally follow the line which the adjective indicates as appropriate—to picture immediately a relationship originating from man as its source. A representative sums up, so to say, what exists in those whom he represents: he acts for those who stand behind him in accordance with the inspirations and instructions they transmit to him, translating these into whatever speech or action successive occasions may require; and such a relation is constructed and construed, be it noted, along a line which starts from the *constituency*, not from the *representative himself*. That is in fact the essence of the matter. Can the relation between man and Christ be properly described by a phrase with such an implication as that? We have seen before that some do actually take Christ to be the perfect working out of the possibilities of human nature, in some cases going so far as to hold the very process of God's incarnation in Christ for no more than the representation on a higher scale of a similar process going on in man. Certainly those who so look on Christ are warranted in speaking of Him as the "representative man," and in attaching the ordinary meaning to the epithet they use. The phrase fits their thought as a glove fits the hand. But it must at any rate be recognized that in doing this they part company from Paul. With the apostle's conception of "Christus Redemptor" as signifying the *restored* immanence of Christ in man the phrase "representative man" has in its normal interpretation nothing in common: the two ideas are poles asunder—so far asunder, indeed, as to be antagonistic with no conceivable prospect of coming to terms. And another New Testament phrase, one of Christ's own, makes itself heard by no means irrelevantly just here. "Ye did not choose me, but I chose you." If we are to speak at all of

Christ as "representative" in this connection, we must speak of the "representation" He makes as one writer has spoken of it, and call it "representation by One who creates by His act the Humanity He represents, and does not merely sponsor it" [43]— and when we once get thus far, it would really be more accurate to speak of man as in some sense representing Christ, or at least as appointed to do so, than of Christ as representing man. For in proportion as "Christus Redemptor" performs and perfects His re-creative redeeming work in man, will man progressively reproduce and reveal—represent—Christ's nature, Christ's mind and heart and will. So, once more, in so far as the phrase "Christ the representative man" has any truth at all, it stands, not for what *is,* but for what *is to be.*

The other phrase, "Christ the Federal Head of the Race," is equally misleading if an attempt is made to use it in what would be its ordinary signification, as descriptive of the relation between humanity and Christ. It is indeed very doubtful whether the analogy which the phrase brings to mind can be worked out at all to any clear issue. At any rate it leads us, as does the "representative man" suggestion, in a direction diametrically opposite to that in which Paul's conception of "Christus Redemptor" points the road. A "federal" government—to take what is perhaps the commonest use of the epithet —is a supreme government set at the head of a number of other governments in such wise that, within its appointed range, its single act shall count as, and in effect be, the collective manifestation of the acts of the federated group. It is a coalescence of the federated members whereby each single member loses its separate status, its very being, in a new entity which becomes in a way the *totality* of the federated members, holding them all within itself. And yet, while including them, it is constituted by them: their existence is the indispensable pre-condition of its own; and it has no other reality beyond that which their self-surrender bestows. They are essential to it as confluent streams are essential to the lake wherein they are lost. As in the case of the "representative" phrase, we find indicated in this "federal"

[43] Forsyth, *The Work of Christ,* p. 182.

phrase a relationship constructed and construed from the *constituency,* not from the *head.* If now we take the phrase "Christ as the Federal Head of the Race" and attempt to mould its meaning into a shape more or less correspondent with that which other phrases, built round the "federal" adjective, take on in our general usage, we find ourselves committed to a very difficult task. What can a federated humanity or a Federal Head of humanity really mean? How can we fashion a mental image of either? If, determined not to be vanquished by the difficulty, we summon up all available reinforcements of the mind and go on with the wrestle, we shall be compelled at last to picture to ourselves a sort of mysterious totality of humanity in Christ, even a totality of humanity *constituting* Christ. To think the "federal" idea through to its logical issue in connection with humanity's relations to Christ is to arrive at a conclusion which for practical religious purposes threatens both the individuality of man and the individuality of Christ. It is true that the majority who employ the phrase leave it in half-light instead of forcing it plainly to reveal its content under investigation's searching lamps. But in this very vagueness, too, there is danger. For those who use the phrase at the present time [44] and yet shirk any close dealing with it are too likely, succumbing to a sort of emotional atmosphere which it will throw around them, to entertain *unconsciously* a suggestion which, were they to face the issue, they would have *consciously* either to accept or to reject, and which many of them, one hopes

[44] The qualifying words "at the present time" are inserted advisedly. For before the theory of Christ's ineradicable immanence in man had obtained so prominent a position upon the field, older theologians could and did use the phrase "the Federal Headship of Christ," even though they left it wrapped in vagueness, without feeling the temptation alluded to. I do not forget that even so comparatively recent a writer as Dale speaks of Christ as "the Federal Head of the Race" and, while only very partially dealing with its significance, seeks to use it for "orthodox" purposes. His explanation of the phrase so far as concerns Christ's Headship over the *new* race—the race of the redeemed—is indeed clear enough. But in respect of Christ's Headship over the race *as a whole,* he goes no further than a suggestion that Christ's eternal relation with the Father showed the ideal relation of the race to God. (*The Atonement,* Chapter 10.) Yet, spite of this very imperfect unpacking and display of its inmost contents, the phrase is pressed into the service of what may be termed the "orthodox" theory of Atonement. But so far as I know, this line has not been much pursued by later thinkers.

and believes, would reject. There is certainly prevalent in many quarters something which might (if a corresponding word to "pantheism" may be coined for our present purpose) be termed "pan-Christian." Christ is in man and man is in Christ: Christ is the race's "Federal Head"; and in the end it comes to this, that neither is man an individual face to face with Christ, under an inescapable compulsion to accept or to repel Him, nor is Christ a Person making a personal appeal. That comes to be, if we must not say the thought, at any rate the undefined impression moving up and down the border-line between thought and feeling. Better, after all, if the implications of the "federal" phrase were thought out to the end. So we should be freed from self-ignorance and self-deception, and it would become clear, at least, that the moment we start out on the road along which those implications conduct us, we have turned our backs upon Paul and upon his "thought-series," and upon his "Christus Redemptor" faith. But if "Christus Redemptor" be taken as Paul took it, as involving the *restored* immanence of Christ, then for those who accept that restored immanence from Him Christ *becomes* the Head of the race in truth and fact, because each member of the new race successive acceptances create refuses to live any longer from self as centre, and finds a fresh source and centre in Him. We may, to be sure, keep the epithet "federal" if it be deemed precious; only it must pass beyond its generally-accepted meaning now, and be taken as signifying, not that Christ derives His Headship from men, but that men accept His Headship as the ground and constitutive agent of their whole life. And certainly of this phrase, as of the "representative" phrase, it may—nay, it must—be said that in so far as it has any truth at all, it indicates, not what *is,* but what *is to be.*

If our interpretation of Paul's "thought-series" has been on right lines, we can answer now the question put at this chapter's beginning, and can call Christ's redeeming ministry "cosmic" in a far wider sense than that in which we applied the term before. We have traced a vital and organic connection *backwards from* the earthly and subsequent ministry of Christ into the

remoter past as well as *within* the incidents of that earthly and
subsequent ministry itself. We have found one and the same
Christ to have been and still to be the operative and energizing
agent for God's creative, sustaining, and redeeming purposes
through the entire range of historic time. It was by Christ the
Eternal Son that God made the world. It was by the immanence
of Christ the Eternal Son that God from the beginning sustained the world and sustains it still. It was by a further immanence of Christ the Eternal Son that God sought to bring
humanity into a higher development from its position at the
apex of created things, and to lead it into a consciously-accepted
union with Himself. And it was by a new immanence of Christ
the Eternal Son, offered in the historic Christ of the New Testament when that earlier immanence had failed of its end, that
God sought (as He seeks still) to make that union come to pass.
Christ is grounded in the eternal order—or rather, as it should
more correctly be phrased, the eternal order is grounded in
Christ. His redemptive ministry is the vindication of His original sovereignty over the eternal order, not His intrusion into it.
And we may note incidentally that this affords at least some clue
as to the spiritual destiny of those whose days were done before
the historic Christ appeared. They did not live *before Christ
came,* as the ordinary phrase has it, for Christ was always here;
and it was through Him that the saintliness of the old-world
saints, no less than that of later saints, had, perhaps throughout eternity, to be wrought up nearer to perfection's sacred
height.[45] Also we may re-assert that from Paul's "thought-
series" there emerges some hint of answer to that ultimate and
age-long problem of human thought of which we spoke before.
It gives us a glimpse, to say no more, of how all that has ever

---

[45] I have never come upon a satisfactory answer to a question which, on the
extreme "objective" theory of atonement, refuses to be silenced. If Christ's death,
as an event in historic time, was an indispensable prerequisite to God's will-
ingness or power to redeem—if that in itself *constituted* the Atonement—what
of those who died before it took place? To confront the question with a Scripture
quotation as to Christ being the "Lamb slain before the foundation of the world,"
as is sometimes done, and then to suppose the question effectually settled, seems
to me a delusive playing with words. Indeed, it appears to involve a repudiation
of the very doctrine it professes to defend.

been, all that is, and all that ever will be, may be gathered into a unity out of which all emerges, within which in spite of the emergence all is nevertheless retained, and by which all is to be reclaimed in the final act—how "after Last returns the First, Though a wide compass round be fetched." [46] And as redemption is itself a part of, deeply embedded in, the offered reply to that ultimate and age-long and searching problem, we are entitled to add to all else, that in the suggested interpretation of Paul's "thought-series" the opportunity of a Christianity and a Christian gospel at once philosophical and evangelical may perhaps be found.

5

But now, at the close of this study, we may perhaps find the question raising its head, "What is the use of all this?" At the commencement of the chapter, it may be remembered, it was suggested that the question might possibly intrude. Some one may say, "You admit that much of this is tentative: you admit also that neither thought about these things nor any definite opinion about them is necessary for a true Christian experience; and you admit, still further, that even a preacher need not fail in the presentation of his message just because he leaves these topics undealt with in the pulpit or unexplored in the study. Why then should we be called upon to vex our minds with things confessedly non-essential?" By some, indeed, the point is much more strongly put. One most able writer, speaking specifically of the "Christus Creator" conception, declares that he declines to "hamper" himself with it, and compares speculation upon it with an effort to "enrich astronomy by guessing hard what the back of the moon may be like." "It may be a Christian duty," he proceeds, "to be icily indifferent to such affirmations." [47] To me this dismissal of the topic appears somewhat cavalier. At any rate, while we remind ourselves that the question "What is the use of it all?" gave us a hint of its

[46] Browning, *Apparent Failure.*
[47] Professor Robert Mackintosh, *Albrecht Ritschl,* pp. 256–258.

possible intrusion when our study began, two answers also gave us a hint of their possible entrance close upon the question's heels. It is better, surely, to listen to whatever pleas these answers may have to put in rather than to remain "icily indifferent" to the entire case.

The first answer suggested as possible was this—that such a study as the one we have been following will help the student and preacher to "think things together," to view the various items of his religious belief as parts of an inter-related whole. Paul's "thought-series," as we have read it, at least binds into a connected volume what might have been but scattered leaves, and into a volume with a meaning which could never have been deciphered from the scattered leaves taken each in its isolation from the rest. That such a correlation of ideas is an inestimable advantage in constructive work on any topic is almost universally confessed, however often in practice the fact may through haste be forgotten. The larger the framework within which idea after idea, as each in turn proposes itself, can be satisfactorily fitted in beside other ideas already in place, the better. With a large framework, and with its contents "fitly framed together," the thinker (and every preacher must be in measure a thinker) is conscious of a system behind him instead of a mere collection of fragments lying around him—so establishing his faith more firmly, and bringing, one may confidently expect, a note of more emphatic conviction into his voice as he proclaims it. Neither thinker nor preacher will fear lest, while he affirms this supposed truth or that, some other truth should spring from its ambush and with an unexpected but undeniable challenge put the supposed truth to the blush; for he has subjected this particular truth to the test of compatibility or incompatibility with all else his "framework" holds, and has found that the test is successfully met. And he will feel very sure that in affirming any one of the truths he cherishes, he is not pursuing an *ignis fatuus* which may lead him and his hearers into a swamp and then go out and leave them mocked; for all the lights he follows have their places in some shining constellation set steadfastly in a wide-stretched sky, so that with tremorless assurance he can say "What first were guessed as points, I now know stars." [48]

The second reply suggested as possible, if a doubt as to the utility of the whole discussion were raised, was of a different order, and, if it can vindicate its claims, comes closer home. It was suggested that from a consideration of the topic there might emerge something fitted to waken in the preacher a keener realization of what man requires and of what Christ has to bestow, and fitted as a natural consequence to inflame to more passionate heat the preacher's zeal for souls of men. Has any idea with such a quickening impulse throbbing at its heart actually shown itself as our study has gone on? Looking back upon Paul's "thought-series" as we have sought to reconstruct and interpret it, surely we must admit that such a quickening idea has made itself felt and heard. For if that "break" in the immanence of Christ which so often shadowed the apostle's mind and heart mean what we have taken it to mean, then *every man is definitely either Christian or Christless; and unless the new appeal of the Christ who lived and died is heard and responded to, it is among the Christless that a man must be ranked.* Paul's synthesis—at least one outstanding factor of it —flings us into contact with a truth which must be counted as not merely in "a real if indirect" connection with salvation and redemption, but in a connection with them most startlingly direct. If Christ withdrew His former indwelling within man at the Cross, if along another line of approach He offers man a new indwelling to-day, the alternative clutches fast and hard —every man is Christian or Christless according as Christ's newly-offered indwelling is accepted or refused. That last word may indeed be made milder, though only to render the issue more stern. For there needs no stubborn refusal: mere neglect will suffice to stamp any man with the "Christless" sign. We are forced back upon those clear-cut distinctions which have been so blurred in recent decades, from which our sensitive delicacy shrinks away. "Black" and "white" must come once more into use as terms descriptive of a man's spiritual condition; the

[48] Browning, *A Death in the Desert.*

"grey" with which a mistaken hesitancy or an inveterate colour-blindness has been content must be recognized for what it really is. Converted and unconverted, Church (the real Church, not the nominal) and world, all those varyingly-phrased antitheses in which the essential antithesis of Christian and Christless has been dressed—they must all become significant and vocal again. Our shrinking from definite classification must give way if we are to range ourselves beside Paul, to think his thoughts and speak his words. Our tendency to envisage men and women as placed along a far-stretched line graduated to mark *more or less* Christian degrees, rather than as standing on one side or the other of a boundary fixed between Christian and un-Christian territories, must be overcome—if we are to think and speak with Paul. Of course on the Christian side of the boundary there may be a more and a less—degrees in which individuals are given up to the new immanence of Christ. But of every one it remains true that on one side or other of the boundary he finds his place—so we must affirm if we are to think and speak with Paul. Christ is either within a man or still knocking vainly at his heart's locked doors—so we must read the case if we are to think and speak with Paul. All the old distinctions must rise to our lips again—unless we are prepared to say that Paul was wrong. Nay, it is with a greater than Paul that one thinks and speaks when one uses them; for one remembers a judgment-scene, pictured by Christ Himself, in which the sheep and the goats, with no third group intermediate between the two, stood severed from each other on either side of a clear-drawn dividing line.

It is through failure to realize the existence of this definite "dividing line" that urgency such as Paul's has disappeared from so much of the religious thinking and preaching of our day. We need not wish for a reversion to the forms in which the persuasiveness and the warnings of bygone years were embodied or to the language in which they were clothed. But regret must grow keen that nothing more consonant with the facts and spirit of the Christian gospel, more relevant to the real meaning of the Christian redemption, has stepped into their empty places. The preacher is not possessed of or by any "theology of crisis," [49] and consequently cannot with adequate urgency persuade men to the definite decision which such a theology would render imperative. How shall he preach except he be sent? And the commission which, inscribed in letters of fire, would send him forth equipped with a flaming message and with himself aflame to tell it, has not been given. Men and women do not stand before him as definitely "saved" or "lost"; and enthusiasm cannot maintain itself when the once-burning issue has died down to mere ashes spent and grey. But if Paul's "thought-series," with that factor which speaks of the "break" in Christ's immanence and of the necessity for its repair prominently displayed—if that sweeps in regnancy across the theologian's or the preacher's mental horizon, surely the old persuasiveness must return. *Christ's immanence was withdrawn from humanity at the Cross. Christ, dead and risen, offers a new immanence to man. Every man is therefore definitely either Christian or Christless; and unless the new appeal of the Christ who died and rose again is heard and responded to, it is among the Christless ones that a man must be ranked.* The theologian, framing thus his statement of the case, must feel himself stirred with evangelistic fervour even as he sits in his study chair; and the preacher, as he faces his hearers, will be moved with eager evangelistic passion because he will know that he is setting them at the parting point between the way of life and the way of death. Of course the preacher must exercise all needed restraints. He will not judge individual cases in arrogance or haste. While he will be insistent to every man that Christ and Christlessness constitute and exhaust the inevitable alternative, he will not without sufficient knowledge pronounce as to any man's place on either side of the partition line. Only when some

---

[49] The phrase "theology of crisis" is chiefly used in connection with Barth and his school. Professor Emil Brunner, an authoritative exponent of Barth's system, while informing us that the title was not bestowed upon the group's doctrine by either Barth or himself, nevertheless admits its aptness. (*The Word and the World,* p. 6.) One cannot but wish that the decision so insistently demanded by Barth and his followers might once again resume its prominence in Christian preaching and in Christian discipleship, whether or no one thinks the Barthian method of recalling it the best.

one has openly and flagrantly judged himself will he sternly declare "Thou art the man!" He will be primarily and always the warning herald, only secondarily and seldom the accuser or the judge. He will remember that some degree of unconscious contact with Christ is possible, especially in the more or less Christian atmosphere of a professedly Christian land, and that perhaps even an indirect contact with Christ may be possible through some personality whose contact is direct. Nor will he be hopeless of those whom he knows or fears to be Christless; for he will have the abiding assurance that the Spirit pleads still in the hearts of men. But none of these things will abate one jot or tittle from his zeal. Always it will be a present fact to him that if Christ has withdrawn His indwelling from man, then, unless Christ comes back, man has lost both Christ and himself. Always there will seem to be wandering through the air around him the notes of the solemn refrain, "Christ in all men, ah yes! for in Him all things consist—yet Christ not there!" That "thought-series" of Paul's—that "break" in Christ's immanence over which the apostle mourned—that new immanence of Christ on which for life or death humanity's fate depended—if theologian and preacher are gripped by the reality of it all, how often must there rush like a mighty wind through their souls and burst with the noise as of a trumpet-call from their lips Paul's own great word "Woe is me if I preach not the gospel!"

A theology both philosophical and evangelical we seemed to find suggested as Paul's "thought-series" was reviewed. May we not now add to the two epithets a third in further justification of our study, and speak of a suggested theology philosophical, evangelical, and *evangelistic* too? Surely the old urgencies come back, even though it be a new language they speak and a new garb they wear?

CHAPTER VII

"BY THE FAITH OF THE SON OF GOD"

We pick up now our main thread where at the end of the fifth chapter we laid it down. We laid it down upon the fact that by His Cross and His Resurrection Christ became for all the world and for all time the Giver of His own life to men. We pick it up to ask, and if possible to answer, the question which follows in natural sequence, "How is man to take hold upon the proffered gift?" Of course the immediate answer is easy enough to find. The word "faith" leaps at once to one's memory and one's lips as being the great New Testament word descriptive of the means and method whereby man is brought into touch with the redemptive power of Christ. But what does the word mean? The theologian cannot complete his system without settling upon some adequate interpretation for it. The preacher cannot, unless his conception of its significance be so clear in his own thought as to become in his expression clear enough for all to understand, offer any gospel to disquieted hearts. However much the fact may be obscured during more or less prolonged periods by the necessity of concentrating upon apologetic or doctrinal revision along particular lines, it remains true that for both theologian and preacher the Christian message comes to its completion and its climax in their reply to the inquiry "What must I do to be saved?" And though the theologian in the retirement of his study may succeed in evading the inquiry, the preacher has no such way of escape. For his business is to win and nourish the souls of men. If he shies from a plain enunciation of faith's essential character, or if he contents himself with vague replies, he may be a successful lecturer on many theological themes (though even so the broken column, type of unfinishedness, might well stand as the symbol of the gospel he proclaims), but an evangelist he cannot be. And it is perhaps not far from the truth to say that for many a preacher—specially for those who have moved away from the older theological positions and for whom in consequence the older formularies have lost their savour—the conception of faith is hung round as if with a veil he cannot draw aside. The statement that "faith is acceptance of the finished work of Christ" rings unconvincingly now. Conceded that it may still awaken in some an emotional response not quite valueless, nevertheless, for those who in their quest after the "way of salvation" would fain meet with clues which the mind can follow as well as with emotional currents to which the heart may yield, it raises more questions than it resolves. To most, it seems a specimen left over from an ancient coinage which religious speech once issued from its mint, and a specimen so worn and battered that the inscription telling its value cannot be deciphered any more. No sincere preacher can be content simply to let the matter go at that. The conception of faith must have its clinging mists dispersed, else the preacher can be but a blind leader of the blind, merely linking hands with his hearers for a common groping through the enveloping dark.

What is faith?

I

Faith is a word of many meanings, meanings which as it were constitute a ladder having mere belief for its lowest rung and utter self-abandonment to faith's object for its highest. Yet, for all its multiplicity of meanings, it should not in any given case prove very difficult to determine the significance which the term must bear. The sufficient principle for guidance is always this. What faith is, in any special sphere or context, depends upon the object in which it is to be placed. The interpretation of faith in regard to any particular relationship must be governed by the *kind* of relationship into which faith is to introduce us; for faith is always a response; and the character of a response necessarily depends upon the character of the appeal. Faith

may be purely an act of intellectual belief or assent, as with the
faith we place in the multiplication table. In a case like this,
faith—if we care to set so great a word to a comparatively
slight application—is neither more nor less than saying "yes."
But pass a step or two up the ladder. On a higher rung we find
ourselves speaking of *faith in* a man. And to have *faith in* a
man is a quite different thing. We should hardly use the phrase
"I have faith in that man" to indicate merely that we have
accepted as true a statement which he has just made concerning
the shortest railway route to a certain destination or the time
of a train's departure. Or if we did employ the phrase in connection with such things, it would be only as an emphatic expression of our reliance upon our informant's proved knowledge, as
against somebody's scepticism real or supposed; and we should
really be using it as a sort of testimonial to our informant's
character rather than as indicating our belief in the statements
immediately in question. Our faith would be our response to
the appeal which his character, in the relevant section of it, has
made. And as we climb further up the ladder of faith's meanings, we find the same principle holding good. Faith is always
a response to an appeal, and in framing a satisfactory description of faith in any particular instance the character of the
appeal must be the decisive thing.

Bearing this in mind now as we stand on the loftiest rung of
the ladder and deal with man's faith in Christ, asking "What is
the faith that saves?", we fall back upon our guiding principle,
and answer, "It depends upon the character of the appeal to
which faith has to make its response." We go back accordingly to the fact that Christ offers the new life-dynamic, offers
life, to man by offering Himself; or, using terms with which the
immediately preceding chapter has made us familiar, we remind
ourselves that Christ brings a renewed immanence of Himself
in man within man's reach. The appeal, therefore, is that of a
life-giving Personality seeking to take man into itself. And, in
consequence, the response—the only possible response if a vital
and organic connection is to be established between the idea of
Christ's part in the offering and that of man's part in the receiv-

ing—must be the surrender of man's personality to Christ's.[1]
For that is the answering and corresponding Christward movement on man's part to the movement which Christ has made
toward man. A life offered from one personality can only be
appropriated into another personality through the surrender
of the personality which is to receive: if one cares to make a
sort of paradox of it (which may occasionally assist our thinking) the personality which is *giving* itself must *take* the other,
and the personality which is *receiving* must *give* itself to the
other. Faith *vis-à-vis* a life-giving Christ becomes an altogether
different thing from what it would be if Christ brought only a
new revelation, be that revelation never so resplendently glorious. It must be more than an intellectual assent to certain facts
or doctrines concerning Christ and His work, more than a reliance upon the efficacy of any ministries which He may have
performed or may be performing on our behalf, though these
things must certainly be present, laid down as the first stepping-
stones over which faith passes to its goal. It means, not merely
an adjustment of the mind so that new truth may enter in, not
merely an adjustment of the will so that new commands may be
obeyed (even Tennyson's "Our wills are ours to make them
Thine" does not adequately cover the ground), not merely an
adjustment of the heart so that new encouragements and inspirations may be received, but an adjustment of the whole
nature so that the new force may transform and re-create it.
Faith is really a matter of giving up self-adjustments altogether,
except that one self-adjustment whereby the entire content of
one's nature is brought into the grip of the new force. Faith is
a movement of the whole man, undivided and with everything
that constitutes him unanimous and simultaneous in assent. To
an actual life-force a man must submit, not his intellect alone,
not his heart alone, not any single element alone, but *himself*.
Faith is not taking something *from* Christ, but *taking Christ*—
which means, when we go deep enough, Christ taking us. Faith

[1] I have in this paragraph used here and there, in scattered fashion, a few sentences from the chapter on "Faith" in my previous book, *The Philosophy of
Christian Experience.*

must be the actual movement of man's entire personality to identify itself with, and to lose itself in (albeit the losing is the real finding too) the personality of Christ.[2] To some extent, at least, parallel experiences may be found on lower planes. In any case where there is the giving of any quality of character or mind, of anything inward and temperamental—and such giving is a quite possible thing within the limits of our ordinary human experience—the giving can be effective only through the surrender of him who is to receive to him who is to give: the inferior personality must identify itself, at any rate in that range and department of it that is to be enriched, with the superior; and no mere intellectual conviction that the superior personality *is* superior, no mere expectancy, nothing in short except the real moving up of the lower personality into the higher, will secure the boon. Of course the bestowal of external and tangible gifts need involve no such intimacy of relation. For that the mere stretching out of two hands is enough. Nor does exchange of thought call for it either. The movement of the lips in speech on the one side, and the hearing of the ear on the other, will suffice for that. But to give qualities of character or endowments of mind is a totally different matter. Those other relations are merely those of two circles which remain external to one another, though at a single point their circumferences may touch: this relation implies one sphere contained at any rate partially within another. And since between Christ and man it is a question of giving and receiving, not some qualities of character only, but *life,* the sum total of all qualities, it is the *whole* personality of man that must be enclosed within the personality of Christ. One sphere—the smaller and subordinate one—must lie *wholly* within the other's circumference. The one effort of the human soul is to be *in* Christ so that Christ may be *in* the human soul. He is to dwell in our hearts by faith. The loftiest ideal that our faith keeps in view is to possess its Christ, not as

[2] Compare Didon's striking phrases. *"L'essence de la foi est de nous livrer tout entiers à celui qui en est l'objet. Le croyant ne s'appartient plus, il renonce à ses pensées propres, à ses intérêts, à son initiative personelle, à tout, et il appartient sans réserve à celui à qui il croit. Il meurt à lui pour vivre moralement dans un autre, il échange sa vie contre la vie d'un autre."* (*Jesus Christ,* I, 452.)

companion only, however close and faithful He might prove—not as dearest friend only, however changeless His friendship might be—not even, one may dare to say, as Saviour only in the limited sense of rescuer from doom—but to possess Him as soul of our soul, life of our life. A vital faith (it is hardly putting it too strongly) makes exchange of personalities with Christ. Christ's own words may be cited as strong support of the saying. He spoke of belief, but He spoke of belief *in* Him or *on* Him almost always. And these phrases must be taken as synonymous with other phrases which Christ employed to define the disciple's true relation with Himself. "Coming to Him," "receiving Him," and the like—they all mean this veritable union of personalities, or exchange of personalities (it matters not which way we put it) between the disciple and Christ. Indeed, all those utterances, cited in a previous chapter,[3] which show that Christ held His own right relationship with men to be one of self-communication, might be cited again as showing that He held man's right relationship with Himself to be one of self-identification; to use them thus would be but to make them repeat from the other end of the connecting line the same message as before. Faith is the actual passing of our nature into the nature of Christ Himself. It is man's contribution to the establishment of Christ's restored immanence within him. Faith, like the love for which it is really another name, smites the chord of self till it passes in music out of sight. To faith every moment is a Christmas moment, with Christ new-born within the heart whence faith proceeds. The soul which yearns after faith's sublimest experience voices its aspiration thus as it looks toward its Lord—

> Thus would I live; yet now
> Not I, but He
> In all His power and love
> Henceforth alive in me!

And the soul which in answer to its yearning after that sublime experience attains to any measure of it knows, in proportion to

[3] Chapter IV, § 2.

the degree of its attainment, first the death and then the resurrection of being "dead to herself and dead in Him to all beside."

If we are to *live* by faith, or are even to aspire after that experience—thus matching our spiritual programme to that of Paul, who declared that the life which he lived in the flesh he lived by the faith of the Son of God—it is only on these lines that a satisfactory conception of faith can be framed. Faith must do more than look back towards a historic event, with whatever splendour the historic event may gleam down upon us across the distance and however intense and expectant the backward look may be. No backward look, with all the utmost possible light of trustfulness shining in the eyes that fling it forth, can be an instrument for the making or the sustenance of a present life in the soul, any more than recollection of food that once nourished the body can make or sustain the body's life to-day. And faith must be an attitude ceaselessly repeated or, better still, maintained. To live by faith cannot mean to live under the impulse and impetus communicated to us in response to the faith of a single by-gone hour. A faith whereby we live cannot mean a faith which merely gives us a start and then retires from the field because its work is done. A faith which is to make life can only be a faith which holds us in perpetual oneness with the Christ who is Himself life's source, who is Himself the life-dynamic for the world. It is true, certainly, that inferior kinds of faith may have some real and spiritually valuable effect. A faith which gets no further than to lay a finger on the hem of Christ's garment is by no means a vain thing, and cannot fail to draw some virtue from Christ's store. We are the better, doubtless, for an imperfect relation with Christ, so that it be genuine and cherished in the spirit's love. But even a genuine relation, if it be of inferior rank, becomes a snare to the soul when it prevents the soul from seeking a higher relation still. Here, as elsewhere, the good may be the enemy of the best. And the inferior kinds of faith do not make full use of God's provision in Christ. They do not cause us to *live* by faith. Even that great word "love" may lead us astray if taken as descriptive of the bond between us and Christ—will do so unless we recognize that utmost love and utmost faith are one and the same thing, and that self-surrender is the meaning of both. A man may love Christ with one of the lower brands of love, and the love may reach to a pitch of almost consuming intensity while yet leaving him who loves Christ unidentified with the Christ whom he loves. If so, he is not *living* by faith. We may trust Christ in the sense of believing that He has secured all good for us, that He will permit no hurt to befall us, that He will save us through all life's storms and at last bring us safely to the desired haven, and yet may remain makers and masters and managers of our own lives. Such a trust as that does not necessarily involve self-identification with Christ. It may still be we that live, not Christ that lives in us. We may imitate Christ; but the very phrase seems to imply that we are *outside* the Christ whom we seek to imitate. If imitation be all, then it is still we that live. All these things are right and good, of course, so far as they go; but they do not come within measurable distance of Paul's transcendent idea and ideal of *living* by faith. It is not until all these inferior relations between Christ and ourselves are gathered up into and abolished in the supreme relation which makes His very Personality take the place of ours—not until we step off even the very highest of these other relationships and stand upon the platform of an absolute identification in heart and spirit and mind and will of ourselves with Christ—that the line of our experience runs parallel with Paul's, enabling us to say with him, *"The life which I live in the flesh I live by the faith of the Son of God."*

With this conception of faith, we may well call the experience to which faith introduces us by the name of a "new birth," and may without any sense of inappropriateness use all the great phrases which, if faith be reduced to smaller dimensions, seem almost like an exaggerated caricature of its effects. It means a new birth indeed. It means life from a new centre. It means conversion. The great words need no longer be whittled down, as under imperfect conceptions of faith it has been necessary to whittle them down. And it says at any rate something for the truth of our conception of faith that it enables us to tune our voices, as they seek to tell what our faith has done for us, to the pitch which the ringing New Testament voices reach. All the New Testament expressions which speak of "putting on the new man" or of "being a new man in Christ Jesus"—these move far nearer, faith being thus construed, towards claiming an almost literal interpretation than they do under any other conception of faith and its results. It is difficult to see how on any conventionally "orthodox" views of atonement and faith and redemption, views which make the issue of the matter turn primarily on a judicial acquittal or at any rate on a free dismissal from the judge's bar, there can be any justifiable use of the phrase "a new birth" to describe the experience of the redeemed soul. Equally difficult, perhaps even more difficult, is it to see how on "moral" theories of atonement and redemption such a phrase can be employed; for these seem to provide no more than new inspirations, new ideals, a new Example, at utmost and closest a new Companion and Friend; and they lack any suggestion of such a transformation in the very substance of the soul as a "new birth" implies. But on the conception of faith indicated in the previous paragraphs, this and all its kindred phrases recover their relevance and keep their reality, and can be employed, not as poetic similes or metaphors or exaggerations thrown up by the heavings of a turbulent emotional sea, but as phrases which in truth and soberness and with almost literal exactness fit the facts.

By the light of this conception of faith, moreover, we begin to see a little way into the meanings of those phrases of Paul's, phrases so profound and strange, to which reference was made at a previous stage—phrases in which the apostle exhorts his readers to remember how they have died *with* Christ, have been baptized into Christ's death and have risen with Christ again. For the exercise of a faith which so identifies a man with Christ that all his life is Christ-derived and Christ-constituted must necessarily detach his entire personality from the secular process of things, from the "world," to use the New Testament expression; and as Christ (if the previously-offered interpretation of

Christ's death to the world and to sin be correct) died away from and out of the older order, so in the very act of uniting himself with Christ does the man who lives by faith drop out of his former relationship with that older order too, just because he is *in* Christ. For him, as for Christ Himself, the new era has begun. The change in relation to the world, which was cosmic for Christ, is repeated on the smaller and personal scale for a man as he begins the life of faith; and in a very real sense he dies with Christ, dies the death that Christ died. The older order will no longer constitute the environment wherewith he is immediately surrounded: his environment will be Christ Himself. The relationship with Christ into which his faith has introduced him will not mean an additional adjustment *within the framework of his adjustments with the world* or an additional adjustment set up *alongside* of them in a sort of partnership: it will mean that all those adjustments have given place to the one adjustment wherein his whole life consists. In the world he must still be, but not of it. He must *go out upon* it, not *derive from* it. He will have no roots in its soil, no homeland in any one of its territories: its speech will be a foreign tongue to him, and all its programmes and its standards and its values, through all the range of them, will be things which he surveys as if across infinite spaces dividing his own new world from the world where the writs of these things run valid and regulative still. To all this he, being *in* Christ, will have died as Christ died to it all; and from his death to it he, being *in* Christ, will have risen in his act of self-surrender to the Christ who rose again from the dead. Perhaps, to prevent misapprehension, it is well to state that to live thus by faith does not imply spiritual arrogance or even asceticism. As has been said, the man who lives by faith must go out upon the world, though he will not derive from it. In Christ he passes into severance from it: then from Christ, yet still in Christ, he returns into whatever relations with it the inevitable conditions of humanity compel him to sustain. But it is nevertheless true that to him who lives in that self-identification with Christ which true faith brings, all relations with the world will be *indirect*. For him

who lives by faith, as Paul intended the expression to be interpreted, the line of connection with all the world's concerns will
run, not directly from him to the world and back, but from him
through Christ to the world and *through Christ* back to its
starting-point again. He will be the world's master with a mastery which the very externality to it of his life's source wins for
him: he will not be mastered by the world. He will know by experience the meaning of that great and at first sight not easily
understood scripture, "Who is he that overcometh the world
but he that believeth that Jesus is the Son of God?" Detachment
from the secular process of things so far as all life's initiatives
are concerned—to that, in summary, it comes. In the life of
faith the Christian dies to it all because of his union with the
Christ who died to it all at the Cross. Let us say again that
Christ's cosmic death to the old order is repeated on the smaller
personal scale for him who lives by faith. So the seeming paradox is resolved that Christ died *for* us and that nevertheless we
die *with* Christ, that His death was substituted for ours and that
nevertheless we share it; and so, having to some extent known
the fellowship of Christ's sufferings (for that divorce from the
world is not often an easy thing; that dying to live seldom brings
a painless passage through death's shadowed valley) we attain
with Christ to the resurrection from the dead.

All that has here been said as to faith and its methods and its
effects stands, of course, simply as the picture of an ideal. With
Paul, any one who reads these pages must say, as the writer of
them must say, "Not as though I had already attained." But
the first partially successful effort after such a faith as has been
described contains within itself the promise of a perfect attainment, is the seed from which the perfect flower may bloom, and
needs but to be sustained and multiplied in order to bring forth
a perfect manhood in Christ Jesus. Sanctification is the progressive realization of faith's initial aspirings, and comes by greater
faith *of the same order* as the faith which first passed the soul
through redemption's door. Of other kinds of faith than that
consisting in self-identification with the life-giving Christ no
similar statement can be made. We saw earlier how the view

which makes saving faith direct itself solely upon a transaction
finished at Christ's Cross, and takes redemption as being the
offering to the soul of relief and release from a threat which
hung over it before—we saw how this view necessitates an entirely fresh start when the question becomes one of developing
the flowers and fruits of holiness in the nature which faith has
freed from its impending fate. If the faith that saves be such as
that view of things declares it to be, then faith cannot be the
means and method of sanctification too. One may turn the old
word to new purposes, certainly, and call the sanctifying programme by the name of faith if one so chooses; but in its fresh
context the old word does not and cannot carry the same meaning as before. No influence dynamic for sanctification can
emerge *directly* from a conviction that the day of wrath has
passed; and if salvation denote the acquiring of that conviction
and faith be the means of acquiring it, then when the man who
has been saved looks longingly toward the heights of sainthood
whence all the Christian graces beckon him, the prayer "Lord,
increase our faith" will scarcely serve his turn. The largest increase of the faith which saved him could do no more than in-
tensify and seal his assurance of being saved. For growth in
grace he must begin all over again.[4] But if faith mean that we
are living in Christ and that Christ is living in us, then the whole
question of Christian advancement, up to the final point of
Christian perfection, resolves itself into a question of what
Christ is and of what Christ can do. If Christ live in us, there
are no ideals ultimately impossible—how can any ideal be impossible to Him? All the limits which hedged in our spiritual

[4] Some theologians actually deem it important to emphasize heavily the utter
separateness of the two processes, to make the gulf between them appear as wide
as possible. Thus B. Weiss puts it—"*Die Gerechtigkeit des Menschen zu beschaf-
fen, war das eigentliche Ziel der Gnadenstalt des Christenthums: Gott beschafft
dieselbe aber auf zweierlei Wegen, durch die Rechtfertigung und die Neu-
schöpfung und darum auch in verschiedener Weise. Es ist von entscheidener
Bedeutung für das Verständniss des paulinischen Systems, jene beiden göttlichen
Heilsthaten und darum auch diese beiden Resultate derselben nicht zu ver-
mischen.*" (*Lehrbuch der Biblischen Theologie des Neuen Testaments*, p. 338.) And
by way of still further underlining the warning, Weiss adds in a footnote on the
same page, "*So wenig die Rechtfertigung die Heiligkeit, welche nichts anders ist
als die factisch hergesteute δικαιοσύνη, voraussetzt, so wenig ist diese die noth-
wendige Folge von jener.*"

possibilities before are overleapt in proportion as we can truly declare "I live; and yet no longer I, but Christ that liveth in me." And in this connection it must be insisted that growth in grace is a greater thing than growth in "practical virtue." We may keep tally of the "practical" virtues drawn one by one within our achievement's reach till the total over-runs the bottom edge of the account-book's page; but it will be no proof of deepening sanctification, of any high tides of grace flooding us within, in the real sense of the terms "sanctification" and "grace." Doing the things we ought to do, leaving undone the things we ought not to do, may on its negative side signify merely submission, more or less reluctant, to restraint, and on its positive side merely a response, more or less willing, to a command. Neither action nor inaction *necessarily* spring from character's essential deeps. Sanctification and grace point to a spiritual enrichment spreading itself through the depths of personality and welling up thence in every word and deed, in every look and gesture—a spiritual enrichment which does not wait for its self-manifestation till the hour strikes for the discharge of some specific duty or the vanquishing of some specific temptation, but which shines itself out along the chain of the successive hours in time's procession as incandescence shines itself out along the electric wire. Grace, as it grows, not only transfigures the capital and critical actions of life, but passes down the descending ranks of life's actions till it transfigures at last the most trivial and commonplace of them all; [5] and it does this because its growth is in personality's depths, and because, growing there, it streams livingly through all life's activities as the blood courses livingly through the veins. It is by faith, therefore, by the same faith that constitutes the first step in the experience of

[5] In a work of fiction, I find a speaker represented as saying to his friend, "If you are a Christian, you are preaching more sermons than pulpits can ever hold each moment of your day. They all see it. The office boys and the girl who gets your lunch know it. Or if that is too prosaic a way of putting it, read *Pippa Passes.* . . . There are porters, newsboys, servants, clerks, type-writers, waitresses, that you meet every week—the very way you smile at them and wish them good-morning shows the stuff you are made of, and pulls them down toward hell, or lifts them up nearer heaven." (*Love—and The People,* by Edith Anne Stewart, pp. 229, 230.) It is hardly an exaggeration.

redemption, that growth in grace and sanctification are won. There need be no second start, no waiting for the heavens to open in a new quarter and shed a fresh shower of blessing abroad. For that passing of self into Christ, feebly carried out at the halting start of a Christian experience, must, as it draws nearer to becoming the habit of the soul, draw nearer also to securing for the soul all that Christ has to bestow when His personality takes the place of ours. "For me to live is Christ—" that is faith's earliest aspiration after an ideal hanging un- counted miles away in its sky. But the first step towards it has a promise of all the intermediate steps safely overpast and of the last step taken for the gaining of the goal, if faith does but follow the star which shone upon it at its birth.

2

It is not difficult to foresee that the reproach of "mysticism" —that word which scorn so often uses as its missile against any searching presentation of the Christian programme—may be flung with eager hand at the conception of faith offered here. And because it is liable to be labelled as "mysticism," it is liable to be labelled also as "unpractical," in the sense of giving the "go-by" to philanthropy, social reform, duties to one's neigh- bour, missionary enterprise, national righteousness, and the rest, and of swamping all "good works" under a torrent of self- ish zeal for the salvation of one's own individual soul. The critic may say "Does it not all come to just another way of put- ting the old mystical expressions such as 'the ecstatic Vision' or 'the marriage of the soul with Christ'? Mysticism, of course— rank mysticism! And must not the consequences work out as the consequences of mysticism have ever worked out—in a reluc- tance to face the ordinary demands of life and duty, a closing of the ears and eyes to the call and misery of the world, a settling down into mere selfish enjoyment of spiritual sweets? Must not, indeed, these faults become more and more accentuated in pro- portion as the aspirant after the supposedly perfect spiritual experience finds his prayer and his aspiration fulfilled?" One need be no inspired prophet to anticipate such criticisms as these. What is the reply?

It can be easily found. Though in one sense the title "mysticism" is beyond dispute applicable to this idea of faith, yet in its application it must be carefully guarded from misuse. For it is "evangelical mysticism" it must fairly be called.[6] It speaks of and points to a mystic union with God—yes, but only as the divine life is mediated through Christ. Whoso lives by faith, as faith has been interpreted in these pages, will assuredly not follow a mystical programme which consists in mere contemplation or in mere ecstatic abandonment to the Holy Vision. But an "evangelical mystic" he will be. For one thing, he will avoid the mistake into which mysticism has sometimes fallen—the mistake of supposing that growing spiritual progress means the growing realization of an already existing fact rather than the creation of a new fact, a growing realization that God and man *are* one rather than a growing realization that they are *being made* one. Even this mistake, by the way, might be more accurately charged against mysticism as one which it has often *seemed* to make than as one which it has often actually made; for mysticism's account of itself has very frequently failed to fit precisely upon the experience it was intended to expound; and it is in the exposition, not in the experience itself, that the flaw has lain. Those who have travelled furthest along the mystic road and taken deepest soundings in the mystic sea have surely yearned with straining eyes and eager hearts toward something which seemed, like the rainbow's foot, to keep at almost undiminished distance however swift and sure their advance. Still, let it be granted that even the highest mysticism has often mistranslated itself both *to* itself and to others, and has sometimes repeated the error of the Greek theology and taken the oneness of man and God as a fact to be realized rather than as a yet unborn fact, so to say, awaiting its birth into actuality. These things may have been. Nay, a careful student of mysticism must

[6] This expression was, I believe, used by Dr. Alexander Maclaren a good many years ago as the title of an address delivered to a joint assembly of the Baptist and Congregational Unions. It obtained fair currency at the time; but so far as I know, it has been little heard of during recent decades.

admit, I think, that the case can be made out. But the man who lives by the faith whereof these pages have spoken can never fall into a similar error. His mysticism will deserve the "evangelical" name. For if mysticism of this description be mine, I shall know—as Paul, the Church's supreme evangelical mystic, knew—that self will make no swift or easy retreat from its strongholds within me nor readily lift the white flag of surrender to the diviner self that seeks to capture it, and that however passionately union with the divine life may be desired, there must be a striving even unto blood before it can be attained. I shall realize the imperative necessity of taking a grip upon myself in order that the self which clamours so insistently to be and do something great may be subdued; and my whole soul, I shall be reminded by many a resurrection of old impulses which I thought were dead, must not lie bathed in trance nor even wrapped in adoration, but must gather together all its energies in order to give them up again. And evangelical in a yet stricter sense my mysticism will deserve to be called—for it will look, not to a once-distant but now nearing God upon Whose breast, if I continue to climb up the ladder of contemplation and rapture, I may some day hope to lie in utter bliss, but to a God Who has been manifest in the flesh and Who in Christ has come down the ladder of Incarnation to make Himself one with me as with the whole world. For this mysticism Christ remains the one Mediator between God and man; and this mysticism will still say with Christ Himself that no man knoweth the Father save the Son and he to whomsoever the Son willeth to reveal Him; and it listens with full assent and consent to Christ as He declares "I am the Way, and the Truth, and the Life."

Nevertheless, the title of "mysticism" is, as has been admitted, applicable to the conception of faith here set forth. And indeed the title may well be welcomed, not merely accepted or endured. For the nature of man is a strangely mixed affair; and amid the drab pattern of its desires to be "practical" and its tendencies to tie itself down to the tangible "realities" of life, there runs, as if worked in by a protesting hand, the coloured thread of an aspiration after union with something beyond those "practicalities" and "realities" which in ordinary hours appear, and at every hour claim, to be all in all. The most "practical" man sometimes surprises one by drawing aside a veil behind which he conceals a shrine wherein the lamp of something very like mysticism is burning. In most of those whom the "contagion of the world's slow stain" has not utterly spoilt, there lies the instinct which demands union with the Eternal, a sinking of self into something higher and greater than self, a raising of the individual life up to a plane whereon the individual life and all its interests are linked up with the Life that is from everlasting to everlasting. The instinct does not strive nor cry nor cause its voice to be heard in the streets; but it is far more prevalent than the casual observer suspects. How is it to satisfy itself? Christianity should assuredly offer it food for its hunger and water for its thirst. If Christianity does not do so, there are other systems which at any rate claim to answer to the instinct's need. Theosophy is for no inconsiderable number a new star in the east; and theosophy holds up absorption into the "all" as the final paradise into which its "Masters" have already penetrated to such an extent that their voices only come back upon us faintly and far, and which faithful devotees, now picking their way through many repetitions of the painful ordeal of individual existence, may hope at last to attain. Eddyism, seeking to raise and revivify the ancient Neo-Platonism and Gnosticism which serious philosophic thought discarded and buried centuries ago, lays down as a fundamental tenet what it terms the "allness of God"; declaring not only that the individual is to lose himself in the one and only Mind, but that already, if he only knew it, no such thing as his own personality exists; and bidding him think his own separateness away. "Higher thought" systems instruct us to search into the deeps of our own nature, promising us that there, if the search be earnest and thorough, we shall come upon a sort of reservoir of life wherein Eternal Being has permitted some of its streams to be collected and stored, so that we may leap in and find ourselves by losing ourselves there. And on the *motif* of being "in tune with the Infi-

nite" book after book of quasi-philosophical and quasi-religious
cast rings the changes, the dominant note through all the variations being that the individual must perfect himself, not by ac-
centuating and developing his individuality, but by blurring its
outlines and so opening its upper and lower sluice-gates that in
the rush of the infinite sea it may be overwhelmed. Must Christianity leave the satisfaction of the mystical instinct to systems
like these? Any lower conception of saving faith than that here
presented must, I think, turn aside in silent refusal when the
mystical instinct asks for an audience. But by proclaiming the
faith in which "evangelical mysticism" is implied Christianity
can conquer these inferior mysticisms on their own ground and,
while offering to the mystical instinct a satisfaction at least as
complete as that whereof they advertise their proprietorship,
triumphantly avoid the devastating disability which besets them
all. For they all, be it noted, while professing to link personality with the Eternal, do so only at the cost of depreciating personality's value and of finally extinguishing it in proportion to
their success. On the other instinct, the instinct which demands
the assertion and *conscious* completion of personality—the instinct equally clamorous and equally worthy with that which
demands the union of personality with something greater than
itself—they can only frown. But a true Christian faith (if our
reading of faith be true) gives all that these other systems profess to give, and conserves personality by making it *consciously*,
not as in trance or in dreamless sleep, share the divine life
through a personal union with a personal Christ—a union *consciously* striven for and *consciously* maintained. Mysticism, but
evangelical mysticism—that is the mysticism which enables personality to lose itself and simultaneously to find itself again,
thus answering, not only to one, but to both, of personality's
persistent demands. It is assuredly not as a reproach whose
shame it must endure, but as a distinction wherein it can well
take a legitimate pride, that faith may bind the title of "evangelical mysticism" across its brow.

Does the critic (seeing, as he thinks, an invitingly open door)
at this point take up his parable with a view to urging the "un-

practical" charge against the proffered conception of faith? What if he says, "At any rate, you have given the case away on its practical side. You have admitted that the faith you advocate may fairly be called mysticism, whatever modifying adjectives be added to the name. Well, but does not history declare with unmistakable emphasis that mysticism of all shades and shapes fails to produce a religious life rich in impulses to philanthropy, to great movements of social reform, to everything which the general term 'good works' can include? Must not this 'faith' of yours come under the same reproach? Does it not in the last analysis come to a matter of saving one's soul and of *laisser faire* as to all else? Is it not, for all its profession and appearance of selflessness, in an inactive religious self-coddling, a sort of hot-house pietism, that it will find itself landed if and when at last it reaches it goal?"

The faith which merits the title "evangelical mysticism" may run eagerly and fearlessly to pick up the gage thus flung down.[7] We may, as we did on a previous charge, first of all make a concession to the critics and admit that historic mysticism has sometimes led to aloofness from the world's life, to cooling down of interest in the world's needs and sorrows and sins, to an avoidance of tasks and ministries ameliorative of the world's sad lot. But when, this concession made, we will go on to say to the critics, "Your complaint of mysticism's frequent failure in this regard is true enough. But your diagnosis of the failure's cause does not go sufficiently deep. Mysticism, in so far as it has incurred just blame on this score, has incurred it, not because it has been too mystical, but because it has not been mystical enough." If this assertion sound startling, it can nevertheless be made good. It may be truly said that mysticism has too often conceived itself to be simply a substitute for *reason* in the quest for *knowledge* of God. Conceiving itself to be merely this, it has allowed its self-surrender to go only to such measure of completeness as would bring a consciousness of God's *reality* and *nearness* to flood the self with its tides. It has been a self-

---

[7] I have attempted, in the first three chapters of an earlier book (*The Christian Method of Ethics*) to deal more fully with this question.

surrender possessed certainly of ample depth, but of hardly sufficient breadth; flinging a *part,* and a large part, of the self *wholly* into God, but leaving another part, and a large part, unparticipant in the offering made. The *active* faculties of the self, meanwhile, have indeed been saved from running loose on the ways of sin (the intensified consciousness of God's reality and nearness would touch them sufficiently close to keep them from that), but have not been *consciously* linked with or made the instruments of the activities of God. Mysticism has too often failed to be the *whole* man surrendering himself to the *whole* God. From this error and its consequences the "evangelical mysticism" implied in our definition may confidently claim to be free.

For in the act of faith which this mysticism calls for, together with the response the act of faith receives, we have (of course the phrases are used under the qualifications obviously imposed upon them when relations between finite man and the infinite God are in question) the *whole* man moving out upon the *whole* God in Christ and the *whole* God in Christ moving down upon the *whole* man—the activity of God thus by inevitable consequence supplanting the activity of man, and the activity of man thus by inevitable consequence being transformed into that of God. And the life of God which Christ brings near and instils is a life ceaselessly working, ceaselessly seeking to realize itself through every detail of the history of the world and of human life; so that man's self-abandonment to that life must mean, not that man's activities remain unaffected or that they are allowed to sink in sleep, but that they are progressively heightened and intensified, in proportion as self-abandonment becomes complete, upon the line of perfectness. It means, when it becomes complete, that man's ethical programme will be all that it ought to be, failing neither by inclusion of the wrong nor by exclusion of the right, from the smallest matters of personal conduct up to the most complicated affairs of inter-relations among individuals and families and societies and States; for through His use of a surrendered man the perfect and active God will be enabled to will and to do something of His good pleasure. So far as the man is concerned, the moralist will be lost in the saint; but the saint will be no trance-wrapped emotionalist, but a worker through whom the works of God are wrought. The cheap reproach of "saving one's own soul and letting all else take what course it will" has no thrust nor relevance against evangelical mysticism, however sharply its point may pierce the armour of a mysticism which mistakes a part for the whole. It is true, as has been said before, that for the man who lives by such a faith as that which evangelical mysticism requires all relations with his fellow-men and with the world will be indirect, even the relations depending upon and constituted by love; but they will be none the less active for that. Rather will they be all the more active, and all the more redemptively active, for that, because man's relations with his fellow-men and with the world in general will be a part of that larger complex of relations which God maintains with both. Faith of the true order means a relation with God in Christ wherein the *whole* man moves out upon the *whole* God and the *whole* God moves down upon the *whole* man. If it be said that the Christian programme, ringing with mysticism as it is, is out of relation with practical life, one may answer boldly, "Not if it be interpreted mystically *enough!*" And in so far as mysticism has failed to be a practical force, it is because it has been mystical only half the way. The faith implied in evangelical mysticism provides for every ethical perplexity and problem not *in spite of,* but *because of,* the fulness of its mystical content. Precisely because it pushes its mystical element to the final and furthest point, it carries an inevitable implication of that ethical perfection which mysticism is sometimes, and not always without warrant, supposed to ignore.

3

But does this conception of faith shape itself, or can it be shaped, into a gospel for the common man? We have more than once said that the preacher, as well as the theologian, is in our view; and the preacher may with every right put the question just set down. For he has the plain man before him face to face.

It is with the plain man that the preacher's business lies. It is the plain man that the preacher has to persuade and rouse— and bring to peace again after he has roused him. The preacher must seek first of all to prick and sting or woo the plain man into asking "What must I do to be saved?" But it is of small use to waken questions to which no satisfactory answers can be given; and the preacher must have his answer ready and must be able to communicate it intelligibly to the plain man on demand. He must not lay himself open to the accusation, "You have propounded, and made me echo, a riddle by which you are baffled yourself." "Faith," of course, is the answer condensed into and concentrated in a single word. But then the plain man will want to know what faith is and how he is to exercise it. This is by no means the same thing as saying that he must understand the *rationale* of the Atonement. It does not even mean that he need be instructed in the entire process of thought followed in this book. The clearer a preacher can make his own thinking on these high themes the better; and in his quest for a partial understanding of what he knows to be ultimately un-understandable in its fulness, he should be prepared to explore any and every promising road. But in regard to the "common man" this does not hold good. It has been one of the errors of much "orthodox" evangelicalism that it has not only professed itself able to see far into the unfathomable depths of truth on this topic, but has required the Christian neophyte to make an intellectual acceptance of its findings much as he would accept the implications of a mathematical formula. It has forgotten that a man "may be unable to explain the bearings of the Sacrifice on the Cross on the mind and heart of God, and yet by faith and love lay hold of Christ as his personal Saviour." [8] It has made the beginning of faith, at any rate, to consist in an understanding of the "plan of salvation"; and through this as a sort of anteroom must the aspirant for Christian enrolment pass before

[8] Griffith-Jones (*The Ascent through Christ,* seventh edition, p. 338.) Dr. Griffith-Jones adds in a footnote, "To affirm the contrary is to make a purely rationalistic statement: and yet this is often done by some extreme representatives of the 'orthodox' Evangelical school, who practically make an acceptance of the substitutionary and 'legal' theory of Atonement a condition of salvation."

reaching the inner chamber where the Book of Life will enter his name upon its lists.[9] Nothing like this is meant when it is said that the would-be disciple must know what faith is and how he is to exercise it.

But most assuredly his *own* part in establishing the desired relationship between himself and the saving Christ must be clearly grasped, else he will be but as a wanderer to and fro among the tangled paths of a maze whose centre obstinately refuses to be found. It is possible to press too far the idea that no theory of the Atonement is required. In the sense already indicated it is an idea of price, and an idea which brings emancipation from fretting chains to souls perplexed about many things when only one thing is needful. But if it be interpreted to mean that the soul may rest content with relinquishing all care about the question of its own redemption, trusting that in some mysterious way everything has been made right for it—if the soul is encouraged almost to wave the matter off and actually to make a merit of doing so, disguising its lassitude under an appearance of complete reliance upon Christ—then the idea becomes a delusion and a snare. Nor can "orthodox" evangelicism, in spite of its claim to possess a clear-cut view of the "plan of salvation," afford to throw stones on this charge at others who thus go astray. For the "orthodox" evangelicism which has often demanded of the candidate for discipleship's badge that in one direction he should know too much, has just as often, and for companion error, permitted that same candidate in another direction to know too little, and has substituted the repetition of formulas for the working of clear thought. It is very difficult to

---

[9] At the first International Congregational Council, held in 1891, Dr. Conder observed, "It would not be fair to say that in the preaching and religious literature of fifty years ago the Method of pardon and justification was presented as the immediate object of faith in place of the Saviour Himself. But it must be allowed that there was a dangerous tendency in that direction. The phrase *'the way of salvation'* (which, by the way, occurs but once in Scripture, and that from heathen lips) was made to bear a meaning which few would ascribe to it to-day, and in which certainly the apostles would not have used it: *q.d.*, as signifying the divine plan or method by which in the Atonement effected by our Saviour, God saves sinners, and is 'just, and the justifier of him who believeth in Jesus.' The knowledge of this Method was deemed essential to sound conversion." (*Report of the Council*, p. 196.)

attach a really luminous meaning to such phrases as "appropriating to oneself the benefits of Christ's death" and others of like
kind. The idea of applying to oneself, by an act not very particularly defined, the benefits of some transaction which Christ
carried through long ago—the whole matter being professedly
based on analogies (in their turn very mistily discerned) with
the cancelling of a debt and similar things—is far too meagre
in connection with the redemption of souls in the Christian sense
and on the Christian scale. Not much more than a dim guess is
possible as to what the soul's part in the programme really is
according to these presentations of it; so that in the half-lights
there almost seems to be a touch of magic in the thing, scarcely
in place in the Christian gospel. The conception of faith must
be more definitely outlined than this. Not many things may be
needful to set the soul into saving contact with Christ, but the
one thing that is needful the soul must surely grasp. What the
soul has to do with Christ (if that phrase be allowable), and
what the soul has to do with itself, in order to establish itself in
a redemptive fellowship with Him—that much the soul must
surely understand. It is true that faith has its exceptional sea-
sons when any labouring to understand itself or to explain itself
appears waste of strength and breath: it may be a spontaneous
response to the insistent call of Christ, an upward flight wherein
the soul is unconscious of even the beating of its own wings and
only knows that it is being carried effortlessly through the em-
pyrean. Nay, faith may even misunderstand itself, misinterpret
an experience which is intrinsically genuine; and so long as the
misunderstanding and misinterpretation are only temporary,
no harm is done. And certainly faith at its highest does not stop
nor need to stop for self-analysis or to explain itself *to itself* by
way of self-justification. But granting all this, it remains true
that for the permanent maintenance of its relationship with
Christ faith must know its own programme, plan its own route,
be able to give an answer when it is asked about the method
whereby it works. The ecstatic hours pass away—so soon!—
leaving reactions of spiritual gloom, perhaps disaster, unless
faith can feel its sure foothold when they depart. And even if

it were otherwise; if it were the case that faith could live contentedly without understanding the *rationale* of its own action, it will be put to the test and touch some day by questionings from the curious or scornful outside world—questionings to which it must reply or else in its silence stand ashamed. The preacher, then, standing face to face with those who put the vital inquiry "What must I do?" must be prepared to satisfy them with something more than vague generalities or phrases wreathed in fog. He must himself understand, and must be able to make his hearers understand, what is meant by this faith on which salvation depends. We must ask, then, whether the conception of faith outlined in these pages is one which will be found intelligible by the ordinary hearer, by the common man who is the preacher's principal concern, as it is borne to him upon the preacher's voice. Does it shape itself into a gospel preachable to man, woman, and child?

The answer may be boldly given. The conception *is* an easy one for the plain preacher to deal with, an easy one for the plain hearer to grasp. As to its root idea—the idea of a Christ who lives and who, while in one sense He has done His work once for all, nevertheless repeats and renews it in the experience of every one that lets Him—as to the comprehensibleness of that, at any rate, there will be no quarrel. That Christ is here—the great fact which came home to Dr. Dale one Easter day with all the force of a new revelation [10]—there will be no difficulty about that. It will indeed come with the force of a new revelation to many even of those already within the Christian ranks, as it came to Dr. Dale; but just because it comes as a self-vindicating revelation, it will not even to the slowest hearer cause any knitting of the brows. Wonderful the idea of the Living Christ must ever be; mysterious or puzzling, in the sense of offering something which the brain must twist and torture itself to seize, it is not. But then that conception of self-identification with Christ, losing oneself in Christ, and so drawing one's very life from Christ, what of that? Is not that puzzling to the plain man? Surely not. How can he be made to understand? He will

[10] A. W. W. Dale, *Life of Dale of Birmingham,* pp. 642, 643.

not, I think, require much making. After all, there are analogies enough on the plane of our common living. Let it be remembered that the matter is not one of kindling enthusiasm and affection for a Christ of centuries far behind us, though of course it must be largely on the historic Christ that any conception of the present Christ is founded. Were it a question of making a bygone Christ *seem* living, we might well feel chilled by Jowett's warning that this is in the last analysis an impossible task.[11] But it is a question of relationship with a Christ as real and as close as any human presence can be. And so the preacher can remind the plain man that we have friends sometimes (and that when we have them their friendship is one of the most sacred blessings of earth) who without avowedly teaching us make us wise; who without obtruding detailed counsel upon us make us strong; who, simply by the life that is in them, grip the life in us and impart to us something of what is in themselves. The preacher can go on to remind the plain hearer that we obtain the benefit of such friendships, not by offering these friends our outward service, not by a hundred feverish methods of winning from them what they have to give, but simply by abandoning our natures to the influence of theirs. We set ourselves *in* them, and so possess them *in* us; and thus, so far as it is in their power to do so, they make us live. The preacher can, further, appealing to the sublimest relationship of purely human experience, bid the plain man remember how Browning's lover speaks to the one he loves— [12]

> I would I could adopt your will,
>   See with your eyes, and set my heart
> Beating by yours, and drink my fill
>   At your soul's springs—your part my part
> In life, for good and ill—

[11] "Is it possible to feel a personal attachment to Christ such as is prescribed by Thomas à Kempis? I think that it is impossible and contrary to human nature that we should be able to concentrate our thoughts on a person scarcely known to us, who lived eighteen hundred years ago." (Abbott and Campbell, *Life and Letters of Benjamin Jowett,* II, 151.) The truth of this may be allowed. But the question as Jowett puts it has no relevance to the conception of faith dealt with in these pages.

[12] *Two in the Campagna.*

and bid him so voice the aspiration of his faith toward the
Lover of his soul, only adding that he may stop short of Browning's final phrase, since to the soul wrapped in the great Lover-
soul ill there cannot be. Difficult! Nay, the human heart knows
this thing by a thousand experiences and in a thousand ways!
And for evidence that this is so, and for a consequent greater
ring of assurance in his tone as his message goes forth, let the
preacher be mindful of this—that the plain man, who does not
know what the word "mysticism" means, becomes without effort
a mystic when he sings his hymns or prays his prayers, in so far
as mysticism is implied in this conception of faith—

> And that a higher gift than grace
>   Should flesh and blood refine,
> God's presence, and His very Self,
>   And essence all divine!

What is that but God in Christ taking hold on man? If the plain
man can sing it, the preacher may assuredly preach it to the
plain man without hesitation or fear! Difficult! Why, it is a conception of faith which may be preached at street-corners and in
alleys to people who have hardly heard Christ's name before—
and preached with assurance that it will be understood! Ay, and
though the preacher thinks and ought to think chiefly of the
plain man (for he is the preacher's chief concern when all is
said), he may take it also as a glory round such a conception of
faith that it is equally suited to all ranks and conditions of the
human race. The philosopher may find in it that union of the
First and the Last—that returning sweep of all creation to its
Source—for which he is always seeking: the poet may find in it
the way to that transfiguration of the temporal into the Eternal
of which he ceaselessly dreams: the saint may find in it the secret
of those baptisms of holiness wherewith he passionately yearns
to be baptized; and—to come down to common earth again, and
to that classification which includes us all—the sinner may find
in it the supreme miracle whereby even the vilest may be made
white. Difficult! Nay! It is this message, I believe, for which the
world in all those most serious hours when its mind and heart go

questing—the world, itself so often all unknowing of what it needs and seeks—the world, tired of itself and of its flaunting pride, tired of all the half-religions and tired no less of the half-Christianities which offer it stones for bread and mirage for living water—it is this message for which the world waits and longs.

4

How does this conception of faith stand in regard to an experimental test? It may be quite legitimately called upon, one notes, to face it; for its claim is that it sets him who exercises faith into contact with a dynamic force; and to an experimental test an offered dynamic force must always be prepared to submit. Over and above any theoretical likelihood the conception may possess, can it adduce on its own behalf any evidence drawn from experience? How far is it possible to say of it to a perhaps hesitant if not actually sceptical questioner, "It has been tried and proved by others: try it yourself and see!"?

In calling upon the argument from experience to play a part in the discussion we must make sure that the experimental test it implies is rightly proposed and adequately made. Quite apart from the mistaken readings of it to which allusion has been made before, there are pitfalls to be avoided, notably one lying in wait at the initial formulation of the test to be applied. The question to be faced, it must be clearly understood, is this— Can the man who exercises faith of the kind described become conscious of a real dynamic life-giving power coming down upon him from Christ in response to the faith he puts forth? Can he, from the unimpeachable witness of something felt as a *fact brought into being within himself,* affirm that a veritable process of re-creation is proceeding within his own personality? Assuming the man's part to be done, can he, as a matter of developing and ever-intensifying experience, know that he is being made a new man in Christ Jesus and that Christ is being *formed in him?* The test, to have value, must take the word "experience" in its larger sense—in its longer sense would perhaps be a more exact expression, if the grammarians will let it pass without cavil. It must concern itself, not with the spiritual experience of selected and exalted moments, not even with that of a series of moments in which an identical spiritual experience is reproduced, but with a spiritual experience going on from strength to strength and deepening through stage after stage of vividness and warmth and colour as the common days and hours pass by. It is upon the exceptional moments that the argument from experience has too often taken its ground. The ecstatic transport in which the soul it visits is swept into realms so far and strange that whether it be in the body or out of the body it cannot tell, and in which the world and all worldly things become suddenly attenuated to a translucent veil behind whose shimmer the present Christ is clearly seen; or the flood of power which in an hour of temptation miraculously arms the soul when it cries to its Lord for help against the hard-pressing fiends of hell and finds that Christ's promises are fulfilled; or the sound of the Master's voice as it breaks through from the further side of some obstructing wall of difficulty or floats across the seas of sorrow or weaves its music of peace and hope into the dark background of the grave's sad silence—it is these experiences and such as these that are almost invariably recited and called on to bear their witness when the argument from experience is at the bar. Valuable their testimony undoubtedly is; but they can hardly take the entire burden of proof upon themselves. Without belittling what they have to offer, one cannot but remember that, were their evidence left unsupplemented—or were it even set in place of first importance—they might be looked upon as perhaps the result of thoughts and feelings, carried up to a quite exceptional level of intensified heat, *about* Christ rather than as signs of the presence and working of *Christ Himself*. And besides, there is the difficulty that experiences like these fall to the lot of comparatively few. Must the majority, whose wings never grow strong enough for such soaring flights, be debarred from making a sufficient proof of Christ's re-creative power? That, surely, cannot be. Further still, these experiences will not come at call, but must be watched and waited for; and since this is so, there would, if they were the only armoury whence the argument from experience could draw its weapons, be a temptation to force them, with the result that an artificially-manufactured experience might easily be mistaken for a true. And finally, the experiences of the exceptional hours, even putting at its highest their value as evidence that Christ is present *then,* cannot suffice as proof that Christ is the soul's very life in the intervals between the departure of one and the arrival of the next. Yet that is the test which, in connection with the faith here offering itself for judgment, has to be met. It cannot be *only* on the high peaks of transfiguration that Christ the Life-giver proves Himself as such to men.

The real test as to whether faith can and does draw a veritable life-dynamic from Christ, and so prove Him to be in the fullest sense a Life-giver indeed, has to be made in less sensational ways. It is to be made in the quiet hours, not so much in the special ones—though these, when the quiet hours have borne their witness, may be taken as confirmatory of what the quiet hours have said. To test faith, to test the life-giving Christ, there needs the cultivation of receptivity towards Christ amid the whirling roar of all life's crowding concerns, not merely the opening of the soul's gates when from some cause or other the spiritual tides beat up against them strong and high. As has more than once been said, faith is a consciously maintained attitude towards Christ on the part of the entire personality, and is therefore not a thing to which we give ourselves with sudden recollection when now and then a pause in the noise of the grinding wheels provides us with the chance, but a thing kept unbroken at the retired centre of the soul even while the machinery whirs and clangs its loudest. True faith does not wait to practise itself till it can find a field cleared of all else. It runs parallel with and pervades all the common activities of the common day. Just as a man, whatever his immediate engagements may be, is a loving or an unloving man, a wise or a foolish man, a brave or a cowardly man, an upright or a morally feeble man, through and in them all—the central qualities of his being remaining unchanged and energizing however the moment's activities may change—so in and through all of them he can be a man of faith, with his entire personality turned towards Christ's. All this is of course implicit in what has been previously set down. The testing question comes finally to be, Do we, assiduously cultivating though not fully attaining the required attitude of receptivity towards Christ—practising it without hurry or fuss, and without intermission so far as may be—gather the fruits of it in an awareness of Christ's life as more and more penetrating and permeating ours? Is there through the humdrum days—putting aside the days whereon the soul makes high holiday as it were from all the common concerns and passes into a different spiritual clime—is there an increasing change in the very spiritual fibre of us; a change signalizing something beyond a more successful self-discipline or a swifter subsidence of once clamant passion or a stiffened adherence to duty's summons; a change only to be explained as the progressive enfolding and re-creating of our self by Christ's? The test is whether Christ is making us by actually homing in us, and whether we can ever more and more clearly see Him occupying the seat of the Master of the house and discern His presence in every room. One can set the test question, if variations of it will make it plainer, in many forms. Is Christ, one may venture to put it, to any extent in our blood? Is it more natural to us than it used to be to think of ourselves as being within Christ as the branch is within the vine or the scent within the rose or the wave within the sea? Are all materialisms becoming less obtrusive and tyrannical because we have a Vision which makes them all shadowy by contrast with its shining, and of which we can say—

> That one Face, far from vanish, rather grows,
> Or decomposes but to recompose,
> Become my universe that feels and knows? [13]

These are the tests by which a faith claiming to have found the secret of a life-dynamic, and offering an argument from experience in confirmation of its claim, must content to be tried.

How then does the suggested conception of faith stand in

[13] Browning, Epilogue to *Dramatis Personae*.

regard to the argument from experience when "experience" is interpreted in this way? To turn our glance upon the preacher once again, as he comes face to face with the common man, can he say confidently to a hesitant and perhaps sceptical inquirer, "This faith has been tried and proved by others: try it for yourself and see!"?

It must be admitted at once that while an affirmative answer is entirely justifiable, it cannot be made as triumphantly as one would wish. Only a little flock has entered into possession of that lofty spiritual kingdom whereof this faith can make us free. The fully-enfranchised citizens of that kingdom—even if there be more walking unrecognized among us than one suspects— make but a small band. The confession must, however reluctantly, be made.

And yet, with all this admitted, it remains true that the argument from experience holds good. The faith here advocated, and its power to bring a re-creative life-dynamic in power from Christ upon the soul, have been proved over and over again. For one thing, we are entitled to point to what faith at some of its lower temperatures has done, and to say, "How much greater things would a warmer faith achieve!" Of course, we leave out of the reckoning the simply intellectual assent to truth *about* Christ which constitutes the faith wherewith so many are content: if that operates at all, it can only do so through a reminder brushed occasionally and lightly across the surface of the mind, felt for just a moment and then forgotten again. But there are degrees of faith, far higher than this and yet far lower than the highest, which do by their results go at any rate some distance in supporting the claim made for the highest faith of all. They do secure a real, if not a full, union with the life-giving Christ, and thereby strengthen all that has been said as to what a full union with the life-giving Christ would achieve. It is indeed to be expected that this would be the case. For the life-giving Christ is Himself an appealing Christ, a Christ who moves toward man in invitation long before man moves toward Him in prayer; and the feeblest movement that the feeblest faith makes toward Him is met by and enveloped in the advance

which Christ from His side has already made. It cannot but be
that from such a contact, be it on its human side imperfect as it
may, some baptism of Christ's rich life should be bestowed. His
re-creative life must necessarily possess within it a self-communicativeness which will find its way through any door that
any personality sets so much as barely ajar. One meets constantly, as one tarries in private home-circles or passes through
the more public streets and squares and halls and market-places
where men and women congregate, with some whose lives and
characters, far as they may be from reaching to the measure of
the stature of the fulness of Christ, nevertheless show something of Christ's transforming power. When they can be
brought to break the silence they impose upon themselves too
often, they tell of temptations conquered and of evil habits
broken down and of aspirations set aglow; and we see deeply
enough into them, or feel vividly enough the electric current of
sympathetic understanding speed over and bridge the gulf between their souls and ours, to know that their professed experiences are real. Their half-faiths have tested only so to say the
half of Christ; but that at least they have done; and in view of
what the half-faith has accomplished we are entitled to trust
the promise of what a perfect faith would do. Further, although, as has been said, the full exemplars of a full faith make
but a scanty folk to-day, most of us meet once or twice in a life-
time with some few whom we would set upon the list—not that
they themselves would do anything else than shrink from putting in such a claim, but that in almost every look and word and
gesture they bear witness to a formative Personality behind
their own. Their silent impact upon all who are not quite insensi-
tive announces them for what they are. Of more than one in our
own time it has been truly said that "at his very entrance into
the room it seemed as though Christ came in"; and most of us
have encountered now and again a man or woman far too
remote perhaps from the public eye to have such a verdict
pronounced about them in the public ear, but known to us as
deserving it with the best. It is not that one could cite any one
grace for the distinguishing mark of people such as these: it is

rather that they are compact of an ineffable and nameless grace wherein all nameable and unnameable graces are summed. The man or woman whose life is manifestly homed in Christ and equally manifestly comes back upon us out of Christ may be and is too sadly rare; but occasionally he or she appears white-robed and shining, and taking no contamination from all the soiled and soiling surroundings, on the dustiest or most miry road. And in view of all the testimony to what faith at its various heights and depths can do—testimony given by both folk of half-faith and folk of fuller faith to the presence and working of another "formative Personality" behind their own—it may be repeated once again that the preacher of the full faith here advocated *can* say, "This faith has been tried and proved by others, in part by many, in its fulness by at any rate a few: try it yourself and see!"

Yet the "cloud of witnesses," one bethinks oneself again, should be greater than it is. And one passes on from that sharply-pointed reminder to say that if the company is to be enlarged the Church must revise her reading of faith's meaning, and must preach the revised reading in such wise as to lead men to faith in its fullest sense. For the Church, it must be confessed, has not in this matter soared sufficiently high nor dug sufficiently deep. Faith as the veritable interchange of personalities between man and Christ has hardly been the Church's message. She has not actually decried that experience of "vitalism" with which we have been occupied, though individual theologians have even done that; but she has looked upon it as super-normal, as an experience not possible to ordinary men and women who ply their tasks in the work-a-day world, but the monopoly of a special spiritual race or class. And the Church's attitude towards it has usually been one of admiration or wonder, tinged with a feeling that to the general company of wayfarers along the Christian road it can scarcely be a matter of practical concern, however much it may merit praise. It has been taken, in its successive manifestations through the saints of all the ages, as a sort of miracle which happens when heaven so decides, as a revelation of what Christ can do for His favourites when He puts forth some extra grace for their behoof, not as a revelation of what He offers to humanity's common races and ranks. The faith which has raised the saints so high must be of a different order from that whereby ordinary men and women are saved. That has been the assumed implication of the Church's attitude. Nor has faith in its loftier ranges, and the experience of self-identification with Christ to which its great exemplars have been led, been taken by the Church as rational in the sense in which even spiritual experiences must be rational. That is, these things have not been looked upon as matters of which the Church must render some reasonable account to the rank and file of her membership—unless indeed to put them aside in a class of things not to be explained by ordinary spiritual processes can be called the giving of an account. They have not been fitted into the Church's general theological scheme as lower conceptions of faith and its results have been. The theologian has more or less respectfully bowed them out as material too intractable for his use : he has looked upon them much as a regular practitioner looks upon unorthodox medical methods, holding that while they may win an occasional success, they have no title to be accepted as standard. They have been pointed to— if the terms be not too harsh—as almost religious "sports" or "freaks" lying alongside of, but not really placed in, the system of established religious thought. Whatever is to any extent "mystical" must bear the reproachful label of "irrational" or at least "non-rational" as well, and must be left to plead its own case without any aid from theology strictly so called. It is probable, I know, or at least by no means impossible, that many of the things written in this book concerning the levels to which the ordinary Christian should aspire will be greeted with the lifted eyebrows—some sort of pitying smile beneath them perhaps— with which "extravagances" in any field are always met. "Not practical politics" in religion—that has been too much the attitude towards such things as these. No wonder that the "cloud of witnesses" is so meagre! For naturally enough, this strict severance between the lower faith and the higher, between a first experience possible to everybody, of salvation by faith, and richer experiences, possible only to the few, of something more than salvation, works a "spiritual inferiority complex" in the masses of religious men and women, and tends to make them content with the lesser things, or at any rate hopeless of the greater. If the argument from experience in regard to union with the life-giving Christ is to exert all the power of which it is capable, if the number of those able out of first-hand knowledge to confirm it is to be multiplied till their voices ring compellingly across the world, then the Church must take what has hitherto been held for an exceptional Christian experience, open only to those spiritual mountaineers before whose challenge the sky-kissed peaks are conquered, as open also to those who at present dwell cramped in the lowlands: she must proclaim that seemingly exceptional experience, and the faith which wins it, as setting the common standard of faith and experience for all: she must accept the ideal thing as being the only rational thing as well, and this not *in spite of being,* but just *because it is,* the ideal; and she must preach as the one true faith that faith which is from its very beginning at least an aspiration after a veritable exchange of personalities with the life-giving Christ. If the Church does this, a contagion of faith will be started that may and must spread far. Those who know anything of faith in its fulness, anything of what a full faith can achieve, will more readily break their silence and tell what they know, no longer restrained by the sense of strangeness and loneliness that earlier sealed their lips. The loftier conception of faith, delivered from its reproach, will become magnetic for many to whom, sad to say, it has hitherto been merely odd; and the contagion of it will spread in widening circles, each soul that accepts and lives by it becoming central to a new series in its turn. And so the great "cloud of witnesses" will assuredly at some time or other come thronging into the empty spaces which have been vacant and waiting for them so long.

"At some time or other"—for all one's hope and desire, the phrase with its suggestion of an unfixed waiting period must be set down. For however ardently the Church might take up the preaching of faith in its fulness, she would not find the present time propitious for a new spiritual crusade of the kind called for. The outside world is certainly not in the mood, and drops ever further and further away from the mood, to listen with any particular attention or even with patience to the summons of a religion which bids man lose himself in Christ: the utmost it is disposed to yield is a sort of half-patronizing admission that Christ may hold a subsidiary partnership in the management of its life so long as He does not interfere too authoritatively or present too sweeping demands. The outside world, for certain, would turn with a shrug and a sneer from a Church which preached the fulness of faith. Well, the Church, abandoning the futile compromises in virtue of which her very *locus standi* as Christ's representative is lost, must accept the situation, and realize that her standards and the outside world's are at eternal war. But there is still more to say. Of her own professed adherents, if the Church begins the new spiritual crusade, not a few will forsake her and flee, or, short of that, will raise their voices in angry protest against a reading of religion which so wantonly disturbs their ease. Many will show themselves successors of him who went away offended because Christ's requirements were too searching for him to meet. It was not, forsooth, to be put about in this fashion that they gave in their adhesion! And the Church, mourning her dwindling membership as she does, must perhaps be content to see her muster-roll become yet smaller before it turns to increase; for there may have to be a purification of it from many names that cannot be allowed to stand. This too the Church must accept. Acceptance of it may indeed be lightened to some extent of its painfulness for her if she remembers that it is enough for the disciple that he be as his master and for the servant that he be as his Lord. For Christ Himself knew that faith would prove a plant of feeble growth; and He spoke of its future now and again in very minor key. He knew it too sadly well. There it stands, that pathetic utterance of his, written "as if in starfire and immortal tears"—to borrow Carlyle's phrase about a piece of John Sterling's; "When the

Son of Man cometh, shall He find faith on the earth?" [14] Nor do I know of anything Christ ever said with the implication that within the time-bounds of the present world-system the faith He so desired to see would draw a majority of men to its practice. The echoes of those warning words of His, quoted before, as to the narrowness of the true life's way, re-awaken. *"Few they be that find it."* That Christ will somehow and somewhere see of the travail of His soul and be satisfied, we may be sure; but we may be sure also that "How long, O Lord, how long?" will break over and over again from some who eagerly desire to see the great day but must die without the sight. Christ Himself knew it too sadly well. And the Church, if and when she calls her hearers to fulness of faith, must hold herself prepared to find her message scorned. "The Church was born crucified," said Lacordaire; and the Church of to-day will find that a re-birth into fulness of faith may mean, through despisal from the world and from her own children, that she must in part fill up that which remains of the sufferings of Christ. If the "argument from experience" is to be inscribed on the banner under whose folds the Church wants to march to victory and to set Christ's life-giving power beyond denial or doubt, the Church must pay the price. Let it involve what it will, the Church must re-learn what faith is, must experience it, must teach it, whether men hear or whether they forbear. And she must listen, her soul possessed in patience, for "as it were the sound of a going in the tops of the trees," for the first faint rustle which will be a sign that the rushing mighty revival-wind is at hand at last.

It may be well to say a few words—many are not required—on an objection which still sometimes flourishes its sword somewhat boastfully against the argument from experience, notwithstanding the really conclusive counter-thrust wherewith it has repeatedly been met. "You say that the experience of the Christian is valid testimony to his faith"—so the objection runs. "Well then, why may not the adherent of some other of the

[14] Luke xviii. 8.

great world-religions make a precisely similar claim? May not the follower of Mohammed or Buddha steal your argument and turn it against yourself? Is not your argument from experience in fact a playing with double-edged tools?" The effective reply is that Christian experience is experience of contact with a living Person, and that while Mohammedan or Buddhist might conceivably plead that his experience proves the *teaching* of Mohammed or Buddha to be true (though our lack of knowledge as to Mohammedan and Buddhist experience leaves even this not much more than a shadowy possibility), he could not and would not claim that it brings him any consciousness of a personal communion such as the Christian claims. The reply, effective enough even for a Christian experience based on the less intense forms of faith, becomes tenfold effective in connection with the faith (and its resultant experience) which connotes entire self-identification with the life-giving Christ. There can be no parallel between the experience of Mohammedan or Buddhist and the experience of the Christian who can truthfully declare "To me to live is Christ." Can one imagine a Mohammedan saying "To me to live is Mohammed"? The supposition at once stamps itself as grotesque. But the experience resulting from fulness of faith enables a man to use with added emphasis language such as this—"If I am not to be an absolute Pyrrhonist, doubt everything, and renounce my own reality, I must find my practical certainty in that which founds my moral life, and especially my new moral life. . . . Now, my contention is that my contact with Christ is not merely visionary; it is moral, personal, and mutual. Nor is it merely personal, in the same sense in which I might have personal intercourse from time to time with a man in whom I am little concerned between whiles. Because what I have in Christ is not an impression, but a life change; not an impression of personal influence, which might evaporate, but a faith of central personal change. I do not merely feel changes; I am changed. Another becomes my moral life. . . . He has not merely passed into my life as even a wife might do, but He has given me a new life, a new moral self, a new consciousness of moral reality." [15] Such experiences as these are too flamingly incandescent for any alleged Buddhist or Mohammedan parallel not to shrivel up in their burning and searching light. He who makes experimental test of the faith with which we have been dealing need have no fear lest any other religious experience in the whole round world should produce credentials able to challenge comparison with those his own faith can show.

5

But what of the Cross in such a faith as this? It is almost impossible not to anticipate that the question will be asked. Does not the conception of faith here advocated belittle the Cross? Does it not at the very least remove the Cross from the outstanding position which the legalistic theories of atonement and faith accord to it? Must the Cross pass to the rear of the redemptive scheme instead of holding, as it has held, the central place? The question cannot be lightly dismissed. For it must be granted that in many of the reactions against the legalistic theology the importance of the Cross has shrunk. It has often been with sad reluctance that the framers of the non-legalistic systems have watched the shrinking; but they have been powerless to avert it. We have seen how vain have been their efforts to give to the Cross a significance as great as that which is surrendered. [16] Is the conception of faith opened out in these pages exposed to the same reproach? Could "orthodoxy" curl its lip and, launching a shrewd dart, say of this conception what it certainly can say of some forms of Christian thinking on this theme, "See what you come to when once you quit my side!

[15] Forsyth, *The Person and Place of Jesus Christ*, p. 197. See also in this connection Dale, *The Living Christ and the Four Gospels*, pp. 64–68. Among other forceful observations Dale has this: "The devout Christian has an immediate knowledge of the Living Christ as the Saviour of men. This is not an inference from experience: it is *given* in experience." In his primary construction of the argument from experience Dale lays too much stress, I think, upon the exceptional hours. But on this particular point of comparisons, or rather contrasts, between Christian experience and the experiences of non-Christian devotees, he is extremely effective.

[16] Chapter V, § 4.

You have practically abolished the Cross from your scheme, or at any rate you bestow upon it only a casual glance and a half-patronizing bow, as you pass by!"?

We have previously vindicated the indispensableness of Christ's death for the line of thought which this book pursues, shown it to be an essential factor in the redemptive scheme as this book conceives it. But that hardly covers the matter. Thus to vindicate the indispensableness of the Cross is indeed to secure for it an established footing in our theology, to make it stand out prominently in the foreground for the student who seeks to trace the historical sequence of events whereby God wrought out the salvation of the world. The death of Christ must have been an antecedent fact if the faith of which this chapter speaks were to become possible at all; and for the theological thinker as such the Cross retains a prominence as pronounced as under any other system it could possess. But this—if this be all—does not make the Cross a reality, *present and vivid in the very act of faith,* for the soul that accepts Christ. So far as the mere theory of the thing is concerned, it need not follow, from recognition of Christ's death as a historic fact whereof theological system-making must take account, that the soul's consciousness plays round it in the moment when it sinks its selfhood in Christ. The Cross might be firmly established in a theological scheme, and might be found standing safe and steadfast there whenever the mind chooses so to say to pay a visit to the spot, without being also actually part of the vision which through all time faith beholds. But for New Testament writers it undoubtedly was this; and unless the Cross does thus form part of faith's constant vision, the faith exercised is not the faith which the New Testament knows. This statement involves no withdrawal of statements made on an earlier page, some of which might be superficially taken as looking the other way.[17] While, as was said, neither the early apostolic preaching nor the utterances of the first Christian centuries concentrated on the Cross as though it were the one determinant factor in Christ's redemptive work, yet the authors of the New Testa-

[17] Chapter V, § 3.

ment epistles and the Christian writers of early times all set and kept it high before their eyes. Faith, for the New Testament writers especially, was assuredly always *conscious* of the Cross, and most vividly and passionately conscious of it, though not exclusively centred upon it; and therefore any faith which is to keep in step with the faith of the New Testament must be able to claim that same vivid and passionate realization as an abiding possession of its own. Can the faith we have been describing make the claim?

In point of fact, the question answers itself—one might almost say laughs at itself—for those who practise the faith described. Only in theoretical, almost academic, speculation and analysis could any severance be made between that wholehearted self-abandonment to Christ in which fulness of faith consists and a vivid apprehension of the place occupied by Christ's death in the redemptive scheme. In the actual *experience* dealt with in this chapter the abiding vision of the Cross and the permanent close clinging of the soul to it are assured.

For the faith called for by our definition is faith in a living Christ *known to be living because He died and conquered death,* and consequently a faith which in its every movement must be most keenly conscious of the Cross. Let the vital and organic connection, made in earlier chapters from the Christ of Calvary and the Resurrection to the Christ who is through all time the re-creative life-dynamic for the world, be recalled. The soul surrenders itself to Christ; but Christ is there to receive its surrender only because He died and rose again; and the soul must, in its very act of surrender and in every repetition of it, realize and freshly realize that it was by way of the defeated Cross and the forsaken tomb that Christ became and remains the Christ ever present with His life-giving power to welcome the surrendered soul. We cannot receive Christ in His response to the surrender we make without remembering that He gives Himself to us only because He first gave Himself *for* us. We cannot—if it be to a really risen and living Christ that our surrender is made—look upon His living face without catching sight also of the print of the nails in His hands and feet and the wound in His side. These are in a manner the guarantee to us that He was dead and is alive for evermore; and it is as these with their meaning are borne in upon us that we are encouraged to be not faithless but believing. Every act of self-identification with the living Christ carries us back to the Cross, or rather brings the Cross forward from the past to face us on our present standing-ground. Indeed, in this connection phrases about thought's travels from present to past, though one has to use them, are more or less misleading. It is not a matter of thought's pendulum swinging backward and forward between the Christ who lives and the Christ who died. The Christ who died is not *remembered* from the Christ who lives. The first is *given in* and *with* the second. Christ's very livingness speaks of Christ's death, as one side of a shield speaks of and vouches for the other. The Cross becomes present as it were in successive beats of self-emphasis, struck out in time with the pulses of faith (if faith be what it should be) whereby the soul gives itself to the Christ whose open arms it sees stretched waiting for it now. There is more than gratitude for a great Sacrifice implied in this, though of course passionate and adoring gratitude will be there. What is meant is that for the soul which practises fulness of faith the Cross will necessarily stand out regnant and royal in the redemptive scheme, formative in it, part of it not merely as an accompaniment *to* it but as a constituent *in* it, asserting itself wherever and whenever the redemptive scheme comes into play. For faith such as that which these pages have described all these things hold good. It is not *exclusively* upon the Cross that such faith will centre; but in the practice of its faith the soul will be conscious that without the Cross its faith could never be. As by Christ Himself, in order that He might become Life-giver, death and Resurrection were taken *together*, constituting in their conjunction one single enacted fact in His redemptive work, so faith's act of attachment to Him will be a single act *simultaneously,* not *successively,* embracing Him both in His risen life and in His death. Each act of faith is so to say a sacramental service without the actual presence of the symbolic bread and wine. Indeed, it is illuminating to notice how the sacramental service itself (so much more full-charged with meaning, I think, on our reading of faith than on any other it can be) gives opportunity to faith, or rather makes a demand upon faith, to intertwine past and present into one, sets both the Christ who died and the Christ who lives simultaneously before faith's eyes. It is precisely because it carries faith so far beyond the Cross that it makes the Cross so vividly real. For those who gather at Christ's memorial table in the true spirit of faith, the service is emphatically a memorial of Him just because it is very emphatically so much more. We break the bread and remind ourselves of the body broken for us; but we remind ourselves too of that breaking unto us of the Bread of Life which moment by moment He performs on our behalf; and yet the second recollection, so far from supplanting the first, takes it up and thrusts it in equal co-partnership with itself to the front again. We take the cup in remembrance of the blood He shed; but we take it, too, in the certainty that He is continually pouring into our soul's veins life's heavenly wine: yet the certainty keeps the remembrance glowing at its heart. The symbols speak, not only of what He gave, but of what He gives; but they none the less remain penetratingly and poignantly vocal as to what He gave. So in the sacramental ordinance the past and the present—and for that matter the pledge and promise of the future too—are twined into one. So the sacramental ordinance by its acted symbolism reads us its lesson as to what faith should be and do. And every act of faith must of necessity—if it be faith after the meaning we have given to the word—be a sacramental service, whether or no the symbolic elements be there.

It was thus that the New Testament writers came to find the Cross so vividly present that they could not let their pens run through many lines without setting down its title. We noted at an earlier stage that in the first apostolic preaching of the Gospel the Cross stood out far less prominently than it does in the epistles of Paul and Peter and the rest. We are faced, indeed, with the fact that while in addresses intended to persuade men into acceptance of Christ mention of His death is made merely as a preliminary to mention of His Resurrection, in letters to established Christian Churches its shadow slants almost from top to bottom across every page. For those who wish to defend the view of Christ's death traditional in the juristic theology, which would seem to demand precisely the reverse order of things, the fact constitutes an awkward intrusion among their data, protruding at an angle not easily to be smoothed away. But it drops with exact fittingness into its place in the mosaic of thought which we have been attempting to piece together. It was the very reality and intensity of their experience of Christ's livingness, of His self-communication to them, that made the Cross so prominent to the minds of these New Testament writers, and would make it equally prominent (so they assumed) to the minds of those to whom they wrote. For He lived, and He gave Himself to them, only because He had died. But that fact won so close and strong a grip upon them only because faith had *previously* (though again one regrets using the inappropriate time-succession word) made for them a vital contact with the Christ who lived. In their contact with the Christ who lived they came to realize that the contact was also with a Christ who had given Himself to death on their behalf. Then, not till then, the Cross became a glowing, piercing point of light that caught and fixed their magnetized gaze, for it proclaimed as it stood there the cost at which their Life-giver was redeeming them: then, and not till then, they understood in all its sad and glad poignancy the truth that they had not been bought with corruptible things such as silver and gold, but with the precious blood of Christ: then, and not till then, they realized (which is more than knew—that much they may have done before) the length and breadth and depth and height of the love wherewith they were loved, the love which had made their Lord obedient unto death, even the death of the Cross.

Of Paul, so persistently put forward by many as the champion *par excellence* of a saving faith set exclusively on the Cross, all this is pre-eminently true. The supposed swing in Paul's writings between "two theologies," one mystical and the other legal, does not really exist. Two lines of thought are certainly discernible; but they are parallel and complementary, not opposed. They form two streams deriving from the same spring, and flowing along side by side. To look upon Paul as one who in calmer moments insisted on the death of Christ as the one matter of supreme importance in the redemptive scheme, but who in more enraptured moods took his flight into ecstatic rhapsodies about Christ living in him and about himself living in Christ—and moreover as one who in his more exalted times troubled himself little or not at all as to how far their utterances harmonized with those to which he had given expression when he walked in the lowlands—is to misconceive the facts and consequently to create wholly artificial difficulties. No appeal can lie, nor is any appeal necessary, from Paul the rapt mystic to Paul the sober theologian. It was just because Paul was so mystical—with the evangelical mysticism we have talked of—that he came to set so much emphasis on Christ's death: it was the fulness of mystical experience, brought to him through his faith in the living Christ, that made the Cross, with Christ hanging upon it in the greatness of His redeeming love, so ever-present and so real. Any effort to read the process in the reverse direction is doomed to fail; in part because there is no natural passage leading from insistence on the Cross as the one object of saving faith to an experience of a personality exchanged with Christ's; and in part because the ascertainable facts are demonstrably against reading the process thus. In Paul's accounts of his own conversion no reference to Christ's death is found—a startling fact if a faith centring on that death was really for the apostle the all-embracing secret of salvation; while the phrase he uses to the Galatians as descriptive of his great change, "When it was the good pleasure of God to reveal His Son in me," indicates beyond cavil that it was in a realized union with the living Christ that his Christian experience had begun. Through and in this union he had passed into so vivid a vision of the Christ who died that thereafter, whether it were of the Christ who lived or of the Christ who died that he spoke, it was both of whose reality and presence he was ardently conscious all the while. Still more startling is the fact that, repeatedly as Paul mentions the Cross, enthusiastically as he glories in it, passionately as he adores the sacrificial love it embodies and displays, in no single line of any one of his epistles does he point to the Cross of Christ as the object of saving faith.[18] The traditional theology, I think it is fair to say, has never reckoned with this remarkable fact, unchallengeable as it is, but has rather chosen to pass it by. Indeed, it quietly assumes the opposite—as it is almost forced to do if its chief position is to be maintained. Yet a fact it is, as a careful examination of Paul's writings will quickly prove. Whenever the object of faith is specifically indicated, it is Christ's Resurrection, not His death, that is selected for mention expressed or implied. Evidently it was with the living Christ that Paul held Christian experience to begin: it was thus that he had begun his own; and he had no dread lest emphatic stress upon that fact should rob the Cross of its due meed of honour and praise: on the contrary, he took it as certain that for those to whom he wrote it would prove the case, as for himself it had proved the case, that the fulness of faith's experience could not fail to uplift the Cross high and haloed on the sky-line of thought's loftiest mountain-peaks. And by the spell its revealed love cast over the

[18] The only passage which could with even a superficial show of plausibility be cited in opposition to this statement is contained in Romans iii. 25 (Authorized Version). "Whom God hath set forth to be a propitiation through faith in His blood." But it is agreed by practically all competent scholars that the correct rendering is that of the Revised Version—"Whom God set forth to be a propitiation, through faith, by His blood." That is, "by His blood" goes with "propitiation," not with "by faith." Alford's Greek Testament defends this rendering, or rather takes it as unquestionable, first because "through faith in His blood" would be unexampled, and next, decisively, because $\dot{\epsilon}\nu$ $\tau\hat{\omega}$ $\alpha\ddot{\iota}\mu\alpha\tau\iota$ requires a primary, not a subordinate, place in the sentence, since the next clause $\epsilon\dot{\iota}s$ $\ddot{\epsilon}\nu\delta\epsilon\iota\xi\iota\nu$, &c., directly refers to it. Sanday and Headlam, in the *International Critical Commentary,* also support the Revised translation for very similar reasons. They add (what would have to be remembered even if the Authorized rendering were kept) "Blood was regarded by the Hebrews as essentially the seat of life. Hence the death of the victim was not only a death but a setting free of life: the application of the blood was an application of life." And Alford also remarks that $\alpha\ddot{\iota}\mu\alpha$ does not equal $\theta\dot{\alpha}\nu\alpha\tau\sigma s$, but refers to the typical use of it in sacrifice. Even with the older translation, therefore, it is the living Christ, of whom the passage speaks. But scholarship is practically unanimous that the Revised Version is the true one.

minds and hearts of Christ's own, it would become the sufficing symbol of all that Christ had done and was still doing for the redemption of mankind.

So we can answer our original question now. Does the Cross, on our reading of faith, maintain the prominence which the New Testament writers accord it? In the very practice of the faith described, and in the experience it brings, the affirmative reply is given; and thus, also, it is reached along the path which the New Testament itself suggests. The historic Christ, in all His words and works, in His life and in His death, is none the less—rather is all the more—real to it because it knows also a Christ "not after the flesh." Law's words may be echoed by all who practise the faith which makes Christ live in us and us in Him. "Let no one here think to charge me with disregard to the Holy Jesus, who was born of the Virgin Mary, or with setting up an inward saviour in opposition to that outward Christ, whose history is recorded in the Gospel. No: it is with the utmost fulness of faith and assurance that I ascribe all our redemption to that blessed and mysterious Person that was then born of the Virgin Mary, and will assert no inward redemption but that wholly proceeds from and is effected by that life-giving Redeemer, who died on the Cross for our redemption. Was I to say, that a plant or vegetable must have the life, light, and virtues of the sun incorporated in it, that it has no benefit from the sun till the sun is thus inwardly forming, generating, quickening, and raising up a life of the sun's virtues in it, would this be setting up an inward sun in opposition to the outward one? Could anything be more ridiculous than such a charge? For is not all that is here said of an inward sun in the vegetable, so much said of power and virtue derived from the sun in the firmament? So, in like manner, all that is said of an inward Christ, inwardly formed, and generated in the root of the soul, is only so much said of an inward life brought forth by the power and efficacy of that Blessed Christ that was born of the Virgin Mary." [19] He who has fulness of faith, or at least aspires to have it, will, even while his lips frame his spiritual programme

[19] William Law, *The Spirit of Prayer* (edition 1814), part I, pp. 40, 41.

thus, "The life which I now live in the flesh I live by the faith of the Son of God," keep this also for his heart's constant undertone beneath his spoken words, "Who loved me and gave Himself for me."

6

Passing reference has necessarily been made here and there in the progress of our study to that conception of faith, so different from the one set forth in these pages, which takes the death of Christ as being exclusively and in itself the one object on which "saving faith" is to be set. It may be well, however, to devote a little space to making still clearer the main points at which that conception appears to fail. It is the more advisable to do so because that conception is the only one seriously competitive against the conception advocated here. For it is difficult to see how, on the so-called "moral" theories of the Atonement, faith in Christ can be anything more than acceptance of His authority as a teacher and of His ideals and example as regulative for the programme of human life; and for a trust so rigorously limited in its scope the term "saving faith" can hardly be used. Such a relation with Christ would be heavily overloaded by a title so imposing. But the system which, however near to or far from the line of strict "orthodoxy" it may lie, is known as "evangelicalism" claims with considerable show of right to be the preacher of "saving faith" in the fullest connotation of the words. Some sort of salvation it certainly does offer; and some sort of faith it certainly does require. The "legal" theology from which it derives is in broad outline familiar enough, with its assertions that in some way Christ endured on the Cross the penalties justly due to sinful man, that God accepts this voluntary suffering as clearing man's account and making forgiveness possible, and that it only remains for man to claim his share in the benefits of Christ's "finished work" and plead it before a God who turns from wrath to favour and from judgment to mercy as He listens to the plea. This is of course evangelicalism's strictest formula, and many of its representatives shrink

from repeating it precisely in that shape. Some protest that its
explanatory clauses must undergo sufficient qualification to remove from them all cause of offence, though it is not always
easy to attach a clear meaning to the qualifications offered or
to any new clauses suggested in substitution for the old. Some
drop explanatory clauses altogether, contenting themselves
with a simple assertion that the Cross is the one and only
source of salvation and the one and only object of saving faith.
But however the detailed terminology of the system may be
varied by one or another of its representatives, the fundamental idea always remains that the sinner is to shelter himself
under the "finished work" of Christ (that is, under the fact
that Christ somehow suffered in his stead) from an otherwise
inescapable doom. Even in the least crude enunciation of the
system's content, it is the Cross which, exclusively and alone,
makes possible the change from wrath to mercy in God's attitude towards man.

I am not going to pause long over the violence which, in the
opinion of very many, the theory in its crudest form offers to the
moral sense. It is scarcely a matter for argument. It may perhaps be worth while, however, to reinforce the protest which
the moral sense makes against the theory by reminding ourselves
of what the message of the earliest apostolic preachers must
necessarily have been if for them the theory had held good.
We saw in an earlier chapter that their message ran on totally
different lines. If they had held for true the doctrine under
notice, they would have been compelled to speak somewhat as
follows. "Men of Jerusalem, you have committed one of the
greatest crimes of history. You have crucified the Son of God.
Nevertheless, you have made it possible for God to forgive and
redeem the world, and it now remains that you, while repenting
of your crime, should take the offer of salvation which you have
brought within reach of all mankind." If the mere statement of
the theory, thus reinforced, does not startle the conscience into
spontaneous protest, no amount of subsequent discussion is
likely to convince the mind of anyone whose conscience has slept
while the statement was being made. And the converse is

equally true. I will content myself with saying that for my own part I remain wholly unmoved by the answers sometimes offered to protesting consciences in their recoil. To say that our notions of justice cannot be held valid for God seems to me equivalent to charging God with having mocked us by planting a lie in our souls. The attempt to draw a fine distinction between chastisement and punishment, with the assertion that Christ underwent the first but not the second, appears to me to be idle playing with words. The contention that the transference of penalty from man to Christ involves no moral difficulty and need give no moral shock, because Christ is Himself God and consequently in His sufferings we really see God taking man's penalty upon Himself, goes far towards making God as it were blindfold Himself and then act out an almost theatrical representation of justice in order to evade the demands of His own laws; and besides this, it marks the suicide of the very doctrine it is intended to support, the doctrine that God the Son made it possible by His death for God the Father to forgive. But the matter must finally be left for each individual—mind and conscience jointly working—to decide for himself. Perhaps this may be added—that we do well to suspect, and to test under particularly searching tests, any theory which, because it offers at small cost to ourselves an easy escape from dangers with which we cannot otherwise grapple, it is in our selfish interest to consider true.

If, however, these cruder forms of the theory be put aside, there are two objections making strongly even against those forms of it in which the crudeness is more or less refined away. All alike make salvation to reside in something else than an immediate and personal relation with Christ; and all alike make saving faith affect the external and legal status rather than the inward spiritual state. The implications under both counts are serious.

The "saving faith" which directs itself *exclusively* upon the Cross travels back through nineteen and more centuries of history, and at its travelling's end settles down, not into a personal association with Christ Himself, but into reliance upon something which Christ accomplished in those far-off times. True, it is always assumed, when the way of salvation is thus formulated, that personal fellowship with Christ will follow; but there is nothing in the programme laid down that makes this sure. Entrance into a personal fellowship with Christ is not actually a part of the saving experience, not actually implicit in it. A man who places his faith exclusively in the death of Christ at the most takes hold upon a boon procured for him long ago. And even that really overstates the case. For the boon was not provided for him as an individual, but for mankind in general to secure if it will: the individual merely asks for his share from a store of blessing which Christ laid up for whatever claimants might present themselves as time passed on. The whole thing is without any suggestion whatever of a personal relationship, *inherent at the very moment and in the very article of salvation* —between the saved man and the saving Christ. It is scarcely to be supposed that the adherents of the doctrine would agree with that one of their own number who—so it is reported—admitted that so far as he could see the Atonement could quite well have been wrought out on the planet Mars; but grounds on which they could dispute the statement are not easily discoverable. For, on the theory under review, a man can obtain Christ's salvation without coming into contact with Christ. Which means also that there can hardly be on the part of the man in question that consuming love for Christ whereof the New Testament is so evidently full. You cannot love Christ, in the large and rich sense of the word, unless He be a living Person present here and now. You cannot love a memory, though you may feel toward a memory emotions bearing a pale resemblance to love. And a theory of salvation which does not within its four corners assign a definite place to passionate love for the Saviour from the saved—nay, which does not *demand* such a love as an integral element in, not as a mere adjunct to, saving faith—is surely suspect.

In fact, a faith directed *solely* upon Christ's death can in the last analysis be nothing else than an intellectual assent to the statement that the event took place. Of course the assent may have an emotional accompaniment or reaction in greater or less degree; but *essentially,* intellectual assent, nothing else and nothing more, is all that such a faith can be. You cannot identify yourself with an act done either in the near or in the far-back past *between two parties of whom you yourself are not one* except by accepting the fact of its historic happening as true, and, if an emotional accompaniment or reaction makes itself felt, feeling approval of it. Of course we may profit by some law passed long ago and extending its grip over all the subsequent years down to to-day, and may avail ourselves of all the permissions or protections it bestows; but in this there is no analogy whatever with "appropriating" the benefits of an atoning transaction begun and ended between God the Father and God the Son. It is true, also, that under some circumstances—in times of religious revival, for instance—the emotional accompaniment or reaction just spoken of may become so strong that faith itself rises from the purely intellectual to a loftier stage. But under normal conditions an intellectual act must constitute the sum and substance of a faith directed solely upon Christ's Cross and death. Indeed, some defenders of this view of saving faith employ language which amounts to a confession of the fact. Candlish's nakedly straightforward statement runs, "There is room for His (God's) arranging that, through the gracious interposition of His own Son, meeting on my behalf the inviolable claims of justice, His wrath should be turned away from me; and if from me, from others also, willing to acquiesce in the arrangement." [20] So bald a setting out of the matter would not be approved by every advocate of the view we are examining; but whatever terms be used, "acquiescence in an arrangement" is in the last resort all that a faith of this kind can be or perform. And the consequences of this are serious indeed. For as he hears this theory of faith proclaimed, the ordinary man under ordinary circumstances does not feel himself confronted by any all-important religious alternative on which his

[20] Quoted by R. H. Hutton from an address delivered by Dr. Candlish, in reply to Maurice, to the Young Men's Christian Association (*Theological Essays,* pp. 415, 416).

spiritual fate depends: he does not feel himself called upon for a decision that goes to the very roots of his life. And the intellectual assent which seems to be all that is required of him is easy to give, the flinging of it out in answer to the demand for faith being but a moment's work and costing little or nothing at all. Under these conditions religion inevitably and quickly becomes nominal. It must be remembered, too, that the danger of a merely nominal religiousness becomes ever more pressing as the years and decades and centuries pass on. The historic event on which faith is bidden to concentrate fades further and further into the distance behind; and each newly-completed year of the ageing world piles up another bank of mist in addition to those already heaped between the present and the past. More and more insistently the misgiving will haunt, "How can an act done so long ago be the means of rectifying my spiritual position to-day?"; and more and more in consequence must the assent, when given, pass into a mere matter of form. One would suppose that a divinely-appointed scheme of salvation would take account of psychological facts; and conversely, it is hard to believe that a theory of salvation and faith which ignores these facts can be divinely ordained. At any rate, the theory of faith which makes Christ's Cross, as it stands behind us in the process of history, the *exclusive* point to which faith is to take its flight and at which it is to settle down, may fairly be asked to produce its defence against the danger of letting faith drop down to a merely nominal thing.

The other point of failure in these theories of faith lies here: they look upon saving faith as affecting external and juridical status rather than inward and spiritual state. Faith's essential purpose is to secure for the sinner, not indeed an acquittal at heaven's judgment-bar—that is in the nature of the case impossible since all have sinned and come short of the glory of God—but at any rate a certificate of discharge. In the essential article of salvation, whatever may be looked for subsequently, there is no necessary implication of any cleansing touch laid upon the sinner's personality and character, no assurance of any spiritual change. One cannot but be startled to realize how this reading of faith and its effect verges perilously near to superstition; for the essence of all superstition is the effort to change God's attitude towards man without changing man's inward attitude towards God. That holds good, to take a few instances out of many possible ones, of the idol-worshipper who hopes to propitiate the object of his worship by laying a number of gifts on the temple-shrine; of the fanatic who mutilates himself in order to placate a savage god; of the dervish who tries to dance his way into his deity's good graces; of the heathen ritualist who gives a certain number of turns to a praying-wheel so that his god may veer from frowns to smiles. They all seek to change the attitude of the gods to men without changing the inward attitude of men to the gods. It must surely give one pause to find a theory of Christian faith making even a distant approach to superstition's errors, blindfolding itself with the same bandages that superstition binds around its eyes. Superstition of course starts from fear; but while a genuine Christian experience may sometimes start from fear, a Christian theology cannot, and becomes merely a thinly-veiled paganism if it does. At any rate, whether starting from fear or not, the theory of faith under consideration is akin to superstition in that it sets itself to deal with external status rather than with spiritual state. It is not going beyond the facts to say that this theory makes salvation possible without a single movement of genuine spiritual aspiration in the saved. The soul, in its dread of the divine wrath and in its haste to escape, may "acquiesce in the arrangement" whereby safety can be secured, and may do so with the most ardent enthusiasm, while at the same time remaining as aridly bereft of any holy desire as the desert sands are bereft of water-springs. Certainly repentance is always presupposed when these theories of faith and salvation are advanced. But even if repentance be present and genuine, that is not the same thing as a desire to be spiritually cleansed; and a repentance springing from fear of punishment will often, under the assaying flames, turn out to be many grades below fine gold. Further, not only does this theory of faith fail to make any imperative demand for spiritual aspiration; but if a yearning for a spiritual deliverance, rather than a juridical one, has been kindled in a soul hitherto sunk in sin's horrible pit and miry clay, the theory offers nothing in the first instance to satisfy it. To spiritual hunger it makes no immediate offer of bread. Salvation *quâ* salvation is on this theory freedom from threats that overhung the soul before: if more than this is promised, it is promised as the result of a second and supplementary process timed to be set going when salvation has been won; and the soul that hungers and thirsts after righteousness is not, by salvation as such, set down where the table is spread. It is only to fear that this conception of faith offers its gifts. It would almost appear, indeed, as if to come within its ambit a soul must *make itself* fear, or else simulate a fear it does not feel. Juridical status, not spiritual state, is the primary interest; and the soul whose overmastering desire is to be perfect, and which would gladly suffer the loss of all things if only its desire might be achieved, is warned, as it approaches the treasury where all sacred riches are stored, that it is not putting first things first, and that its scale of religious values must undergo drastic change.

Once again the danger that faith will sink into a merely nominal affair rears its head. For status, and the regulation of status, can be concerned only with *acts;* obviously no legal scheme has power (nor, for that matter, right) to pierce beneath the surface movements to the streams of character that flow below; and a theological scheme based on juridical ideas, however indignantly it may protest its negative in its endeavour to prove itself free, is hampered by a similar limitation. It follows almost inevitably that where no great acts of sin send their ghosts to haunt a soul, both repentance and faith will be languid and lukewarm. Men cannot persuade themselves and will not be persuaded, that culpability for minor sins rises to the same thermometric level as does culpability for major ones, or that relief from appointed penalties calls for a repentance and a faith at equally high temperature under both heads. Nor can they be blamed.[21] Psychological facts, being what they are and presumably what God intended them to be, surely claim their right here, as previously, to be taken into our reckoning. The average man, unconscious of anything approaching criminal guilt, cannot be expected—if the whole thing is a matter of *acts* —to feel himself in such great danger, and by consequence cannot be expected to work himself up into such a fever of effort after escape, as the man whose record shows out muddied through and through with foulest stains. Were the average man told (as on the view of salvation and faith this book advocates he would be told) that salvation is a matter of exchanging personalities with Christ and that faith is the act whereby that exchange is made, it would be clear as day that for people of all the varying degrees of moral attainment up and down the entire scale, whether blameworthy or blameless or something of both according to the world's legal codes, faith must be the same—in quantity and quality and all else. But so long as *acts* remain the ruling consideration, faith will in perhaps the majority of cases let the mists of unreality wind their chill folds around it till it well-nigh reaches the freezing-point. It has to be admitted that many have been moved into a warm Christian experience even by such presentations of faith as those termed questionable here. The fact cannot be gainsaid. But it is usually in times of revivalism that this takes place, when, as was previously suggested, faith passes into something higher and more intense than intellectual assent. But at these times those with whom the whole matter is as "the early dew of morning which has passed away at noon" at least equal in number those who persevere; and any explanation must cover both sets of facts. For my part, I venture to think that the steadfast converts have really, unknown to themselves, acted upon a larger conception

---

[21] Occasionally the old fallacy still is heard, that even the smallest sin is infinite, and merits infinite punishment, because it is done against an infinite God. The idea involves to begin with the absurdity of a finite creature performing an infinite act. Apart from that, the saying is as meaningless as would be a saying that a sin committed against a tall man must itself be tall or that a sin committed against a monarch must itself be royal.

of faith than that which has been pressed upon them and which they supposed themselves to entertain, and have exercised a truer faith than they knew: they have really, brought face to face with Christ and His redeeming love, flung themselves *into* Him: the Christ who waits for and blesses even the most imperfect faith, and who responds lavishly to faith's most stammering prayer, has taken hold of them; and they have, while fancying themselves to be receiving something *from* Christ, received Christ Himself. It has all been good, so far as it has gone. But how much greater good if these converts had of set purpose and with conscious understanding bent themselves to the deeper thing! For the ordinary man in ordinary times, at any rate, it remains true that a faith which aims primarily at the rectification of legal status before God must by its very nature take account primarily of acts, and is for that reason liable—as it is liable for the reason that it ensures no personal contact with Christ—to sink into a feeble and nominal thing.

"But sanctification follows as the night the day, when once status has been rectified"—so the defensive parry is always made. "Spiritual aspiration cannot but be kindled, and kindled, cannot but be satisfied then. The operation of the Holy Spirit ensures the growth of the justified soul in all Christian graces. When the salvation obtainable at the Cross is once possessed, then the process sets in, not indeed as a part of the essential saving experience, but as an inevitable sequence following in its train." Listening to this defence, we find ourselves again in company with that conception of a twofold redemptive process which we met before.[22] In its first section the experience it brings is that of salvation from penalty: in its second section it is that of salvation from sin. A strange reversal of the order in which one would expect to find them placed!—the consideration is almost bound to flash across the mind.[23] It is certainly startling to see escape from punishment promoted in the list of the soul's interests over the head of deliverance from sin. But not to pause

[22] Chapter V, § 4.
[23] I believe that I have somewhere met with this point very forcibly made; but if this is so, I have no note which will enable me to identify its source.

upon that, and putting aside also the indisputable fact that in many instances sanctification has most lamentably failed to follow rectification, or at any rate supposed rectification, of status, emphasis must be laid upon the risk lurking in this division of the soul's experience into two chapters. Of the difficulty which, by its breach in the unity of things, it makes for thought, we have spoken before; but more serious still is the difficulty it makes for the spiritual experience it professes to safeguard and make so sure. Does the coming of the second phase of experience depend upon the *conscious* realization that the first phase has been passed through? In other words, does sanctification come to the soul only when and while it is "appropriating to itself the benefits of Christ's death"? Then the soul is called to an impossible task. It cannot be incessantly repeating the act of intellectual assent (or, though admission or denial that it is this makes no difference at this point, let us say simply the act) in which the initial stage of spiritual experience consists and upon which the second stage must follow: its escape from penalty cannot be re-enacted over and over again, cannot even be constantly present to memory as an accomplished fact. Besides, just as faith of this kind must inevitably become more difficult for the world at large through the process of the centuries, so must it become more difficult for the individual through the process of threescore years and ten; and under increasing difficulty attempted repetitions of faith's first act may easily end as colourable imitations of the genuine thing. But what if the answer to our question runs thus, "No, the second stage of the experience does *not* depend upon the conscious realization of the first. The rectification of status once accomplished, the Christian's name is registered in heaven's books as that of one entitled, inasmuch as he has satisfied the first test, to pass on to the taking of the next degree: so long as the name stands unerased, he retains his rights, and all other things shall be added unto him." Well, then there opens a further inquiry. That clause in the reply, "so long as the name stands unerased"—what exactly does it mean? Can the name *ever* be erased? Can the newly-acquired status be forfeited? If it cannot, Anti-

nomianism has free licence to run rampant as it will—a danger
whose existence many defenders of the "orthodox" theories
have not denied. A good man once said to me, "Nothing that I
do can alter my covenant relation with God." Fortunately he
was a good man, else one wonders whither the theory might
have led him. It does not seem a safe one to proclaim to the
crowds of passion-seared and conscience-blunted men. Surely
this assertion that status once won is won for ever sets souls
swaying over the very edge of perdition's abyss! If on the
contrary it is possible for those who have once been dismissed
from the judgment-bar to be recalled and have their discharge
revoked, if status be held on a sort of indeterminate lease liable
on any day to be called in, then the soul, under ever-recurring
wonder whether yesterday's guarantee holds good to-day or has
been made void by unwitting violation of the terms, will be
driven into a miasma of morbid introspection by which spiritual
growth will be choked. Whichever way one looks at this conception of faith—the conception which makes faith concentrate
solely on Christ's death and holds salvation *quâ* salvation to be
deliverance from doom—we find it in all its implications leagues
away from the faith whereof the New Testament is redolent
from the first page to the last, the faith which flings the soul
into a direct and personal contact with the life-giving Christ
and which through that contact changes, not status, but the very
substance of the soul.

With the carrying through of the act of faith, as this chapter
has interpreted it, the soul makes its own spiritual destiny
secure, and enters upon a life which, so long as the faith which is
its very breath does not fail, must become ever purer within and
must wax ever more and more fruitful in every good work. But
the soul has done more than this; and before passing on to the
few other things remaining to be said, we want to pause for an
instant and lift up our eyes to behold the greater thing which the
individual soul, through its surrender to Christ, has done or is
doing. For it is contributing something now to atonement and

redemption in the *cosmic* sense, has become a partner with God and Christ in the *cosmic* redemption scheme. We have seen, in passing over the various stages of our thought, how God's purpose for the world was that it should rise out of its primary life-stage into a higher stage wherein man should consciously derive his life, his very self, from God; how through man's sin and failure the life-movement of the whole system of things went astray; how in Christ a life-dynamic powerful enough to reverse the erring movement was offered; how through Christ's Cross and Resurrection the Christ of Palestine became the universal Christ for all time; how in his act of faith the individual man makes exchange of personalities with this Christ of all earth's geographical spaces and all earth's accumulated and still accumulating years. So far down a line connecting the "eternal order" with the single life our thought has brought us. But our thought, having come down to the single life, may well make a swift return journey for a moment to the "eternal order" whence it set out. For the single life, in linking itself with Christ, does something towards forwarding the return-movement of all things to the original source in God. Individual salvation is not a transaction apart from the process whereby all things come back to their appointed end—which was their beginning too. Individual salvation is integrated into that process and finds its proper context therein: individual faith impinges upon it, contributes to it, does something to re-fasten into it that immanence of Christ which the world once possessed and so sadly lost. Let us remind ourselves again how the presentation and interpretation of Paul's "thought-series," as we followed it up, provided a Gospel evangelical, evangelistic, *and philosophical too*. For it binds personal redemption and the eternal process of things—by man deflected, by Christ restored—with close-knit bonds. It shows us how by the individual act of faith the entire system of things is helped to ascend a little higher over "The world's great altar-stairs that slope through darkness up to God." We shall look up to the "eternal order" and its glorious foreseen climax once more in our study's concluding moments: for this moment a reminder that in winning its own redemption the individual soul brings that glorious climax a little nearer may suffice.

God flashed His power into the void,
　And thus His bidding ran—
"Be thou through curve on curve employed
　Of greatening Life, till man,
Last-born, with clear will unalloyed,
　Turn Life where Life began."

In clear-drawn round the line was steered
　Till man's power seized its sway:
Through will unruled and spirit seared
　Was checked the circling play;
And Life fulfilled no perfect-sphered,
　God-born, God-ended way.

God's power flashed forth once more, and lo!
　Whence Life had first begun
Life o'er the gap itself did throw
　To Life whose sweep was done:
God the cleft circle rounded so—
　Man God-grasped by God's Son.

Chapter VIII

DIVINE WRATH AND PARDON

Nothing beyond bare passing allusion has hitherto been made
to God's anger against sin. Yet all history—history outside the
Scriptures as well as the history contained within them—bears
witness to man's undying certainty that there is such a thing;
and every man who will listen to the voice of his own conscience
can detect the certainty echoing there. In any effort to construe
Atonement some account of the subject must be taken. Nor,
though the fact that God cannot offer to man the facile forgiveness which man can offer to his fellows has been stressed in an
earlier chapter, has any positive conception been set forth as to
what forgiveness, when God does offer it, really is. Yet we
surely want to know what meaning we are to extract from the
phrases when we hear or read of a God who forgives iniquity
and transgression and who refuses to remember His people's
sins. If he cannot forgive as man forgives, how does He forgive
at all? The question is natural. Both gaps may well be filled in
the same chapter, since there is obviously a close connection between the two hitherto omitted themes.

I

It will be well to set down two or three preparatory points, by
way of clearing our minds of misconceptions or of preventing
their entrance, before proceeding to the positive treatment of
the topics. These preliminary remarks, however, while throwing
a little light forward to help us in our more positive treatment,
will themselves yield their full significance only under the light
which that more positive treatment throws back. For the moment, then, they are offered as cautions asking for provisional
acceptance till their justification appears.

First of all let it be emphasized that there can be no mere *moods* in God. God is always *activity*. Whatever there may be in God corresponding to what we term emotions in man must be something else and something more than those emotions which so often beat round and round within the walls of man's inner being without finding any outlet or being translated into any definite result. In man emotions very frequently simply feed on themselves, spin round on their own centre, rise to their climax and drop down again in futile alternation without producing any effect outside the subject who feels them. With God it can never be so. One may say that by His own action in the creation of humanity He made Himself liable to the impact of answering action from the humanity He made, and therefore liable to *reaction* toward humanity's answering action; but that *reaction* must always be another definite *action* on the part of God, not a mere *mood* within Him. If humanity's action be wrong, God's reaction towards it may well be one that merits the name of wrath; but it cannot be anything like the "temper" which a wrong action done by man to man so often provokes in the victim, the anger which can find no other way of venting itself than heaping fuel upon its own fires. Indeed, to recollect how extended a scale of emotions the term "anger" may be made to cover in the case of man, from the mere "temper" just spoken of up to the out-flaming of righteous indignation, is to learn caution in employing it of God. Whatever God's anger in reaction against sin may be, it can at any rate never be a mere wrathful *mood*. It must always be a *re-acting act*. To which one may add at once that it must be an act of offensive war and of conquest, since God does not accept defeat.

The second cautionary word is this. As a clear distinction must be drawn between anger in God and anger in man, so as to punishment a similar distinction holds good. Of course in saying this one finds oneself at once in opposition to traditional "orthodoxy," which makes close adjustment between the penalties of earth and those of heaven. Moreover, even freer modern theology, while abandoning much that traditionalism asserts, has been very largely influenced by instinctive repugnance, and has not always thought the matter through. There needs a reasoned as well as an emotional justification for a break with the traditional view; and there needs also something positive to put in its place. It is the first of these needs that these paragraphs attempt to supply. Punishment, it is here affirmed, must be a different thing with God from punishment among men. Minor analogies may perhaps be traced here and there; but God's final and large-scale dealing with sin, when He separates those who have accepted from those who have rejected His redemptive grace, cannot be *literally* represented (parabolic representation as Christ employed it is another matter) by a sort of assize at which God sits as judge and sends those found guilty to something vaguely correspondent with an earthly tribunal's sentence of penal servitude or death. Nor are difficulties at all lessened if for a universal judgment when the present era has expired there is substituted an individual judgment upon each soul in its loneliness immediately after the moment of death. It is in both cases on strictly legalistic lines that the entire conception is shaped—naturally enough in a theology fundamentally legalistic or in a theology only partially freed from the cords of legalistic thought. But man's criminal-law-court procedure can afford no parallel with and can throw no light upon God's penal dealings with sin.

To begin with, we are faced once again with the fact that in writing its chapter on punishment, as indeed in writing most of its chapters that touch on sin and God's dealings therewith, legalistic theology concerns itself primarily, not to say exclusively, with acts. It could hardly do otherwise. Its conception of penalty, shaping itself after the model of the conception prevailing in the courts of men, necessarily circles round the question, "What has the prisoner at the bar *done?*" It is a different kind of indictment, surely, that God will bring against sin. One may qualify this by an admission that in dealing with individuals in the way of "small-scale" judgment (the meaning of this will become clear presently) God may take account of acts, single and in the mass, and may assign some penalty to each of them for their guilt. But in the final and "large-scale" judgment with which we are at the moment concerned the matter stands differently. If for God both righteousness and its opposite reside essentially not in deeds but in the condition of heart out of which deeds are born, then the whole apparatus of earth's criminal assizes, with their indictments recitative of this overt transgression and that, and their sentences proportioned in severity to the number and the degree of proved crimes, become wholly irrelevant in connection with any verdicts pronounced and any punishments assigned by Him who searches below the external surface of every act to its secret springs. Sinfulness cannot be dealt with by methods which suffice for dealing with sins; and it is sinfulness rather than sins with which God's final judgment must deal.

Further, God's administration of penalties cannot have any likeness to that of an earthly tribunal in respect of the nature of the penalties decreed; and the very term "penalty" comes to mean in the two systems two totally different things. The punishments of the law are not worked out within the moral nature of the wrong-doer as consequences originally implicit in the wrong he wrought: they are purely arbitrary in the sense that the wrong does not *suggest* the punishment, far less give rise to it; this has to be *invented* by the framers or custodians of the law as their sense of fitness may dictate. This consideration is in itself enough to make the legal analogy suspect; for the idea of God thus inventing a penalty quite dissociated from the sin seems antecedently questionable. And the consideration sharpens to a point when we remember that all legal punishments—fine, imprisonment, and the rest—are in very many cases of a physical character, and in all cases, whether in themselves actually physical or not, touch the criminal at some spot in the life of his *senses*. It is on one or other of these senses that penal suffering directly or indirectly falls. In God's final judgment—when, with the life of the senses done, the "naked spirit" must bear the test of the "uncreated beam"—any such *invention* of penalties unrelated to the wrong becomes doubly grotesque. The penalties felt by a spirit divorced from the flesh must themselves surely be of a spiritual kind, and must surely be dependent upon and come out of the spirit's condition, Sorrow, unavailing regret, the consciousness of the highest good lost perhaps for ever, shame before an outraged God—these and such as these, heightened to incalculable degrees beyond what we with our flesh-clogged spiritual sensitiveness understand by the words— are the penalties which an "unclothed" spirit can feel. These retributions are indeed the retributions of God; but it is equally true to say that they are the retributions brought by the spirit upon itself. If now we are going to use the legal analogy in this field, we shall be constrained to think of God as making a quantitatively calculated allotment of penalties of this order—so much shame to this soul, so much regret to that, and so on. Of course the idea is absurd. A far truer analogy for the soul's penalties than the legal one might come into view if we said that just as physical illness follows upon a deranged condition of the physical organism, so the soul's penalties follow upon the deranged condition of the soul. At any rate, any attempt to set the legal analogy squarely on its feet is as vain as an attempt to seize a shred of drifting mist. It is baffled at every turn. The laws of men fail completely when they seek to make God's penalties march in step with their own; and the penal procedures which human jurisprudence observes cannot in the smallest degree mirror the judgments and sentences to be pronounced in the courts of heaven.

Moreover—and it is perhaps at this point that the eclipse of the legal analogy comes nearest to being total—the law's penalties have to be thus "invented," and left out of any real moral relation with the offences which have incurred them, precisely because all moral forces have at least for the time being failed. Against these the wrong-doer has shown himself proof. Yet something must in the interest of society's self-protection be done, and the law steps in to do it. Legal punishment is primarily a deterrent, though of course reformative influences may be conjoined with its deterrent ones if that be deemed fitting. It applies what force—non-moral force—it thinks proper: the culprit serves his sentence, fulfils thus the deterrent office to which the law has appointed him, and then, though this is not of the essence of the matter, passes out of the law's grip with a chance of submitting himself to moral forces again. The milder penalties of home and school reproduce the same picture on a smaller scale and in a less highly-coloured medium, the chief difference being that here penalty, though partly intended as a deterrent, is definitely recognized also as an *interim* measure put into use till moral forces resume their sway. In all the given cases alike—legal, family, school—penalties of an "invented" or "non-related" kind are imposed with an eye to their effect upon the future, either other people's future or the culprit's own or both. And this is their only possible justification. Were they held to be neither deterrent against imitative wrong-doing nor a temporarily-adopted means of dealing with a transgressor till other influences take him in hand, they would constitute nothing more nor less than revenge. And here we come upon the complete collapse of any analogy between man's punishments and God's. *God's final and large-scale judgment upon sin cannot, just because it is final, be either a deterrent or the filling of a gap left by the temporary break-down of moral forces;* and hence, unless we are prepared to represent God as acting penally solely for revenge's sake, the whole legal analogy crumbles away. A *final* judgment upon sin can only look back to the past, not forward to the future. Nor, let it be repeated, does the matter stand otherwise if judgment upon the individual soul when death takes it into its Judge's presence be substituted for a universal judgment at the era's close. Such a judgment cannot be deterrent upon those left living because it is transacted on a stage far removed from their vision, and no authentic report of it comes back: it cannot be an *interim* measure for the soul concerned, for it is *ex hypothesi* the fixing of an irrevocable fate. Nor again (to answer another point which may rise in the minds of some) is there any help for the legal analogy if instead of a judgment day or hour immediately after death we speak of an indefinite postponement of the day with the "larger hope" that the soul may be given another chance. When the final judgment, pictured as legal analogy requires, takes place, it will be *ex hypothesi* over a closed era—either for the individual soul or for the whole world—that the Judge's eye will sweep, with nothing but a stabilized condition of things through the eternities ahead: any talk of penalty as a deterrent is consequently ruled out. Similarly, when that final judgment takes place, it can be no temporary failure of moral forces with which the judge is confronted, for—again *ex hypothesi*—there is no future in which they can resume their operation. It must be as one who has lost all power of response to them that the guilty sinner must stand before the final judgment-seat. (Incidentally, the worst punishment God could inflict, and it would be one worked out in the wrong-doer's moral nature, would be to leave the wrong-doer to himself.) *To speak of God as inflicting some sort of "invented" punishment in anything like legal fashion is therefore to make Him act in a spirit of revenge.* The unthinkableness of such a thing provides a sufficient measure of the entire legal analogy's collapse. Punishment with God, whatever it may be, must be a matter totally different from punishment among men.

There remains a third preliminary caution, and an important one indeed, to be borne in mind. Conceptions of punishment, forgiveness, and related matters, must not be so framed as to imply anything like a civil war between opposite sides or opposite sets of attributes in the nature of God. Here we touch the shield of traditionalism with the lance-point again; for such a civil war is precisely what traditionalism affirms to exist. God's justice, with the wrath against sin to which it gives rise, is at war with God's love, the second moving Him to pardon the sinner, and the first imposing its veto upon the proclamation of pardon which love is eager to send forth. The entire "orthodox" doctrine of Atonement has this war of opposing attributes in God for its starting-point; and it represents the war as ending with an arrangement proposed by love, accepted by justice, and therefore satisfactory to both sides. Christ, sent by love, appeases justice; and thus reconciliation between the divine attributes previously at variance is made. God has been at war with Himself; and God the Father's justice has been satisfied by God the Son.

I venture to think that any one approaching the topic with a

mind quite unbiased by theological conventions would say at
once that any such division, not to say antagonism, of functions
between the Father and the Son is intrinsically unthinkable, and
that its unthinkableness is not a whit lessened because the theory
contrives to achieve the healing of the division and the abolish-
ing of the antagonism at the end. A mind which does not trouble
itself whether or no it is likely to incur traditionalism's frown
will protest instinctively that this picture of a God at war with
Himself or within Himself and of a Son of God (Himself in a
real sense God) intervening to set the conflict at rest is altogether wrongly conceived. Thought—so the instinctive protest
will go on—must have permitted itself to be shunted quite off
the real Christian route before this conception could have been
taken as a satisfactory terminus for its travelling. Even Augustine, legalist as his theology was, did not wholly succeed in shak-
ing off misgivings of the kind. In at least one place he stresses
the difficulty of believing that the Father in His anger looked
on the death of the Son and was appeased; and it may perhaps
be taken as significant that Augustine offers no solution of the
difficulty, simply falling back upon a categorical declaration
that, whatever the difficulty may be, God had loved man from
the foundation of the world.[1] The difficulty is very real. Whatever efforts may be made to hide the fact, we are left, on this
line of thinking, on the one hand with a God revealed in Christ
and on the other hand with another God whom Christ prevents
from coming into antagonistic contact with us [2]—Christ thus

---

[1] *"Quid est 'Reconciliati per mortem Filii ejus?' Itane vero, cum irasceretur
nobis Deus Pater, vidit mortem Filii sui pro nobis et placatus est nobis? Numquid
ergo Filius ejus usque adeo nobis jam placatus erat, ut pro nobis etiam dignaretur,
mori: Pater vero usque adeo adjuc irascebatur, ut nisi Filius pro nobis moreretur,
non placaretur? Et quid est quod alio loco idem ipse Doctor gentium, 'Quid' inquit
'ergo dicemus ad haec?' Si Deus pro nobis, quis contra nos? Qui proprio Filio suo
non pepercit, sed pro nobis omnibus tradidit illum, quomodo non etiam cum illo
omnia nobis donavit?' In illa moritur pro nobis Filius, et reconciliatur nobis Pater
per mortem ejus: in hac autem tamquam prior nos delexerit Pater, ipse propter
nos Filio non parcit, ipse pro nobis eum tradit ad mortem."* (*De Trinitate*, xiii. 11.)

[2] Every reader, whatever his theory of the Atonement may be, is shocked when
he lights upon the story of a murderer, professedly contrite, who exclaimed on the
scaffold, "I hold up Christ's blood between me and the flaming face of God."
But however revolting the man's language, it is not clear at what point, according to the traditional doctrine, his theology has gone astray. It surely gives one
pause if in the last resort an utterance of this kind can be criticized only for its
taste, not for its sentiment.

coming to stand in sharp contrast with, and indeed almost as a substitute for, God Himself. Actually, that is how the Christian trained in the "orthodox" view usually takes the matter, though he may himself be quite unaware of the fact. Martineau's contention that the Trinitarian's Son is the Unitarian's Father [3]— the Unitarian beholding in the Father all the attributes of grace which the Trinitarian deems confined to the Son—may be exaggerated, but cannot be waved off as altogether unsound; and with a theory which leads us anywhere near hailing distance of such a position there must surely be something amiss, to put it in the mildest possible way. The idea of a God at war with Himself must surely bring at least uneasiness to the thinker who starts without preconceptions or prejudice to handle the theme. And the conviction that thought has been enticed into strange paths grows deeper as we reflect that this theory makes salvation something very like getting the better of God, or God getting the better of Himself, or God circumventing His own justice—it matters little which way it is put. It will not suffice to thrust the conviction aside as being a piece of human perverseness or as showing human pride setting itself up in opposition to God's revealed will. There is too much of conscience in it for summary treatment like that; and any such criticism would imply that a sensitive conscience and a seared conscience are one and the same thing, or would at any rate make it impossible for men and women to distinguish between the two. But the fatal objection to the whole conception of God at war with Himself, of the Son persuading or placating the Father—to any doctrine which affirms that Christ made it possible for God to do something which was impossible for God to do before—lies here. The theory makes entire havoc of the Christian doctrines of the Trinity and of the absolute Deity of Christ. It is indeed carrying the war into the enemy's country to charge "orthodoxy" with being "heresy" in disguise: yet the charge must be made. The Christian doctrine of the Trinity affirms that the act of any one of its three members is the act of all; but the idea of a "contract

[3] "A Way out of the Trinitarian Controversy," in *Essays, Reviews, and Addresses*, II, 525 ff.

passed in the Council of the Trinity" [4] throws that affirmation
entirely overboard, and shows one member of the Godhead carrying on a sort of bargaining transaction with the other two.
Trinitarianism thus passes into tritheism at once. In the minds
of many, indeed, the thing goes very far. With many there is a
half-formed idea, inarticulate perhaps but none the less real,
that when Christ visited our earth the second Person of the
Trinity quitted His heavenly place for a time, filling the va-
cancy again when His earthly work was done. Nor can it be
said that this is merely a popular travesty of the truth. One
theological writer has in all seriousness set down these words,
"What did it mean to the Godhead—to Father, Son and Holy
Ghost—when the Son passed out and left the Father and the
Spirit behind?" [5] So "orthodoxy" slips down to take its place
in what it must surely consider strange company, beside the advocates of an extreme "Kenosis," such as that which Gess,[6]
though by a very different road, reached for his Christology's
goal. With regard to the Deity of Christ the case is equally
clear. If we say that Christ was God—and "orthodoxy" can
hardly refuse to endorse the saying—it must mean that He was
the *whole* God, not of course quantitatively, but in such wise
as within the limits of finitude God could be revealed. We must
accept all the implications of the phrase; and one manifest implication is that during His earthly life Christ was not in any
sense *severed* from the Father and the Spirit, nor acting apart
from them, but that in all He was and did the Father and the

---

[4] This phrase is well known as one with which Matthew Arnold made frequent
and sarcastic play. Its aptness can scarcely be disputed. But it is incorrect to
represent it as actually occurring in the Westminster Confession itself, as Arnold
in one place says it does.

[5] W. Clow, *The Cross in Christian Experience*, p. 18.

[6] Gess carried to extremes the doctrine of "Kenosis" advocated by Thomasius
about the middle of the nineteenth century. Both men were of the Erlangen
school. Thomasius argued for a partial surrender of His attributes, for instance
omnipotence and omnipresence, by the Logos at the Incarnation. But he did
not think of the Logos as temporarily ceasing to form part of the Trinity. Gess
went so far as to hold that in the Incarnation the Logos renounced His self-
consciousness, converting it into the human soul of Jesus, the life of the Trinity
thus undergoing a break. The controversy marked the reawakening of a much
older one, for in the seventeenth century the theologians of Tübingen and Giessen
had held dispute along similar lines.

Spirit were present and energizing no less than was the Son. Theological discussion as to the Person of Christ, having been for the most part occupied with the relations between the divine and the human in Christ, has to a great extent left the point aside. Perhaps, had it been kept more constantly in view, some difficulties might never have loomed up in the theological sky and some misconceptions might have been avoided. In the Incarnation, though it was that side or "mode" of the divine Being called the Son which it so to say most brightly illuminated and turned towards the vision of mankind, the other two "hypostases" must have shared. I am not unaware of, and not in the least dismayed by, the fact that such a statement may lead to an accusation of patripassianism; but as has been said, "It is by no means clear that 'Theopaschitism' is so impossible a theory as Dorner supposes." [7] On the main point—that Christ must have been the *whole* God—another quotation may be given. "We have (in Christ) the whole perfect action of the Godhead concentrated through one factor or hypostasis within it." [8] With the affirmation that Christ *acted upon* the Father—persuaded or placated Him—His absolute Deity therefore disappears. Arianism or Socinianism enters by a door unguardedly thrown ajar. Clear thinking on this theme is imperative for orthodoxy, or for what claims to be such, lest by its very efforts to strengthen one part of its building, it should bring another equally important part crashing to the ground.

2

We turn now to more positive statements. Though the negatives contained in the cautions just offered themselves to some extent imply their corrective positives, and will enable our dealing with these positives to be comparatively brief, yet something remains to be set down as to God's wrath, God's forgiveness, God's retribution, and kindred themes.

A start may be made from the fact, already more than once

[7] Dr. Sydney Cave, *The Doctrine of the Person of Christ,* p. 181.
[8] Forsyth, *The Person and Place of Jesus Christ,* p. 338.

emphasized, that in His "large-scale" treatment of His redemptive "problem"—that is, in His provision of a redemption for a world gone astray—God had to deal with sinfulness rather than with sins. At the outset of our study we saw how the originally-ordained world-order, which contemplated the return of the world-process to the God from Whom it set out—this return to be consummated by man's progressive reception of a new selfhood coming from beyond himself and from a source in God, not merely by a development *in* man's personality but by a *movement of man's personality into God Himself*—we saw how this originally-ordained world-order swerved from its prescribed lines. It was along other tracks that the dynamic power of sin, made more powerful by man's weakness of will, compelled man to go. The racial life-movement slanted off from its allotted course. Sin—not this act or that act of sin viewed each in its isolation nor an accumulation of such acts viewed in the mass, but sin as *sinfulness*, as a poison in man's spiritual fibres causing them to fester and rot—dared to enter the lists as challenger of God for the final lordship of the eternal order and for the right of determining what the final goal of the world-process was to be. What now must God's reaction of wrath against this usurping power have been? Not a mere reacting *mood* of indignation, but a reacting *action* of antagonism powerful enough to ensure sin's defeat; an attacking counter-force which, descending in full panoply of armour upon the force which has dared to invade God's ordained eternal order, sweeps its temporary proud triumph contemptuously away. *And this attacking counter-force resides in the new life-dynamic which has for nineteen centuries and more been issuing from that Jesus Christ who is the same yesterday, and to-day, yea, even for ever.* We do well to say, and cannot say too often, that Christ's work is the manifestation of God's love. But we should accustom ourselves to utter also the less familiar but equally valid truth, that Christ's work is the manifestation, the veritable *manifestation*—nay more, the dynamic activity—of God's indignation against sin. And we should never permit ourselves to make the false statement that Christ's work is the means whereby God's wrath is lulled to sleep. Christ's work is God's wrath alive and energizing as well as His grace. The work of Christ *is,* in itself and all through, at its beginning and during its continuance until now and through all its operation from now till time's final chapter closes, the *re-acting action* of God's conquering anger against sin. It is God pitting His power against the power of the evil forces which have deranged His world. And it is God doing this victoriously; for God does not acknowledge defeat. Christ's work, begun long ago, continued still, far from ended—nay, never to be ended—means, as to the ranked powers of hell, "He that sitteth in the heavens shall laugh: the Lord shall have them in derision."

Christ's work, then, is God's indignation against sinfulness dynamically displayed. *But it is also a manifestation of God's forgiveness to the sinner.* In one and the same act both are shown. Unless the view of God's "problem" in redemption and of God's redemptive scheme set forth in these pages be radically wrong, we vex ourselves with an artificial, really non-existent, question when we inquire as to how Christ's work, in His life or in His death, enabled God to pardon sinful man. God's forgiveness is not the consequence of the sending and the work of Christ. It is *manifested in* the sending and the work of Christ. For God's reaction of anger against the intrusion of sin into His ordained order might conceivably have taken a different form, perhaps a variety of different forms. Sinfulness had to be challenged and conquered; but (if we may beckon out at least one conjecture from the realm of abstract possibilities) God might have annihilated the world He had made, and so His victory would have been signal and complete. But that would have meant leaving the sinner to his fate, abandoning a wilfully degenerate human race to reel headlong on its course till degeneration's catastrophic end was reached. It would have been God saying "Ephraim is joined to idols: let him alone." It would have been God pronouncing that sternest of all sentences with its harsh clang of final doom, "He that is filthy, let him be filthy still." From such a line of action pardon is of course ruled out: stark judgment has its way. But in that God's wrath reacted against the dynamic of sin by confronting it with the life-dynamic in Christ, God turned His very wrath into a means of making man's salvation possible; and in displaying His indignation, He displayed His forgiveness too. It is not a matter of succession, but of simultaneity, nay, of essential identity. God's pardon does not issue out of any constraint laid upon Him, or out of any possibility opened to Him, by the work of Christ. The work of Christ issues out of a constraint which God's *previously-given* pardon lays upon God Himself. God's *reaction* of indignation against sinfulness became an *action* out of which were to come both the conquest of sin and the salvation of humanity; and God's wrath against sin and God's forgiveness of the sinner are but two sides of one and the same thing.

But, be it noted, this does not mean that God has done what in an earlier chapter we saw it was impossible for Him to do. He did not, in shaping His redemptive scheme, "forgive as man forgives." The "moral" theories of Atonement which reduce Christ's work to a manifestation of a mere *spirit* of graciousness, and fail to read its *dynamic* significance, are as far as traditional orthodoxy from penetrating to the core of the matter. In God's great redemptive act, manifesting as it does both God's indignation against sin and God's pardoning love to the sinner, there is, precisely because it is *redemptive* and because it is an *act,* nothing of the "forgive and forget and say no more about it" spirit which makes human forgiveness sometimes so sweet and often (perhaps just when it is sweetest) so futile a thing. God, in confronting sinfulness with Christ, has dealt with the dynamic of sin as a God Who has "ultimates" in His charge must perforce deal with it—by a counter-dynamic more than sufficient for sin's defeat. He has not shut His eyes or turned them away. He has not smoothed things over. He has made no compromise. On the other hand He has not, as traditionalism would have it, been at war with Himself. There has been no treaty between mercy and justice by which God's policy towards sin or sinner has been deflected from its former course. No judgment has been cancelled or deprived of its sting, nor have any penalties been stayed except on condition that the new dy-

namic offered in Christ be allowed to take effect. Be it noted also
that, when Christ's work is taken as a dynamic manifestation
of both the wrath and the pardoning grace of God, the question
as to its "objective" and "subjective" effect drops out of sight
under the sheer weight of its own irrelevance. All such questions, in fact, arise from a preliminary assumption that God
must do in *two* out-goings of His nature what He has really
done in *one*. Does Christ's work produce a change in God's attitude to man? The question is really misconceived, and could
not raise its head if that preliminary assumption had not been
made. Of course the entire redemptive scheme implies a change
in God's attitude (though *activity* is a better word, inasmuch as
it suggests the dynamic idea) to man; but it is *in* Christ's work,
not as a *consequence* of it, that God's changed attitude or activity appears. And the change is of course "objective" to the sight
and apprehension of man. But this must not be construed to
mean that God has in anything like the ordinary usage of the
phrase "changed His mind." Change in God's attitude in the
sense of activity there has certainly been: change in God's attitude in the sense of a change in His Will or in His disposition
towards man there has been none. Again, is God reconciled to
man by Christ as well as man reconciled to God? Well, reconciliation necessarily implies *movement* on the part of both the
previously estranged parties; and *in the sending of Christ God's
contributory movement of self-reconciliation is made*. In regard
to these and similar questions, traditional orthodoxy, having
created an imaginary breach between two divine attributes
which in the divine nature itself are entirely at one, first winds
itself into a veritable maze of difficulties, and then with infinite
pains devises for the healing of the breach expedients which
only serve to make perplexities gyrate more numerously and
swiftly and noisily behind its furrowed brow. We may shake
ourselves clear of the whole entanglement and recover the broad
freedom of simplicity by taking courage to deny that the breach
exists at all. Complicated questions of this kind disappear if we
realize that God's wrath against sin and God's pardoning love
to the sinner are but two sides of one and the same thing, and

that when God sent His Son He provided in one inclusive act the proof of both.

Within this "large-scale" redemptive scheme, working as it has done and does with its dynamic power during the Christian centuries, God has carried on and carries on still His "small-scale" ministry—redemptive too, or at least with an ultimate purpose of redemption—to all those who successively take their places in the long procession of individual souls while the suns of time rise and set. God's "problem" in redemption has been solved. Christ has lived, died, risen, and lives for evermore. The Gospel is preached. Atonement in its cosmic sense has been achieved, or set on its way to being achieved. The individual soul remains for what dealing God may determine upon in order that through its redemption it may make its contribution to the consummation of all things. It is scarcely necessary to say that the reference here is only to those in whose ears the Gospel message has sounded and to whose understanding its significance has more or less clearly penetrated. God's dealings with those not falling into this category lie just now outside our range. With those who have heard and understood, God's "small-scale" ministry, carried on as an adjunct to that "large-scale" redemptive ministry which He has made available for the whole world, consists—perhaps one might say necessarily consists—in the pressure of His love upon the individual soul, seeking to persuade it into acceptance of the "large-scale" redemptive scheme. In the *pressure* of His love—the word is advisedly employed. For, once again, there are no mere *moods* in God, no emotions contained within themselves. God's love is itself dynamic; and its dynamic is directed to magnetizing the individual soul into that other dynamic, the life-dynamic which issues from the life-giving Christ. By all the countless ways wherein His Spirit works in soul and conscience and mind and will, God's love draws, or seeks to draw, every man to be a sharer in that larger ministry which, because it is a ministry of salvation, includes all else. But—and this is the crucial point to which these remarks, commonplace enough as they are, are meant to lead— just because God's love thus presses itself upon man, man is forced to a decisive response of either "yes" or "no." We are brought back again along this line of thinking to the same tremendous fact at which by another route we arrived before—the fact that there must be a precisely-drawn dividing boundary between acceptors and rejectors of Christ. From our present standpoint, it may be put that there must be a precisely-drawn dividing boundary between those who accept and those who reject that pressure of God's love which invites them to accept Christ. It comes to the same thing. An answer must be given. A love which thrusts itself upon the loved may be welcomed or may be spurned. Ignored it cannot be. It may *seem* to be ignored, but the apparent indifference is rejection wearing the mask of a less violent mood. If God's love is dynamic and aggressive, then out upon every man a spiritual crisis leaps, a crisis perhaps repeated many times as life goes on. We find ourselves, the moment we take adequate soundings into this theme, fast swept into the solemnities of a "theology of crisis," not because God is an antagonist who has to be softened down from His wrath, but precisely *because God is love*.

But if man answers "no," either the loud "no" of defiance or the inarticulate "no" of an indifference more or less assumed, what then? If he rejects the pressure of that love wherewith God woos him into submission to the life-dynamic of Christ, what then? This, let it be said in passing, is through the Christian centuries the one sin which in a manner includes all others, the one constant sin that man can commit, the one sin which in committing any other sin man *must* commit. While in his "large-scale" dealing with the "problem" of redemption it is *sinfulness* that God assails, in His "small-scale" dealing with individual men and women it is *the one sin of rejecting the remedy for sinfulness* with which He deals and from which He seeks to draw men and women away. But if man says "no"? Then man himself puts God against him, *precisely because God is love*. For just as God's anger against sinfulness is the obverse side of God's forgiveness towards man, so *God's anger towards the sinner is but another name for God's resisted love*. It is many centuries since a Psalmist realized the profound truth that God is to each man what each man makes God to be, and added to those previous declarations of his which affirmed "With the merciful Thou wilt shew Thyself merciful; with the perfect man Thou wilt shew Thyself perfect; with the pure Thou wilt shew Thyself pure," that startling climax or anti-climax, "and with the perverse Thou shalt shew Thyself froward." [9] In a very real sense every man makes his own God. Just because God never changes, He must be a changing God to man in correspondence with man's changing attitudes toward Him. Because He never changes, He may, when man changes, actually become man's enemy and fight against him. God's love is God's interference with man, not just God's amiability toward man; and as man refuses to let Him interfere he finds God to be against him, *just because God is love*. God *against* man? Yes, when man makes Him so. If it is His nature to move toward man in love, He must necessarily be felt as an opposing and even hostile influence when man declines to let Him approach: man's resistance to Him turns Him into an influence that resists man inasmuch as He resists man's resistance; and God's anger is God's love reacting against man's refusal to receive it. One halts hesitatingly on the threshold of any inquiry as to what the end of such resistance must be: yet, since the sense of solemn possibilities hovering heavy-winged around us here cannot be utterly drugged, it may be well to draw the hanging veil just a little aside. Through the gap so opened, I think this at least can be discerned. If resistance to God's love and its invitation to acceptance of Christ hold obstinately on its course to the end, if that one supreme sin be repeated again and again till God's last remonstrance falls powerlessly away, the end must inevitably be this—a petrifaction, a lethargy, an incapacity of the soul (the fittest word is hard to choose) in which all power of movement into God's love or into Christ's life is lost.[10] The soul may see the God and the Christ it has rejected, but so far, far off!

[9] Psalm xviii. 26.

[10] I do not here, any more than when the topic incidentally presented itself before, offer or even hint any opinion as to whether a soul may sink so deep into this condition that God's mercy can find no remedy for its doom. But Whittier's words previously quoted in this connection keep returning hauntingly to one's mind.

and be unable to stir; may feel the sense of "ought to have been" and "might have been" beating up in swirling waves of remorse and regret within it, yet find itself entangled in the fetters of a past that permits no new beginning and no change. That is in the nature of things. Active resistance becomes at last a habit with a slave-driver's whip and a relentless tyrant's mastery: passive resistance turns to hopeless paralysis in the end. And that ultimate fate, if it be reached, must be realized by the soul that suffers it as the loss of a personal relationship apart from which the highest blessedness is absent, apart from which the soul must go wandering for ever through desert places, seeking rest and finding none. By that realization such a fate must inflict its most searching painfulness. A light and mitigated penalty—will any one dare to say?—compared with that which an angry God has sometimes been declared ready to impose? Nay verily. In the very act of withdrawing Himself finally from man, if He does so withdraw Himself, God must surely make His displeasure a very present and a very potent reality, under whose resistless probing, as it tears the last rags and tatters of self-deception away, the shame of its moral and spiritual nakedness must shoot in agony through every fibre of the God-abandoned soul. The false suggestion is sometimes made that, if we banish the "invented penalties" of legalism from our theology, we hand man's spiritual destiny over to the operation of blind retributive forces and clear a personal relationship with an estranged God entirely out of the case. (Though even if it were so, it is hard to see why a sinner in the grip of blind retributive forces should be thought less severely dealt with than a sinner in the hands of the living God.) A false suggestion most emphatically; for when the end comes, if it come, it is a *love* that has been resisted and a *living Christ* that has been spurned; and the soul must to its innermost recesses know that it is so. So profoundly right was Dante when he set over the portals of hell an inscription which tells how in hell's making Eternal Love had taken its part.[11] So profoundly

[11] "Justice incited my sublime Creator;
Created me divine Omnipotence,
The highest wisdom and the primal Love."
(*Inferno*, Canto III, 4. Longfellow's translation.)

true is it that God, *just because God is love,* may become a consuming fire.

What has been said by no means excludes from God's "small-scale" ministry to the individual what may be termed subsidiary dealings with particular sins. There is no strain on faith (for those who believe that the God who has worlds on worlds hanging on His hands keeps also in His thought and in His heart the names of every one of His children) in holding that, besides exerting the ceaseless pressure of His love in order to persuade men into acceptance of His large redemptive scheme, and besides dealing with the one sin of rejecting the remedy for sinfulness, God may inflict some special penalty for some special transgression or may on the other hand ward off from the transgressor some penalty which would naturally follow upon his sin. The purpose of piercing a sinner's hard-armoured heart with a sharp arrow-point of warning or of stirring some movement of repentance in the stagnant depths of a sinner's soul might well inspire God's watchful care to measures like these. And it follows that if this is so, the prayer "Forgive us our trespasses" may well go up daily from our lips, though in the one great act of sending Christ the one great act of pardon for the world's sinfulness has once and for all been wrought. In some such ways as these, in fact, God may at times perhaps forgive as man forgives or punish as man punishes; and to this extent some qualification may be requisite for what has previously been said as to the impossibility of God doing these things. But if and when He does them, He does them within the larger frame-work that has been sketched, and does them only because that larger frame-work encloses them and keeps them in closely-dependent relations with itself. Within the "large-scale" redemptive scheme the "small-scale" ministry is carried on. Within the "small-scale" ministry particular dealing on God's part with particular sins may well find room.

But however that may be, the note on which this chapter closes must surely be this. "Large-scale" redemptive scheme—"small-scale" redemptive ministry in which God's love presses the remedy for sinfulness upon man in his sins—particular influences of pardon or penalty as God may choose to exert them —God's love and wrath, God's forgiveness and judgment—if what has been said about such things in these pages be true, then theology must surely become evangelism again, and any one who thinks or writes about such things must make his final note nothing else than this, saying for himself and for those to whom his message goes, "How shall we escape if we neglect so great salvation?"

CHAPTER IX

THE ETERNAL ORDER

Our journey is nearly done. It has consisted in the main in tracing out and following the road over which another journey —the journey of the world-process, in accordance with or in violation of the eternal order—has been made from its initiation to its present stage, and in attempting to discern what that journey's final stage is to be. And we have sought, as we followed that world-process in its long travelling, to establish for each successive section of it the place and function of Christ, of Christ as Creator, of Christ as immanent, of Christ as incarnate, of Christ crucified and risen, of Christ as Redeemer through the ages by the power of His ceaselessly re-creative life offered to man, and therefore of Christ as newly immanent in the world-process after His first immanence had been lost. Also, we have attempted to make "vital and organic connection" among all the various parts and factors of Christ's ministry to man, and afterwards from all those parts and factors of Christ's ministry to man's response of faith. We have seen, as central to man's spiritual history and as marking the beginning of the redemptive era, the Cross with its "two arms outstretched to save" —associated always in thought, however, with the companion thought of that empty tomb which turned the Cross from a symbol of defeat into, not merely a symbol, but the very instrument, of a victorious Christ for evermore able to redeem to the uttermost all that come unto God by Him. We have found along these lines the suggestion of a view of Atonement which, when we are in a dilemma between professedly "orthodox" explanations which make conscience restless and "moral" explanations which seem too facile for a question so great and which appear to solve the problem by looking at it through a diminishing-glass and then averring that it is not there, may perhaps offer us a new and more satisfying choice. And we have, unless our hopes betray us, set our feet upon a road which may lead us to a theology (and, most important for our purpose, to a *soteriology*) philosophical, evangelical, and evangelistic, to a "theology of crisis" which may be preached as a real Gospel of both warning and promise to the common man. In short, we have seen in something of their cosmic significance both Christ and the Atonement He works out. We have seen Christ grounded in the eternal order, or rather the eternal order grounded in Christ; with Christ as its Author, Christ dwelling in it, Christ restoring it, Christ as fulfilling it or as destined to fulfil it, Christ as its Alpha and Omega, its Beginning and its End. Does a fair assessment of all this reveal any gains?

I

Some, both from the religious and from the philosophical camps, would give a hesitating reply. Many profoundly religious men (and under the title both the average religious man and the professed theologian are meant to be covered) are apt to assume an attitude of reserve when anything in the way of making religion "rational" is proposed; and at the term "philosophical" eyebrows rise still higher in question, and suspicion takes the place of reserve. For the average religious man the attitude is perhaps natural enough. Reason and philosophy, and everything associated with either or both, have so often been pointed to as hostile to religion, and have so often justified the reproach, that the hostility has almost come to be taken for granted on both sides. But one has to face the fact that even the theologian has acquired the habit of looking askance upon such a word as "rational" and all its terminological kindred, and is satisfied that to a very great extent theology and philosophy should go each its own way, an armed neutrality being the *summum bonum* to be hoped for in the way of relations between the two. There are so many failures behind: attempts to make theology "rational" or "philosophical" have so often meant the death of vital Christianity! Better leave the whole business alone! Some theologies, such as the Ritschlian, have advocated a final severance (and an almost defiant proclamation of it) of theology from philosophy *in toto;* and the influence they have at least temporarily wielded is enough to show that they spoke the thoughts of many hearts. But short of that, theological thinking for the most part keeps itself aloof from any alliance, so far as its *soteriological* doctrines are concerned, with a reasoned view of the world-process; and while it admits that some of its findings—such for example as the existence of God— occupy a border-land wherein philosophy's writ also runs, it retires into a secluded territory wholly its own when it deals with such topics as those with which this book has attempted to deal. Of course its work upon these topics, both in respect of each item in the list taken simply and of all the items viewed as a whole, is held to be entirely "rational." It is into a reasoned system that the various items are gathered; and *within* theology's "secluded territory" a connected view is (more or less) aimed at and declared to be achieved. But the results attained are not co-ordinated with the results which reason claims to have attained in the larger spheres outside. Perhaps the general situation may be put thus—that while on its purely theistic side Christian theology admits its partnership with reason and reason's philosophic findings, on its definitely Christian side it prefers to work alone. And philosophy in its turn matches the aloofness of theology with an aloofness, at least equally unbending, of its own. It is certainly true that, except as interpreted by an ever-diminishing band of extremists, philosophy no longer looks down upon theology with the undisguised contempt which for a few rampant decades it displayed; but this amounts to little more than the hoisting of a flag of truce. So philosophy and theology proceed each one upon its way. So long as the clash of actual contradiction can be avoided, both philosophy and theology (the latter term is used here, and throughout these paragraphs, as inclusive of theology's *soteriological* sections) are content.

Such a position of things cannot be considered satisfactory.

It is true that it brings no mental disturbance at all to the man of simple religious faith; for him Christ and everything connected with Christ's name have a reality so intense that they carry their own proofs. Yet even he has at the back of his mind a settled conviction that between Christianity and the final verdicts of rational thinking no contradiction can exist. Few people, we may be quite sure, would find their rest in an "objective uncertainty adhered to by the most passionate dedication of inwardness," as Kierkegaard found his at one point of his storm-tossed quest for truth. And however it may happen with the man of absolutely unsophisticated faith, to the professed theologian, when he gets to grips with things, a failure to set his theology into the context of an all-embracing synthesis must surely bring some qualms. Even the Ritschlian school soon had to make some sort of bridge over the theologico-philosophic gap which its founder left unspanned. Against the dualism involved in the failure the mind instinctively revolts. Besides, the challenge from other worlds of thought will sooner or later compel the theologian to face the matter, and to say whether he is going to claim validity for his religious ideas in philosophy's court or to let the case go by default. And this, let it be remembered, is said with *soteriology* in view. It is true that philosophy usually abstains from *direct* interference with theology there, though of *indirect* interference—inasmuch as many philosophic pronouncements make anything in the nature of Christian soteriology impossible—there is no lack. For the most part, philosophy permits theology to retire as it were into the "back of beyond" and to frame its soteriology there as it will. But the theologian, once he sets himself to the problem at all, cannot permanently acquiesce in that as a settlement of the matter. He will feel that philosophy's very permission to him to do as he chooses in this all-important field—its half-contemptuous abstinence, as if *de haut en bas,* from direct concern with it—is in itself a challenge, not a reconciliation at all. A reconciliation that deserves the name must go deeper. So long as theology in its *soteriological* sections remains entirely divorced from the world-process whereof philosophy speaks, a negative reply is given to one of the primary requests of orderly thought. No organic connection has been traced from the beginning of things to their end. There is no true unity in the apprehension of the cosmic scheme; and therefore, so long as theology is content to leave the matter at that, the existence of unity in the cosmic scheme is by implication actually denied.

2

The line which we have been pursuing throughout this book at any rate attempts, if it does no more, to furnish an answer to the mind's desire for a synthesis within whose limits the results of both theological and philosophical thinking may be enclosed. That is of course no proof that in following it we have not strayed on to a wrong track after all. But it may be modestly claimed as conferring a title to consideration upon what has been said, for the chase of a mere will-o'-the-wisp would surely have led us upon more shifting ground than that which we have reached. It is something gained if we can "think things together," if we can provide a background against which each product of our thinking may be fitted into its own particular place in such wise as at the same time to impart additional strength to all the other products and to derive additional strength from them. We have seen before how many ideas fail under that test and refuse to be thus "fitted in," how the setting of them into close company with other ideas is an ordeal from which they shrink shamed away. But the converse is also true. Many thought-products, perhaps difficult to accept if taken in their isolation, become suddenly invested with the seductive glow and masterful force of almost inevitable and axiomatic truths through their ascertained harmony with some other thought-product: this other thought-product may in its turn be helped and further confirmed by the thought-products to which its own helping confirmation has been given; while, against a background inclusive of the two and providing a still larger company of thought-products which both may join, both may show themselves still more amply approved. Also, a philosophic theology prevents the thinker from mistaking bits of truth for the whole, keeps him back from the over-emphasis upon and distortion of truth into which without it he may so easily fall. Surely all this is very real gain! And the more deeply the method can be carried into theology's soteriological section, so much the greater must the gain become. If a philosophical world-view can be shown to be Christian down or up to Christianity's soteriological truths, and this not by a gracious permission it is pleased to extend to theology but by inherent pressure from within itself—if Christianity, down or up to its soteriological truths, can be shown as fitting into a philosophical world-view—if in such a world-view place can be found for an Incarnation, for the Cross, for an Atonement, for all that Christ's name represents—if these things can be shown as being the supreme satisfaction of rational thinking as well as the supreme spiritual nourishment whereby the soul of man must live—if thus the philosopher and the theologian take their places for the advocacy of the Christian gospel and for the evangelization of the world side by side—can the gain be measured or denied? It may all be only a futile dream. The writer of these pages, at any rate, believes for his part that the dream may come splendidly true; and it is in that belief that he has set down everything this book contains.

The lines on which the attempt has been made do not involve any such whittling down of theological terms, particularly of soteriological terms, as attempts at the "rationalizing" of theology have frequently brought about. Certainly such "rationalizing" as these pages have in view does not mean abandonment or denial of the supernatural: indeed, it implies the rescue of the epithet "rational" from the limits within which much modern thought has sought to restrain it, and the enlargement of the territory it may legitimately claim to cover. "Rational" in our usage of the word, so far as it implies any denial at all, implies simply a denial of the non-reasonable. It does not imply denial of any proposition or any alleged fact on the flimsy pretext that proposition and fact are not verifiable by experience reached through any one of the five senses. That is the frowning mien with which a certain sort of philosophy has seen fit to invest the term, but which it does not wear unless under the compulsion of a thought-system arrogantly bent on preventing it from revealing its natural countenance. The line of thought we have followed gives back to the term "reason" and its blood-relations the larger scope whereof they should never have been deprived, makes reason recognize the supernatural as supremely reasonable, makes reason even *demand* the supernatural for its own perfect content. Further, these pages have nowhere sought to substitute for standard theological or soteriological language what may be called Emersonian equivalents, or alleged equivalents, which at a casual glance seem to bear a similar image and superscription, but are found under examination to be but spurious coin. It is worth while to pause for a few moments upon the point in order to emphasize the gulf between the method of this book and the method referred to here. This latter method is always plausible enough; in fact, it is just because it works in half-truths, and because it is with inadequacy rather than with total worthlessness that it must be charged, that it is so dangerous. Goodness becomes "that which promotes development." Sin becomes, conversely, "that which retards development," or in more *ore rotundo* style, "falling out of harmony with the law of the universe"; and salvation is "self-adjustment to that law" or "harmony with environment." Duty means that man "is to assist his fellows and to develop his own higher self." And so on. The flaw in all such "reconciliations" between theology and science or philosophy is the assumption that because each theological term involved can be up to a point *truly* translated into the offered scientific or philosophical speech, therefore it can be *adequately* so translated too; and such questions as "What *is* the law of the universe with which man is to be in harmony?"—"*how* is the higher self to be developed?"—"what *is* the environment to which man is to adjust himself?"—are glossed over or thrust aside. Theology has its own special answers to all these questions, of course; but in all these "reconciliations" it is not called upon to state them. It has had the high honour done to it of having a few of its phrases stolen, dressed up in scientific or philosophical robes, and sent forth to walk abroad; and with that it ought to be content. Because certain *processional* terms, valid in science or philosophy, can be plausibly employed in reference to the spiritual experience of man, therefore it is somewhat too swiftly, indeed often quite gaily, deduced that these same terms can be comfortably wrapped right round that spiritual experience without leaving anything essential out. Concentration on *process,* which may chance to be to some extent similarly describable in the two cases, prevents care for *essence,* which in the two cases may have nothing in common at all. Whether the starting-point of the process, the road along which it travels, the motive power under which it goes on, its goal, above all, the "entity" with which the process is concerned and which it bears along upon its bosom—whether in regard to man's spiritual experience these things may not be entirely different from what they are in the scientific or philosophical field, and whether in consequence the apparent parallel between the two processes may not be a mere superficial coincidence—these points are not faced. In the end, to declare that this is a kind of "reconciliation" between theology and science or philosophy is much as though one declared that, because two has been discovered to be a common factor of forty-eight and fifty, therefore forty-eight and fifty (especially fifty) both mean two; and the "reconciliation" itself is much like that effected between the lion and the lamb when the lion eats the lamb. God, Christ, redemption, faith, as theology through the centuries has known and handled them, have disappeared. Only a sort of misty wraith hovers waveringly about where they used to stand. Assuredly the coming of Christ did not, in any interpretation of it offered by these systems, mean a new breaking in of God into the impaired cosmic order for the purpose of setting it right. The gospel of these "reconciliations" is that man has but to lay himself down upon the cosmic order as it is, and so be carried safely on its sure tides to his ultimate goal. Both theologian and "average religious man" may well fight shy of "reconciliations" such as these. But this passing glance has been thrown upon them only to make it clear that what has been written in this book keeps no company with them, and need cause no fears nor suspicions such as they naturally excite. Once again, let it be pointed out that the line of thinking we have followed has led us—so at least the writer would fain hope—to a theology at the same time *philosophical, evangelical,* and *evangelistic,* in which the great terms of religion as the Christian ages have used them still speak with their old ringing tones, refusing to demean themselves to the level of mere soft-pedal accompaniments for voices not their own.

3

The claim here made is that the Christian view of the world-order, as that view is built up on the implications of Paul's "thought-series" considered in a former chapter, provides in its soteriological (which is its final) section what non-Christian philosophies cannot offer; that by doing this the Christian view of the world-order becomes a satisfying philosophy in itself; and that Christian theology can consequently stand upon its feet, speak with authoritative voice, and is put beyond the need of any "reconciliations" at all. There is no occasion for theology to adjust itself to other philosophies or to seek shelter beneath their ægis, or to ask them for any certificate of competence or of worth. *And because Christianity's provision of what non-Christian philosophies cannot provide is made in very special measure by its soteriology, and because its soteriology starts from the Cross, therefore it is at the Cross that the final stage of the world-process, as Christian thinking views it, begins; and in the eternal order the place of the Cross is secured.*

The contrast between the treatment of the world-process by philosophy not of the Christian class and its treatment by a theology based on the "thought-series" of Paul lies here. Philosophy, in the common interpretation of its function, seeks to know the facts and workings of the world-order *as that order now exists,* but envisages no *final* fact or stage by which the world-order is passing or will at last pass, is being drawn or will at last be drawn, *beyond* itself; and consequently with all its attempts at knowing, it does not know or even profess to know what the human mind wants to know most of all. It views the present world-process as though it were entirely self-contained and out of all context, detached from anything that may have come before or anything that can come after it: it does not take it as a stage on the way to something else and something ultimate still to appear: it speaks of no ultimate condition of things wherein the world-order shall be transcended and into which it shall nevertheless be taken up, not because it is base but because its work is done. It is true, of course, that philosophy's silence on the theme has varying reasons behind it, ranging from a flat denial that any such final fact is possible to a sense of its own incompetence to utter any illuminating word. It is true also that the idea of something yet to come into being beyond the existing world-order occasionally emerges on the philosophical field; as for instance, when Bergson and Eucken seem to suggest as a possibility that God has not yet completely created Himself. But that hardly calls for any appreciable qualification of what has been said. Philosophy deals with the world-order *as it is*. But Christian soteriology dares more greatly. If our pages have read its meaning rightly, it foresees—nay, *sees being created now*—the final fact of the world-process into which the world-process, when that final fact is *fully* created, will merge. Christian soteriology tells of a *creative activity* now at work and bringing into being the final fact for whose sake the world-process was begun. *Once again, then, because Christian soteriology begins at the Cross, it is the Cross from which the final stage of the world-process, as Christian thinking views it, takes its start; and in the eternal order the Cross finds its place for ever secured.*

To produce in anything like fulness the evidence which would justify what has been alleged as to philosophy's silence on the topic of the "final fact" would require far more space than can be afforded here. A few words may however be said by way of putting the reader on the right track for his search.

It is well, even if nothing more followed, to declare with emphasis that the idea of evolution, taken *per se,* is obviously open to the suggested criticism. It does not even attempt to deal with philosophy's ultimate problem as this was set out in a previous chapter—the problem as to how the existence of the "Many" is to be reconciled with the existence of an all-inclusive "One." The term "evolution" is far too vague as to its content to constitute a philosophy of the world-process: it does no more than indicate a series of successive happenings which unfold themselves without the intervention of any fresh energies, and quite fails to indicate the direction in which the unfolding series proceeds or what the "material" of the series is or anything else of a definite kind. If we clamp ourselves down to the term "evolution," we have to admit in the first place that there is no hint as to what it is that evolves; and we have to follow this with a further admission that the route of evolution may be a line drawn straight on or sideways or upwards or in a curve, or a line which even returns backward upon itself, or a line which does each one of these things in regular or irregular variation; and we have to make the still more fatal admission that as to the direction the line will take in the future, or as to what its ultimate terminus may be, the term offers no faintest clue. Evolution may trace from the first beginning of things—at any rate from the point at which the Unknowable began to transform itself into the Knowable—the course of development which has issued in the present cosmos and which has at last evolved within or upon the cosmos the microcosmos who is its head. But, having reached that point, a philosophy which has only the term "evolution" for its "open sesame" to the secrets of the world-order must confess that its day's work is done, and must retire. This is not to offer a "final fact"; and the questing mind, still repeating "What next?" will have to turn empty away.

Passing now from the term "evolution" and its wrongful claim—so often tacitly assumed as valid and equally often tacitly yielded—to constitute a philosophy in itself, it may be noted next that materialism of the cruder sort [1] also fails to suggest

---

[1] Such as that associated with the names of Büchner, Vogt, and Feuerbach in Germany, of d'Holbach in France, and of Hobbes with his successors down to Bain and G. H. Lewes in Britain. I do not mention Tyndall in this connection, though he is generally looked upon as one of materialism's chief apostles. It

any "final fact" in which the world-order may issue or into which it may be taken up. Indeed, the only sense in which the expression "world-order" can be used at all by a strictly materialistic philosophy is that of movement induced within matter itself by the force dwelling in it, since matter and force in themselves comprise the sum total of all that exists. If these exhaust all the possibilities of actuality, if there are no reserves of possibility either screened in some secret cells within the material system or waiting quite outside the entire material system for their chance to deploy into reality, then further questions concerning what may be beyond this so-called "world-order" are so much wasted breath. To inquire about any "final fact" is to put the foolish question "What will be left when everything is gone?" Unless materialism affirms (as many, perhaps most, of its votaries have done) the eternity of the world-system, and imagines it as perpetually making and destroying, re-making and re-destroying, itself by its own inherent force, and so on for ever, nothingness is the only "final fact" which it could suggest. Büchner seems with something like gusto to picture nature everlastingly imitating Penelope's futile spinning and unwinding of her web; [2] and indeed if a "final fact" must somehow be provided, he had no other choice.

---

should be remembered that while many of Tyndall's utterances seem to point to a purely materialistic creed, he sometimes spoke in a quite different tone. In that same famous Belfast Address in which he made the oft-quoted remark about discerning in matter "the promise and potency of all terrestrial life," he prefixed or appended in later editions observations such as these. "When standing in the spring time and looking upon the sprouting foliage, the lilies of the field, and sharing the general joy of opening life, I have often asked myself whether there is no power, being, or thing, in the universe, whose knowledge of that of which I am so ignorant is greater than mine. I have said to myself, Can it be possible that man's knowledge is the greatest knowledge, that man's life is the highest life? My friends, the profession of that Atheism with which I am sometimes so lightly charged would, in my case, be an impossible answer to this question." And he adds that while at times the claims of the doctrine of "material Atheism" might be found to press him strongly, it is not in "hours of clearness and vigour" that this is so, for in those hours the doctrine "ever dissolves, and disappears, as offering no solution of the mystery in which we dwell, and of which we form a part." Words like these point to agnosticism rather than to thorough-going materialism.

[2] "Gleich der Gattin des Odysseus, welche bei Nacht wieder auftrennte was ihre fleissigen Hände bei Tage gesponnen hatten, gefällt sich die Natur in einem ewigen Aufbauen und Zerstören, dessen Anfang gleich seinem Ende, und dessen Ende gleich seinem Anfang ist." (Kraft und Stoff, p. 240.)

The agnostic evolutionism of Herbert Spencer serves us no better. Materialistic Spencer's system certainly cannot fairly be called. He has himself disavowed the holding of a definitely materialistic belief. "The reasonings contained in the foregoing pages," he declares towards the close of his *First Principles,* "afford no support to either of the antagonist hypotheses respecting the ultimate nature of things. Their implications are no more materialistic than they are spiritualistic, and no more spiritualistic than they are materialistic." [3] But apart from Spencer's own denial, the fact that he so emphatically plants at the back of the visible system of things an Absolute whereof nothing can be predicated except that it is omnipotent Force, and for which the Unknowable is the most fitting name, must at any rate prevent materialism from claiming him as its disciple. Nevertheless, while matter may not be all, Spencer practically compels us to look upon and construe the world-order *as if it were:* matter and force are the only things with which we can have anything to do or which we can know anything about: we may know that there is something else, but that is all the "extra" knowledge we can hope to possess. Obviously no suggestion of a "final fact" carrying the present world-order beyond itself emerges from such a system as this. It is vain to expect that any constructive suggestion is to be glimpsed by gazing into the "dead vast and middle of the night," however prolonged and penetrating the stare may be. As a matter of fact, Spencer leaves us much as Büchner leaves us, with a perpetual cycle of making and unmaking—the cycle being in Spencer's case a repetition of progress from "homogeneity" to "heterogeneity" and of retrogression from "heterogeneity" to "homogeneity" in a never-ending round; so that through a succession of eternities the world-system "spins like a fretful midge." "Final fact" there is none.

With regard to idealistic systems such as Hegel's, a swift glance is sufficient to show that these are as barren as the rest so far as concerns the suggestion of any ultimate issue to which the world-order may conceivably lead. According to Hegel, the

[3] *First Principles,* p. 558.

world-process is the Absolute Mind or Absolute Idea, which is the one Reality, coming to complete consciousness of itself— on its way to an apprehension of itself as it eternally is; this self-apprehension being progressive in proportion as the mind of man realizes that its seeming "otherness" from the Absolute Mind is a delusion. But this process of self-realization on the part of the Absolute Idea is an eternal one for which the world-process merely serves as a mirror in time; so that what we have offered to us is a development which, whatever forward steps of its course it may cover, remains still infinitely far from a goal which is for ever receding like the rainbow's foot. This is hardly a conception of a "final fact" which a mind in earnest about finding one can accept as satisfactory; though it may be added that, even if the goal of the indicated development were advertised as attainable instead of as perpetually moving on, the conception of an Absolute Idea eternally contemplating its own completeness after the last human mind has committed suicide in the Absolute Mind's own deep seas would leave dissatisfaction equally keen. Not the most industrious digging and delving can extract any "final fact" worth the name from systems constructed on lines like these.

The philosophies which lay their stress on the ascent of humanity into union with a timeless life lying round about the life of time—philosophies of which Eucken's may be taken as the type—seem at first to hold out a more hopeful prospect of providing a "final fact." Eucken speaks of an "independent spiritual life" outside of and encircling the visible world, enclosing and embracing it much as the sea encloses and embraces the land, and as it were pressing into its inlets and its bays. In this "independent spiritual life" lies the ultimate source of all creative forces, the fountain whence all the movements of the world-process originally flowed; and this same "independent spiritual life" is the reality whereof man, in that spiritual element of which he is conscious within himself, possesses (if it may be so put) a piece shredded or broken off. Yet no sooner are we presented with the conception of this "independent spiritual life" than we are bereft of it again, or at least find that it has been baptized with too high-sounding a name. This "independent spiritual life" turns out to be not really "independent" after all; for, while "independent" in the sense of not having been produced or created by man, it is itself imperfect as yet, and can perfect itself only as man rises into it and adopts it for his own. The spiritual element in man (which is itself a manifestation and energizing of the "independent spiritual life" *beyond* man) calls on man to satisfy both the spiritual *in* him and the "independent spiritual life" *beyond* him by raising the first into the second and drawing the fulness of the second into the first; and in his struggle between the "inner" and the "outer," between the "natural" and the "spiritual," so far as man deliberately faces the struggle, man answers to the call. The "independent spiritual life" which surrounds the world-order perfects itself, becomes truly "personalized," through the progressive self-spiritualization of man. On this last point emphasis must be laid, for on it Eucken himself lays the principal stress. It is only through the deliberate activity of men that the "independent spiritual life" comes to its own. "Activism" is the term which Eucken approves as the most significant one we can employ if we wish to indicate the chief characteristic of his thought.[4] Man is at the same time *taken up into* the spiritual life and *makes* it: through man's struggle with the "natural" he finds the spiritual life within himself and the spiritual life finds itself in him: the

---

[4] The name of Bergson was a few pages back linked with that of Eucken as representing a philosophy which speaks of an ultimate Reality not fully existent yet. That of William James might make a third with these two. Bergson and James are at one with Eucken, also, in making the completion of the incomplete world-order depend upon an "activism" on man's part. But Bergson takes "intuition" to be the moulding and creative power which man is to exercise; and as it is impossible to tell in what direction this incalculable force will strike off from this or that contact with the existing world, no settled aim or end for its operation can be proposed. And James, seeing behind the world-process a "plurality" of finite deities who, like man himself, are embarked upon a "great adventure," merely bids man adopt the method of "pragmatism" (that is, to act upon whatever truth appears from time to time to be the one which "works" best) and so add his *fiat* and his activities to theirs. Here again, inasmuch as it is impossible to prophesy *what* truth will at any given time and under any hypothetical conjunction of circumstances appear to be the best from the "pragmatism" standpoint, no definite lines of advance can be laid down. Whatever vagueness there may be in Eucken's system is greatly intensified in the schemes of these two thinkers.

movement of the "independent spiritual life" towards its completion has, at the point where man comes upon the scene, reached a stage at which it needs a definite movement toward the spiritual life on the part of man himself. One may put it that the responsibility for carrying on the eternal process rests upon our shoulders now; nor is it by mere acquiescence, by mere settling down upon a "stream of tendency," that this responsibility can be discharged. The curve of development has swept round to this point—we must pick up the thread and carry it forward in our own hands till the circle is complete: we have henceforth to be, not as those who float on the river's bosom to the inevitable sea, but rather as those who, finding themselves where the road ends close up to the edge of the illimitable unknown, are called to be road-makers and travellers too. The system sheers miles away from any idea of lying down upon evolution's tide and letting oneself be borne along; nor is it upon any totalistic self-unfolding of the Absolute, in the Hegelian sense, that we are bidden to look. All this seems to bring us, and actually does bring us, at any rate a good many steps nearer to a "final fact" than to any of the other philosophies at which we have glanced. Yet on closer examination the fair prospect vanishes away. The call "forward and onward" has been sounded, but no real bearings have been taken or given, no clear course set, and we are left wandering in an unlifting fog. What is the "independent spiritual life"? As we have seen, it is not really "independent" at all. It describes itself in Eucken's system as something which does not as yet exist or which exists only partially, and which is to enter upon fuller existence as man's struggle against the "natural order," victoriously carried through, affords it its chance. Which comes to this—that the expression "independent spiritual life" does not in the usage of this philosophy introduce us to any *Ultimate* which is from everlasting to everlasting the same. Nor is this "independent spiritual life" personal, since only through our identification with it and our appropriation of it does it become truly "personalized." In short, one of the constituents of a "final fact"—a source whence the world-process issued and to which it is in the last issue to return, a source which through all the change and movement proceeding from it remains essentially and inherently the same—is absent. What it is, if it exist, is a riddle still. And what, one must ask next, is meant by that "progressive spiritualization of life" which composes man's programme? One finds in Eucken's pages various statements *about* it, but hardly anything that could be offered to an inquirer as *a description of* it. The idea of life's spiritualization, we are told, "should increase our discontent with the life of mediocrity"; should "help us to draw through the confusions of our social life certain clear defining lines"; should "offer us a standing-ground where we can seek to rally our forces," and so on. But these phrases do not suggest any actual practical applications of the idea, though it is under the heading "applications" that they appear.[5] And to affirm and to re-affirm that the "progressive spiritualization of life" points to something different from the "natural order" is only to say that the life into which we are to rise *is* a spiritual life—which does not get us very far. Indeed some of Eucken's most favourable interpreters admit that on this side his philosophy is wreathed in mist.[6] But if in the matter of the programme, as well as in the matter of the goal, the system fails us, what becomes of the "final fact"? We are told what it is *not*. But a mere negation simply flings us off from our present standing-ground into the void, to sink or swim as we may. It is in fact fair to say that we can only read a meaning into the phrase "the progressive spiritualizations of life" by importing into it creeds and ideas gathered from Christian sources: it sketches a mere outline and invites Christian thinking to fill it up. And one cannot but regret that a system which has made such long strides toward a true

[5] They are from the translation (*The Meaning and Value of Life*, p. 139), by Lucy J. Gibson and W. R. Boyce Gibson. The original runs, "*Sie muss die Empfindung der Unzulänglichkeit des Durchschnittsstandes steigern: sie zeigt ein Mittel zur Scheidung des uns umgebenden Chaos: sie gewährt einen Standort von dem aus sich eine Sammlung der Kräften anstreben lässt.*" (*Der Sinn und Wert des Lebens,* edition 1908, p. 154.) It should be said that in later editions the sections from which this quotation is taken have been rewritten and expanded, and these particular sentences are not reproduced. But the new material is really a development of the quotation, not a departure from it; and the quotation might appropriately serve as its text.

[6] For instance, Mr. Meyrick Booth (*Rudolf Eucken,* p. 200).

interpretation of human need should have failed to see how in the Christian facts and their implications the need is fully supplied. For many of Eucken's utterances have a distinctly Christian, a distinctly Pauline, ring. But they are echoes which as it were refuse to recognize the voice which gave them birth. A distinctly Christian, a distinctly Pauline ring but—so near and yet so far! The "final fact" does not emerge.

But a Christian philosophy based on the ascertained implications of Paul's "thought-series," as we have followed them out, provides the "final fact"—leads directly up to it along its earlier stages, *and in its soteriological stage not only tells us what the "final fact" will be but shows it, even although afar off, emerging as a reality into view.* The "final fact" is the return of the world-process which issued *from* God returning to God its source. The world-order came forth from God with God the Son immanent within it, its return to God being secured by the immanence of God the Son, had not man's sinfulness intervened. The world-order then drifted astray through the sinfulness of man; the immanence of God the Son was lost; and the return of the world-order to its source in God suffered check. God the Son offered then a new immanence whereby the world-order should be restored to its right and true lines again; and by man's relationship with the newly immanent Christ, the old relationship restored and more than restored, the world-order's return to God its source became once again a possible thing. So we have ventured to read the implications of Paul's almost unfathomable words. So the "final fact" will be the home-coming of the world-process to God when God the Son, with Himself immanent in man and with man through faith made one with Him, brings it safely and triumphantly back, its former disasters undone. So the "final fact" is the End coming back to the Beginning—not by way of absorption nor by way of "singleness" wherein the distinction between the two is swallowed up, but by way of a "unity" wherein each is both giver and receiver, and wherein, while the two are made one, each eternally recognizes the other for what it is. The "final fact" is the setting up of a mutual relationship which is to endure for ever. And this is a "fact" to which the epithet "final" may well be applied. For in it all the loose ends are gathered up. It makes the world-process subserve a purpose beyond its own fulfilment or self-fulfilment. Yet it justifies and gives value to the world-process while transcending it, the world-process serving as a scaffolding by whose means the "final fact" is swung to its place in a house which is not made with hands and which is eternal in the heavens. That "final fact" the world-order attains to at last for its own simultaneous crowning and passing away.

But (once more) in the soteriological section of Christian thinking this "final fact" is not only spoken of, but emerges, though afar off, as a reality into view; for in the self-identification of man with Christ the Christian and Christ are together making the "final fact" by living it; so that in that self-identification of the Christian and the Christ the eternal order is being borne on to its appointed goal. And, since Christian soteriology begins at the Cross, it is the Cross from which the final stage of the world-process, as Christian thinking views it, takes its start; and in the eternal order the Cross finds its place for ever secured.

If this be so, Christian thinking, worked out on the lines this book has followed, may well speak with authoritative tones, and, claiming to be a satisfying philosophy in itself, feel itself discharged from any need of "reconciliations" with non-Christian philosophies of every shade. It may well echo the utterance of an early Christian apologist [7] and—without joining in his too mournful depreciation of the "bent brows" of the philosophers—affirm that Christianity provides "what they have sought for with utmost eagerness, and have not been able to find." It is a lesson the Christian Church, particularly perhaps those of her children who stand forth as defenders of her faith, greatly need to learn. For the Church is too much on the defensive, content to ward off attack rather than to challenge. It is too anxious to conciliate, too ready to echo other voices

---

[7] *"Gloriamur nos consecutos quod illi, summa intentione, quaesiverunt, nec invenire potuerunt."* (Minucius Felix, *Octavius* xxxviii. See Migne, *Patrolologiae Cursus Completus*, III, 357.)

instead of sounding its own clarion-call. "The Church Apologetic" is a title which might without much injustice be written across its portals. Amid the welter of contending voices the Church is far too eager to make out that in what it has to say there are truths and programmes and ideals common with those of all other competitors for the thinker's ear: the really outstanding and super-important elements of its message are allowed to peep out from somewhere in the rear over the shoulders of less striking elements that hide them, as if in hopes that they will not attract too much notice; and instead of asserting the uniqueness of its position and the absolutely special and final character of its appeal, the Church more or less humbly asks for a place among the prophets or quasi-prophets of the schools. The saving clauses and reserves and parentheses wherewith the Church tries to save its position are not enough to set all this right. Christian thinking must claim its place as the possessor of the "final fact." This is quite compatible, let it be said in passing, with a very real tolerance toward all scepticisms genuine and sincere. If any one should choose to prefer a charge of arrogance against a Church that spoke more decisively, or to make an accusation of trying to bring the dark ages back, the Church need not be particularly anxious to answer the accusers in this matter. At the worst it can endure a criticism which it knows to be false. And if it be said that all this is against the spirit of the time, and that men and women will not listen to a message too heavily accented or under suspicion of exaggerating its own importance, there is the valid and easy reply that men and women run swiftly enough after many self-assertive tongues, attracted rather than repelled by the emphasis these lay upon their uttered words. Perhaps if the Church apologetic became the Church positive and trumpet-toned it might recover much of its lost empire over the minds and hearts of men. It may well dare to speak with emphasis equal or superior to the emphasis any other voices use; for if what has been said in these pages be true, Christian thinking is in possession of what makes Christianity (and this *by reason of, not in spite of,* its capital truths) the absolute religion and furnishes a theology at once philosophical and evangelical, a theology which in its soteriological section provides the "final fact" for which the eternal order waits.

And (once again) since Christian soteriology begins at the Cross, it is the Cross from which the final stage of the world-process, as Christian thinking views it, takes its start; and in the eternal order the Cross finds its place for ever secured.

And the final fact of all? The *"final fact of the final fact"*—if the clumsy phrase may pass muster? The ultimate consummation of all things, when the historic process shall reach its end, and the world-order, its mission fulfilled, dissolve and pass away? What God has prepared against that ultimate hour eye hath not seen nor ear heard, nor has it entered into the heart of man. God withholds that secret. It lies far beyond the utmost bound of the seas of time, and no human gaze can penetrate so far.

Yet Paul had strained his vision toward it, and had caught at least a glimpse. "Then cometh the end, when He (the Son) shall deliver up the kingdom of God, even the Father . . . For he must reign, till He hath put all His enemies under His feet . . . And when all things have been subjected unto Him, then shall the Son also Himself be subjected to Him that did subject all things unto Him, that God may be all in all." [8] That was what Paul foresaw in one of his earlier visions, when for a few moments the veil seemed to lift just a little way. Men have wrestled in hard fight with these words, and interpretations of them have been many—most of them the result of trying to find literal meanings for every word or phrase which Paul "threw out" at something not to be moulded into speech. They have been taken to show that Paul reached conclusions, formally "carpentered" into shape as it were with saw and chisel and hammer and plane, as to Christ's surrender of His mediatorial office into the Father's hands, so that redeemed humanity should thenceforth be in direct spiritual contact with God the Father alone, God the Son having finished the work given Him to do.

[8] 1 Corinthians xv. 24–28.

They have even been taken as justifying the grotesque inference that in the consummation of all things "the Trinity will cease to be." Perhaps indeed Paul's vision passed across his eyes in some such shape as that which the first of these interpretations suggests. But both the first and the second, if offered as definite formulations of a Pauline doctrine, turn poetry into prose, substitute pedestrianism for flight. Moreover, in later epistles Paul tells of another vision, changed in at least one respect from that of earlier times.[9] To the Ephesians and Colossians, for example, he writes of Christ as the One in whom all things are to be finally "summed up"; who is to "sit at His (the Father's) right hand in the heavenly places, far above all rule, and authority, and power, and dominion, and every name that is named, not only in this world, but also in that which is to come"; who has "all things put in subjection under His feet"; "in whom" and "unto whom" all things have been created; who in all things "has the pre-eminence." [10] But changed a little though the second vision may be, as if by the raising of some other fold of the hiding curtain than that which revealed the first, there is no contradiction between the two unless an attempt is made to force one or both of them as slaves into a tyrannous literalism's hands. What emerges from earlier vision and later alike is the suggestion that God the Father, God the Son, and the souls which God the Son has redeemed, will be at last so completely made one that redeemed souls, conscious still of their oneness with the Son, will think of this, not as *leading to or initiating* a further relationship with God the Father, or as being still a *condition*

---

[9] Weiss, under the necessity of finding a literal meaning for every phrase in both the earlier and later epistles, sees a real contradiction between Paul's two views. *"Durch diese Auffassung Christi als des Weltprincips und Weltziels,"* he remarks of the later view *"was nach den älteren Briefen nur Gott selbst ist, geht die Christologie unserer Briefe über die älteren hinaus. Es hängt damit zusammen, dass das Weltziel nicht mehr als das vollendete Gottesreich gedacht wird, in welchem die absolute Allherrschaft Gottes sich verwirklicht im Gegensatz zu der irdischen Mittlerherrschaft Christi, die dieser an den Vater zurückgiebt, sondern als die βασιλεία τοῦ Χριστοῦ καὶ Θεοῦ, und dass die Erhöhung Christi ausgedehnt wird über Alles, was irgend einen Namen hat in dieser Welt und in der Zukünftigen. Es kann eben das Weltziel nicht gedacht werden ohne den in welchem die Weltschöpfung begründet war."* (Lehrbuch der Biblischen Theologie des Neuen Testaments, p. 432.)

[10] Ephesians i. 10, 20–22; Colossians i. 16, 18.

precedent of it, but as *being at one and the same time* a relationship with *both* God the Father *and* God the Son. The oneness of the Son with the Father, realized by redeemed humanity as never before, will make the oneness of redeemed humanity with the Son to be realized by redeemed humanity itself as oneness with the Father too. That is enough for us to foresee. It is truth and poetry and philosophy and gospel all in one. So will come the fulfilment of the Son's prayer in the Upper Room—"that they may all be one; even as Thou, Father, art in me, and I in Thee, that they also may be in us . . . I in thee, and Thou in me, that they may be perfected into one." [11] And in the fulfilment of that prayer the *"final fact of the final fact"* will stand wrought out clear upon the cosmic stage.

That is far, far away. And we may suppose—nay rather we *must* suppose—that before the day of that consummation arrives there must be some revelation and vindication of Christ which will herald the dawn. For it would be a vain thing to imagine that the progress of the world advances in the direction of an unseen but certain goal where such a consummation waits its hour, or that humanity is simply winding itself by a process of natural spiritual evolution up to a level on which such a consummation will automatically appear. What that revelation and vindication of Christ will be we cannot tell. We may hazard guesses if we think it worth while, such as that it will be a mighty revival sweeping the world and turning all the accepted scales of value upside down—a revival whereof both friend and foe would have to say "This is the Lord's doing and it is marvellous in our eyes." But all guesses are really futile, and do but feel round the outside of a casket in which God keeps (and so far as we can tell wants to keep) another secret locked. But the "second coming" of Christ is not a meaningless phrase nor an exploded idea; and it must mean something on a cosmic scale. [12] The old picture of the Son of Man descending on the clouds of

[11] John xvii. 21–23.
[12] See on this the striking chapter on "The Return of Christ" in Dr. H. R. Mackintosh's *Immortality and the Future* (pp. 130 ff.).

heaven in triumphal state for every eye to see has suffered the fading of its colours: geography, if nothing else, has dimmed them. But it stood for something and may be taken as standing for something still. God keeps the secret, and the day of Christ's vindication before the world must tarry for a while. But far, far away though it may be, and loudly as the scorners may exclaim "Where is the promise of His coming?", its coming is sure as God Himself. The vindication of Christ in the eyes of men— and then *"the final fact of the final fact"* in which Christ shall see of the travail of His soul and shall be satisfied.

And with that "final fact" fully wrought out and established, of one other thing we may be sure. We have stood at Paul's side, and shared his *forward* vision. We may rise in anticipative imagination now and take our stand with the company of the redeemed in the high place where when all things are fulfilled they will be ranged. We may stand with them, share their *backward* vision—ay, and hear their song. What will the redeemed soul see as he looks back over heaven's battlements upon the vista of the past? The long historic down-dropping of the world till the swift slope reached its nadir—there, raised in a valley which might have been a valley of despair but which became a door of hope, the Cross, pointing with one outstretched arm back to the sad past and with the other forward to the new glad future it made possible—and then the upward slope to the Eternal Present, as it then will be, wherein he lives and moves and has his being for evermore. And as he surveys the outspread panorama of human history from its entry upon the temporal stage to its merging into timeless life, he will know that it was at the Cross his hope began. *So (once again) since Christian soteriology begins at the Cross, it is the Cross from which the final stage of the world-process, as Christian thinking views it, takes its start; and in the Eternal Order the Cross finds its place for ever secured.* The redeemed of the Lord shall say so. And for his song? As for him and for all the fellowship of the redeemed, ten thousand times ten thousand, the glory and wonder of that Eternal Order and of the Cross which is its re-creative centre surge in overwhelming flood upon their souls, what note can more fitly than this soar and soar upward on their voices in reiterated acclaim to fill with its untiring echoes the resonant vault of heaven, "Worthy is the Lamb that was slain!"?

INDEX

The major topics of this book can be easily traced in the preliminary Table of Contents, and are therefore not mentioned in this Index. Some of the auxiliary themes may also be so traced, because it is at once evident to which of the major topics they are related: and these also are excluded. This Index deals only with auxiliary subjects which are less easily traceable, and which may perhaps be sought for on account of some intrinsic interest they possess.

AUTHORS QUOTED OR ALLUDED TO

317